105

Food Culture in
India

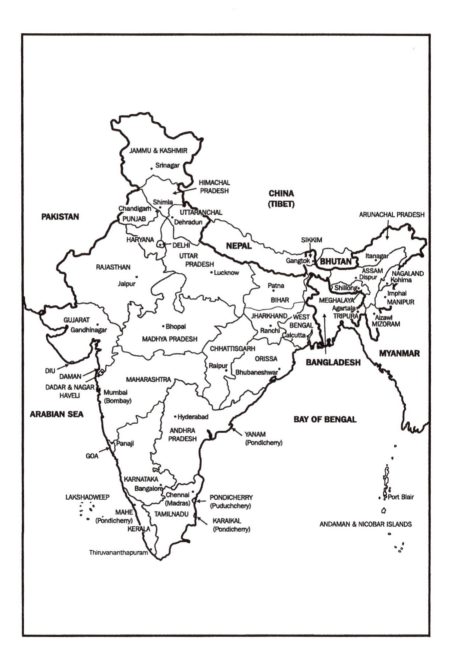

Food Culture in
India

COLLEEN TAYLOR SEN

Food Culture around the World

Ken Albala, Series Editor

GREENWOOD PRESS
Westport, Connecticut · London

Library of Congress Cataloging-in-Publication Dara

Sen, Colleen Taylor.
   Food culture in India / Colleen Taylor Sen.
      p. cm. — (Food culture around the world, ISSN 1545–2638)
   Includes bibliographical references and index.
   ISBN 0–313–32487–5
   1. Cookery, India. 2. Food habits—India. I. Title. II. Series.
   TX724.5.I4S38 2004
   394.1'0954—dc22   2004011240

British Library Cataloguing in Publication Data is available.

Library of Congress Catalog Card Number: 2004011240
ISBN: 0–313–32487–5
ISSN: 1545–2638

First published in 2004

Greenwood Press, 88 Post Road West, Westport, CT 06881
An imprint of Greenwood Publishing Group, Inc.
www.greenwood.com

Printed in the United States of America

∞

The paper used in this book complies with the
Permanent Paper Standard issued by the National
Information Standards Organization (Z39.48–1984).

10 9 8 7 6 5 4 3 2 1

Illustrations by J. Susan Cole Stone.

The publisher has done its best to make sure the instructions and/or recipes in this book
are correct. However, users should apply judgment and experience when preparing
recipes, especially parents and teachers working with young people. The publisher accepts no responsibility for the outcome of any recipe included in this volume.

To my husband Ashish and in memory of Arati and Ashoka Sen.

The life of all living beings is food, and all the world seeks food. Complexion, clarity, good voice, long life, understanding, happiness, satisfaction, growth, strength and intelligence are all established in food. Whatever is beneficial for worldly happiness, whatever pertains to the Vedic sacrifices, and whatever action leads to spiritual salvation is said to be established in food.

Charaka (legendary Indian physician), quoted in Robert E. Svoboda, *Ayurveda: Life, Health, and Longevity* (New Delhi: Penguin Books India, 1992), p. 112

Contents

Series Foreword

The appearance of the Food Culture around the World series marks a definitive stage in the maturation of Food Studies as a discipline to reach a wider audience of students, general readers, and foodies alike. In comprehensive interdisciplinary reference volumes, each on the food culture of a country or region for which information is most in demand, a remarkable team of experts from around the world offers a deeper understanding and appreciation of the role of food in shaping human culture for a whole new generation. I am honored to have been associated with this project as series editor.

Each volume follows a series format, with a timeline of food-related dates and narrative chapters entitled Introduction, Historical Overview, Major Foods and Ingredients, Cooking, Typical Meals, Eating Out, Special Occasions, and Diet and Health. Each also includes a glossary, resource guide, bibliography, and illustrations.

Finding or growing food has of course been the major preoccupation of our species throughout history, but how various peoples around the world learn to exploit their natural resources, come to esteem or shun specific foods and develop unique cuisines reveals much more about what it is to be human. There is perhaps no better way to understand a culture, its values, preoccupations and fears, than by examining its attitudes toward food. Food provides the daily sustenance around which families and communities bond. It provides the material basis for rituals through which people celebrate the passage of life stages and their connection to divinity. Food preferences also serve to separate individuals and groups from each other, and as one of the most powerful factors in the construction of identity, we physically, emotionally and spiritually become what we eat.

By studying the foodways of people different from ourselves we also grow to understand and tolerate the rich diversity of practices around the world. What seems strange or frightening among other people becomes perfectly rational when set in context. It is my hope that readers will gain from these volumes not only an aesthetic appreciation for the glories of the many culinary traditions described, but also ultimately a more pro-found respect for the peoples who devised them. Whether it is eating New Year's dumplings in China, folding tamales with friends in Mexico or going out to a famous Michelin-starred restaurant in France, understand-ing these food traditions helps us to understand the people themselves.

As globalization proceeds apace in the twenty-first century it is also more important than ever to preserve unique local and regional traditions. In many cases these books describe ways of eating that have already begun to disappear or have been seriously transformed by modernity. To know how and why these losses occur today also enables us to decide what traditions, whether from our own heritage or that of others, we wish to keep alive. These books are thus not only about the food and culture of peoples around the world, but also about ourselves and who we hope to be.

Ken Albala
University of the Pacific

Preface

When I started writing this book I was very surprised to discover that there was no comprehensive overview of the cuisine of India. There are, of course, many Indian cookbooks in English and other languages, as well as books on Indian regional cuisine ingredients, festivals, food and caste, food and health, and history. However, no one, except for the late and pioneering Professor K. T. Achaya and Madhur Jaffrey have attempted to synthesize these strands.

It's almost a cliché that India is an extremely diverse country, but it is also a fundamental truth that makes writing about Indian cuisine and culture very difficult. The problem is compounded by the fact that a lot of what is written in English by Indians about Indian food comes from people from Westernized backgrounds and/or from regions that were under direct British rule. As a result, a fair amount has been written about Bengali, Goan, Parsi, and Tamil cuisine, but very little about the food of Uttar Pradesh, Orissa, Madhya Pradesh, or Bihar, for example—states whose combined population is larger than that of the United States. The food of India's scheduled tribes (collectively larger than the population of France) gets even shorter shrift.[1] Moreover, cookbooks are written by and for members of the middle class and tell us very little about the daily fare of the 700 million Indian villagers who represent one out of every eight people on the face of this earth. In this book I've tried to provide balanced coverage but there are many gaps that I hope later writers will fill.

Acknowledgments

Over the past 25 years, I've been to India more than a dozen times on personal, business, and culinary trips, and interviewed people from many parts of the subcontinent. More recently, many people helped in the writing of this book by generously sharing their time, knowledge, and expertise. Special thanks are due to Barbara Dill, Tonse and Vidya Raju, Ashraf Hashim, Mukul Roy, Lata Kalayil, Philip Kalayil, Aparna Krishen, Manju Srivastava, Chef Sumath Das, Shashank and Sumita Goel, Vonu Thakuriah, Bappa and Anu Ray, and to my colleagues at the Gas Technology Institute, Bhupendra Soni, Yvette d'Souza, Alwarappa Sivaram, Suresh and Rosie Babu, Hamid Abbasi, Keyur Pandya, Raj Palla, Adeel and Anita Ali, and Carol Worster. I'm especially grateful to my New Delhi friends Gopal and Pranamita Sarma. Over the years Carol Haddix, Barbara Sadek, Deborah Willoughby, and Bruce Kraig encouraged my writing about Indian food. A trip organized by the Government of India's Department of Tourism gave me valuable information and insights into South India and its cuisine.

I'm grateful to the editor of this series, Ken Albala, and to Greenwood Press Editor Wendi Schnaufer for their very kind and helpful comments and enthusiastic support. Finally, I want to thank my husband, Ashish Sen, for his invaluable suggestions and for introducing me many years ago to the joys and endless fascination of Indian cuisine and culture.

Introduction: India, a Land of Diversity

Attempting to describe Indian food brings to mind an ancient Indian tale about the blind men and the elephant. Six blind wise men had heard about an elephant and wanted to find out once and for all what this strange beast was. They went to the forest, found an elephant, and felt it, each from a different angle. The first blind man touched the elephant's side and declared that the elephant was very much like a wall. The second felt the tusk and concluded it was like a spear. The third handled the trunk and said the elephant was a snake; the fourth put his hand on the knee and declared it to be a tree; the fifth stroked the ear and said the elephant resembled a fan, while the sixth grabbed the tail and concluded the elephant was most like a rope.

The tale is a Buddhist parable to illustrate the futility of arguing over religious differences, but it could equally well apply to food. Many Indians believe that what they eat is more or less what most other Indians eat, whereas in reality there are enormous variations that reflect religious, community, regional, and economic differences. At the same time, from prehistoric times there has been considerable mixing of cultures and cuisines. As Indian Nobel Laureate Amartya Sen writes:

It is futile to try to understand Indian art, literature, music, food or politics without seeing the extensive interactions across barriers of religious communities. These include Hindus and Muslims, Buddhists, Jains, Sikhs, Parsees, Christians, Jews, and even atheists and agnostics.[2]

Today there is no national cuisine in India or even a single national dish. But there are certain ingredients, dishes, and cooking styles that are typical of much of the subcontinent's foodways as well as common ways of thinking about food. This book will reveal both the commonalties and the differences.

LANGUAGE AND RELIGION

The Republic of India occupies most of the land mass called the Indian Subcontinent or South Asia, which also includes the Republics of Pakistan, Bangladesh, and Sri Lanka and the independent kingdoms of Nepal and Bhutan.[3] India is a Federal Republic, consisting of 29 states and six Union Territories under direct Federal rule. Stretching two thousand miles from north to south and eighteen hundred miles from east to west, India is the world's seventh-largest country in area and, with more than a billion people, second in population only to China. Some Indian states are larger than most countries and, like countries, have distinct languages, ethnicities, cultures, and cuisines.

Indians speak eighteen official languages and more than sixteen hundred minor languages and dialects. Although Hindi is the national language, it is spoken as a mother tongue by only about one-third to one-half the population. More than 80 percent of Indians are Hindus, but 12 percent—140 million people—are Muslims, making India the world's second-largest Muslim country after Indonesia. India also has 30 million Christians, who are the majority in several states; 15 million Sikhs; plus small communities of Parsis (Zoroastrians), Jains, Buddhists, and animists (worshippers of nature gods and spirits).

Religion plays an important part in Indian life, and food is inseparable from religious beliefs. On the most basic level, Muslims do not eat pork, most Hindus avoid beef, and many Indians practice varying degrees of vegetarianism. But there are no hard and fast rules: Some Hindus eat no meat, fish or eggs, others eat eggs or fish but avoid onions and garlic, still others eat absolutely everything. A common myth is that Indians are overwhelmingly vegetarian. However, nationwide 70 percent of the population eat meat at some point, although the percentage varies from 40 percent in the western states of Rajasthan and Gujarat to 94 percent in Kerala and West Bengal. However, for economic reasons—meat is relatively expensive—most people are de facto vegetarians who eat meat only on special occasions.

Festive occasions such as weddings, life transition ceremonies, and religious holidays are important social and gastronomic events in Indian life, accompanied by special dishes and meals. Adherents of all religions practice fasting as a means of worship, prayer, and spiritual and physical discipline.

As in medieval Europe, eating habits in India are rooted in moral and medical beliefs. "You are what you eat," is a theme of both ayurveda, the ancient Indian school of medicine, and Unani, the traditional Islamic medical system. Hindu philosophy also assigns qualities to food that are related to caste, personality, and spiritual qualities. All these systems are overlaid with popular beliefs about the "hot" and "cold" properties of food and their effect on mental and physical health.

GEOGRAPHY AND CLIMATE

Most Indian food is still produced regionally or locally, and is highly seasonal. India is a predominantly rural country, second only to the United States in the amount of land under cultivation. More than 70 percent of India's population live in 600,000 villages. Most are engaged in farming either on their own small plot of land or as hired laborers. Much farming is little more than subsistence-level: The farmer produces grain and rice in order to feed his family and sells a small part of his crops at harvest time, using the cash to buy more land, fertilizer, equipment, and household goods. People try to have a few mango trees and in the South tamarind and coconut trees as well as a small vegetable garden where they can grow chilies and vegetables for their daily meals. Relatively affluent farmers own a female water buffalo or cow for milk, bullocks to pull the plough, and a few sheep, goats, and chickens.

In cities, incomes are generally higher and people have access to a wide variety of foodstuffs at commercial establishments. Only 2 percent of India's agricultural input is processed, so most meals are made from scratch. Indian cooking tends to be labor-intensive and in rural areas women spend half their waking hours preparing meals.

Although people often think of India as a tropical country, it is located entirely in the northern hemisphere. A wide variety of altitudes and weather systems give India an extreme diversity of climates. It has practically every kind of soil, ranging from rich alluvial soils formed by the deposit of silt to arid deserts, swamps, and mountain soils.

Geographers divide India into three regions. In the North, the Himalayas (a Sanskrit word that means "abode of snow") extend for fifteen hundred miles from Pakistan and Afghanistan in the northwest to Burma (Myanmar) on the southeast. Here are found the world's highest moun-

Traditional bullock cart. Photo by the author.

tains, including Mount Everest. Over the centuries this forbidding range has served as a barrier to Arctic winds and invaders from the North.

Melting snows from the Himalayas and seasonal rains feed the great river systems of the subcontinent: the Indus (from which the word "India" is derived), the Yamuna-Ganga, and the Brahmaputra. Their basins form the fifteen-hundred-mile-long Indo-Gangetic plain, which was the cradle of India's agriculture and civilization (3000–1500 B.C.). In the past it was covered with dense forests that are now largely depleted, especially in the western portion, the barren wasteland of Rajasthan's Great Thar Desert. Millets and other coarse grains and a few vegetables are all that grow in this region's barren soil.

The northern and eastern parts of the plain are India's richest agricultural region, thanks to the sedimentary soil deposited by the rivers as well as large reserves of underground water. The states of Punjab and Haryana, called the breadbasket of India, produce wheat, barley, rye and other grains, while the eastern states of Bengal and Assam produce two, sometimes three, crops of rice each year.

India's third geographical region, the Deccan or Peninsular Plateau, is separated from the plains by the Vindhyas and other mountain ranges.

They have served as a natural barrier to communication between northern and southern India and allowed the development of distinct cultures, languages, and cuisines in the four southern states of Kerala, Karnataka, Tamil Nadu, and Andhra Pradesh. Running down the west side of India are the Ghats, a mountain range that empties its rivers into the Bay of Bengal. Their alluvial deltas have been the center of many powerful South Indian kingdoms. The rain that blows from the Arabian Sea during the monsoon is caught by these mountains, giving the plateau a hot dry climate. Between the Ghats and the Indian Ocean lies a narrow coastal plain, the Malabar Coast, which is one of India's most fertile regions, thanks to the abundant rainfall. This region, now part of the state of Kerala, is the center of India's spice industry and was the first part of India visited by Europeans at the end of the fifteenth century.

India's climate and seasonal variations are dominated by the monsoons, or tropical rain-bearing winds, that blow from the Northeast in winter and from the Southwest in summer. The timing of the monsoons and the amount of rain they bring have a major effect on agriculture and food supply. Before modern methods of irrigation, the failure of the monsoons could result in widespread famine.

FOOD MYTHS AND CHARACTERISTICS

Many foreigners equate Indian food with *curry*. The word probably came from a Tamil word *kari*, meaning a soupy sauce served with rice, which colonial Englishmen applied to any dish of vegetables, meat, or fish in a spicy broth or gravy. Strictly speaking, curry denotes a meat stew, fried in onions and cooked in a thinnish gravy with potatoes, sometimes tomatoes, turmeric and other spices. At times a ready-made curry powder is used. Curries are associated with the kind of food served at clubs, army messes, and other British institutions during the days of the Raj (British rule, 1857–1947) and even afterward. However, today some English-speaking Indians and cookbook writers use the word in a general sense to describe any meat, vegetable, or fish dish cooked in a gravy, a practice we will follow in this book.

Another misconception is that Indian food is very hot, which comes from equating spiciness with hotness. Hotness, a burning sensation in the mouth, is caused by black pepper and chilies. Spices (the roots, leaves, seeds, and other parts of certain plants) add flavor, which is a combination of aroma and taste. The type and quantity of spices used varies by dish, region, and individual and household preferences: Generally, South Indian food is hotter than that eaten elsewhere, while North Indian meat and rice cuisine is the most aromatic. Some families and individuals use very few spices. Still, spicing is nearly universal: Even the poorest people eat a few green chilies with their simple roasted bread.

Indian meals are centered around a cereal. In rice-producing regions in the South and East, rice is the staple grain, whereas in the wheat-producing North most people eat bread made from wheat flour. Grains are usually accompanied by boiled pulses (beans, peas, and lentils), called *dal*. These two ingredients provide the amino acids (protein) necessary for good health in the absence of meat. *Dal* and rice or *dal* and *roti* (bread) constitute the subcontinent's basic meal, the equivalent of "meat and potatoes" in the Anglo-Saxon world. Relatively small amounts of meat, fish, and vegetables are added to enhance the taste and qualities of the main grain. Condiments complement the flavors and provide essential vitamins and minerals, including fruit and vegetable chutneys; sweet, sour, or pungent pickles; and yogurt and buttermilk.

ECONOMICS, WEALTH, AND POVERTY

From ancient times, the Indian subcontinent was devastated by periods of famine caused by natural and human-made causes. As recently as 1943, 4 million people died of starvation in eastern India. In the 1950s India relied on food aid from abroad. Security of food supply became a major item on the agenda of the new government of independent India. Initial efforts focused on expanding the farming areas but these efforts did not meet rising demand. Thus, the government encouraged the application of improved farming techniques, and the construction of dams and massive irrigation projects. The Indian Council for Agricultural Research developed new strains of high-yield value seeds for wheat, rice, and other crops.

These changes, known as the Green Revolution, significantly increased food production, making India one of the world's largest agricultural producers and an exporter of wheat and rice. Per capita wheat consumption has nearly tripled since 1951 and is replacing other grains, such as barley and millet. Indians consume an average 2,500 calories a day and nearly 60 grams of protein, which is within recommended guidelines.[4] Some 92 percent of this calorie intake comes from vegetable products and only 8 percent from animal products (including milk and dairy products), compared with 28 percent in the United States. India's per capita meat consumption of under 10 pounds a year is only one-fortieth that of the United States.

The percentage of the population living below the poverty line has dropped from 51 percent in 1972 to 26 percent in 2000. However, these general statistics mask substantial differences among states and regions. The percentage of very poor people is less than 10 percent in Goa, Haryana, Jammu and Kashmir, and Punjab, for example, but exceeds 40 percent in Orissa and Bihar. For the landless peasants and laborers in these states, a meal may be roasted chickpea flour or a couple of flat wheat breads accompanied by some raw chilies and salt on the side. Of course, the rich and powerful have always eaten well in India. The rich, meat-based dishes served in many Indian restaurants (a cuisine many non-Indians equate with Indian food) is a version of the haute cuisine served at the courts of the Mughal emperors and local princes and aristocrats, and is in no way representative of the daily diet of the vast majority of Indians.

Today, India is rapidly changing. Better transportation has greatly improved distribution and helped ease local and regional shortfalls. Fruits, vegetables, and fish from other parts of India and abroad as well as processed and frozen foods are sold in Indian cities and large towns. The liberalization of the Indian economy and the creation of jobs in call centers and data-processing industries have generated a dramatic increase in wealth, especially for young, educated, urban Indians. The number of people living in households that earn at least $1,800 annually has increased 17 percent in the past three years to more than 700 million, or some 70 percent of the population, and graduates of elite colleges have an estimated $10.5 billion in surplus cash.[5]

For many reasons, India never had a restaurant culture, but this too is changing. Fast food chains and restaurants serving Western and Indian cuisine are proliferating, and Indians spent 55 percent more on eating out in 2002 than the previous year. Middle-class women are entering the workforce in greater numbers. A surge in the publication of cookbooks, women's and lifestyle magazines, and television cooking shows are also helping to spread awareness of other Indian regional cuisines and perhaps will further the development of a truly national cuisine.

NOTES

1. The term "scheduled tribes" is used in the Indian Constitution to designate communities who are mostly of non-Aryan origin and economically deprived.

2. Quoted in William Dalrymple, "Washing off the Saffron," *Financial Times*, 22–23 March 2003.

3. Although the subject of this book is Indian cuisine and culture, there is not a clear demarcation line between the foodways of India and those of other countries on the subcontinent (including Pakistan, Bangladesh, Nepal, and Sri

Lanka). Punjabis in Pakistan follow a diet similar to that of Punjabis on the Indian side of the border, while Hindu Bengalis and Muslim Bangladeshis also share a common culinary tradition, with a few differences due to religious prohibitions and local availability of foodstuffs.

4. N. P. Nawani, "Indian Experience on Household Food and Nutrition Security," *FAO-UN Regional Expert Consultation, Bangkok, Thailand, August 8–11, 1994.* Available online at http://www.fao.org/docrep/XO 172E/x0172E00.html.

5. Michael Schumann, "Hey, Big Spenders: India's Booming Middle Class," *Time Online Edition, Global Business,* 27 August 2003.

Timeline

Prehistory	Inhabitants of subcontinent start to domesticate animals, including fowls, and cultivate plants. Staples include rice, millet, barley, lentils, pumpkin, eggplant, banana, coconut, citrus fruits, mangoes. Spices include turmeric, ginger, tamarind, and long pepper.
3000–1500 B.C.	Cities develop in Indus Valley based on well-developed agricultural system. The main crops are wheat and barley, baked into bread in communal ovens. Chickpeas, lentils, meat, fish, and buffalo milk are staples.
2000–800 B.C.	Aryan tribes migrate into northern India with their herds of cows. Their dietary staple is barley; later wheat, millet, and rice are grown. Lentils, milk, yogurt, and butter are eaten. Sugarcane, native to India, is grown and processed.
1000–500 B.C.	Hinduism develops and society divides into castes with different food prescriptions. Revulsion against eating meat, especially cows, begins to emerge.
6th century B.C.	Buddha and Mahavira found Buddhism and Jainism, respectively, preaching nonviolence. Jains advocate strict vegetarianism.
300 B.C.– A.D. 300	India is the wealthiest country in world, exporting pepper, spices, and luxury goods to Rome and China.
1st century A.D.	St. Thomas brings Christianity to West Coast of India.

5th century A.D. Practices of ayurveda (the Indian system of medicine) are codified by physicians, including guidance on food.

c. A.D. 650 Rajput dynasties emerge in Rajasthan. Parsis, fleeing Persia, settle on West Coast of India, bringing Persian-style cuisine.

1206–1536 Central Asian dynasties establish Delhi Sultanate, introduce Central Asian and Persian dishes.

late 15th–early 16th century Portuguese explorer Vasco da Gama visits West Coast of India in search of spices. Portuguese found trading posts on East and West Coasts, capture Goa and establish Indian empire. They bring tomatoes, potatoes, chilies, peanuts, and other New World plants to India and China.

1526–1857 Mughal dynasty rules India and creates a haute cuisine that combines Persian and Central Asian dishes with spices and other Indian ingredients.

17th century East India Company is formed in England. Dutch, English, and French establish trading posts in India.

1809–1812 Dean Mahomet operates the Hindoostanee Coffee House in London, the world's first Indian restaurant.

1830–1850 British establish tea plantations in Assam and Darjeeling, coffee plantations in South.

1857 Last Mughal emperor is deposed. British Crown takes over government of India. Britains returning home create curry powder, Worcestershire sauce. Westernized Indians adopt omelets, patties, cutlets, and other hybrid dishes.

1868 N. C. Das invents the rosogolla in Kolkata.

1913 Karim Restaurant opens in Delhi serving the food of the Moghlai court.

1927 Veeraswamy Restaurant opens in London.

1947 Partition of India, independence from British rule as a dominion, and creation of Pakistan. *Tandoori* chicken invented in Delhi.

1977 The first Balti restaurant opens in Birmingham, U.K.

1996 McDonald's and Pizza Hut opens their first outlets in India.

2003–2004 Western and Indian fast food chains continue to expand as disposable income grows.

1

Historical Overview and Attitudes toward Food

HISTORICAL BACKGROUND

Prehistory

Historians speculate that the first humans came to the Indian subcontinent by sea from East Africa and by land from East Asia at different times. Neolithic tools, such as chisels, knives, and hammers made from stones that mark the transition from primitive hunting and food gathering to agriculture, have been found dating back to between 5000 and 4000 B.C.—several millennia after the advent of civilization in Mesopotamia, Egypt, and Persia.

The earliest known inhabitants of India, called Munda or Australoids, lived all over the subcontinent. (Today their descendants, officially known as "scheduled tribes" or, in popular parlance, "tribals," live mainly in central and eastern India and account for 8 percent of the Indian population.) According to a prominent food scholar, archaeological and linguistic evidence indicates that the dietary staple of these early people was rice.[1] Rice is descended from a wild grass that probably was first cultivated in the foothills of the eastern Himalayas and Southeast Asia around 4500 B.C. Other staples were the cereal *ragi* (a kind of millet), lentils, pumpkin, eggplant, banana, coconut, pomegranate, jackfruit (or breadfruit, a large fleshy fruit with a spiky green skin), orange, limes, watermelon, tinda, *parwal* (small green vegetables related to squash), and the edible parts of the lotus plant. Spices believed to be of Munda origin are turmeric, ginger, tamarind, and the betel nut. Oil seeds may have included sesame and mustard. These ancient people may also have domesticated dogs and fowls. The Indian fowl, *gallus gallus*, considered the progeny of the world's domestic poultry, is native to a wide region extending from Kashmir to Southeast Asia and was first bred by these early inhabitants, albeit for fighting, not eating.

The Dravidians

The next people to reach India were the Dravidians, although their origins and time of arrival are a matter of debate. They were mainly hunters and fishermen who spoke languages that are distinct from the Indo-European languages spoken in North India and are not related to any other linguistic groups in the world. Dravidian languages, which have their own script, are today spoken in the states of Tamil Nadu (Tamil), Andhra Pradesh (Telugu), Kerala (Malayalam), and Karnataka (Kannada).

The Dravidians' dietary staples were rice, boiled or prepared as a sour gruel, fried barley, and lentils, accompanied by meat and dairy products, fish, jackfruit, *toddy* (fermented palm sap), and mangoes. An important spice was long pepper *(piper longum)*—the seeds of a dark cattail-like spike that is sharper and hotter than black pepper *(piper nigrum)*.[2]

The Indus Valley Civilization, 3000–1500 B.C.

What many people now believe was the cradle of Indian civilization rose around 3000 B.C. on the alluvial plain of the Indus Valley in a half-million-mile area today located in Pakistan and the Indian states of Gujarat and Rajasthan. Now the land is desert, but in ancient times it was rich and fertile and allowed the production of surpluses of wheat and barley and the technological competence to make the "extraordinary leap from village culture to urban civilization."[3] Called the Harappan or Indus Valley civilization, it contained hundreds of villages and least two walled capital cities, Mohenjo Daro in the south and Harappa in the north, which flourished from 2500 to 1600 B.C.

This was an affluent, commercial society, whose merchants were engaged in an active sea and land trade with the Middle East. They exported cotton and cotton goods, barley, sesame and linseed oils, wood, iron, gems, and copper in exchange for silver and gold. The Indus Valley civilization had a written language that has still not been deciphered and is one of the unsolved mysteries of modern cryptology. Much of our information comes from clay seals and pottery that depict elephants, tigers, the Indian humped bull, and a horned deity seated in yogic posture that may be a prototype of the Hindu god Shiva. The elegance of these artifacts indicates a high level of sophistication and culture. Excavations of the towns and cities reveal well-planned urban centers with grid streets, brick houses, water supply and drainage systems, brick granaries with raised platforms and ventilated floors, and large brick platforms with mortars to pound grain. The dense forests that once covered this arid region supplied the wood that fueled the brick kilns.

Agricultural operations included plowing, furrowing, and irrigation from rivers and raising water from below the surface with water wheels. The main crops were wheat and barley. Bread was a staple of the Indus Valley diet, cooked in round ovens similar to those still used in the Middle East and Central Asia. People also ate peas, chickpeas, and lentils, river and ocean fish, domestic fowls, and meat and milk from water buffalos. They grew sesame, mustard, linseed, and flax and such fruits and vegetables as melons, dates, coconuts, pomegranates, and perhaps bananas.

Around 1500 B.C. the cities of the Indus Valley were suddenly deserted for unknown reasons: perhaps invasion, desertification, natural calamities such as earthquakes and floods, internal decay, or a combination of these factors. In a couple of centuries the entire civilization had disappeared, but it left its mark on Indian culture.

The Vedic Period and the Aryans, 2000–800 B.C.

Starting around 2000 B.C., pastoral semi-nomads living in the region between the Caspian and Black Seas began to move in small tribes in every direction. Natural disasters, plague, population pressure, or Mongol invasions from Central Asia have been suggested as reasons for this dispersion. In the past historians wrote about an Aryan invasion. Today a prevailing theory is that in the mid-second millennium B.C. there was a gradual migration of small groups of Indo-Aryan speakers from the Indo-Iranian borderlands and Afghanistan through the passes in the northwestern mountains to northern India where they settled. The impetus to migrate was a search for better pastures for their cattle and for arable land.[4] They brought herds of cattle, sheep, and horses, as well as their language, which linguists call Indo-European. It is the precursor of the Germanic, Romance, and Celtic languages of Europe; Iranian; Sanskrit; and Hindi, Gujarati, Bengali, Urdu, Punjab, Nepali, Maharashtrian, and other languages spoken throughout the subcontinent today.

This period is sometimes called the Vedic age, from the *Vedas* (Veda = knowledge), four collections of prayers, hymns to the forces of nature and gods, and poems compiled orally around 1700–1500 B.C. and written down around a thousand years later. The oldest and most important is the *Rig Veda* ("Verses of Knowledge"). Some are extremely profound, especially the *Upanishads*—a series of discourses on the nature of reality that was much admired by the German philosopher Arthur Schopenhauer (1788–1860) and fascinates philosophers to this day. Later works that provide information about their daily lives include the *Sutras*, which are manuals of instruction in various fields; the epics *Ramayana* and *Mahabharata* (written down from 200 B.C. to A.D. 200 following centuries of oral tradition); and the *Atharaveda* (1500 to 800 B.C.), a medical work that offers charms, herbs, and dietary injunctions.

Some of these adventurous tribes moved into the Caucasus and the Anatolian plateau; others pushed on farther into Persia; still others, called Indo-Aryans or simply Aryans,[5] advanced across the Hindu Kush Mountains into the Indian subcontinent to the region between the Yamuna and Ganges Rivers. They initially settled in villages in the Punjab and around Delhi. By the standards of the Indus Valley and the city-states of the Middle East, their pastoral lifestyle was relatively primitive. But by 1000 B.C. the Aryans had learned how to make iron, which they turned into ploughs to clear the thick forests. They also had chariots and wielded bronze axes, which enabled them to subjugate the local inhabitants as well as each other. The great Hindu epic *The Mahabharata* is an account of the struggles between Aryan tribes and their consolidation and confederation into kingdoms with regional capitals, including Hastinapura near present-day Delhi. In one battle, a confederacy known as the Bharats defeated another group and gave their name to the entire region east of the Indus—Bharat, the official name of modern India.

Each tribe was ruled by a male raja, just as each family was ruled by a male head. This family pattern, in which the wives of sons live in the patriarchal household, is still a prevalent form of social organization in India. The tribes were divided into three social divisions: the Aryans, which also meant nobles; the priests, called Brahmins; and the *vish*, or common people. "There was no consciousness of caste... Professions were not hereditary, nor were there any rules limiting marriages within these classes, or taboos on whom one could eat with. The three divisions merely facilitated social and economic organization."[6]

Between the twelfth and the sixth century B.C., the Aryans moved east and south, conquering and subjugating the local people whom they called *mlecchas* (barbarians) or *dasas* (servants, subjects). They began to maintain a rigid separation from the conquered peoples, perhaps out of fear that assimilation would lead to a loss of Aryan identity. The original distinction was largely one of color, since the Dasas were darker-complexioned. (The Sanskrit word for caste, *varna*, means color.) To the threefold division of Aryan society was added a fourth group, the *shudras*, who were either Dasas or of mixed Aryan-Dasa origin. They were relegated to performing more menial tasks and not allowed to participate in sacred rituals. People who performed particularly distasteful and "unclean" tasks, such as handling dead bodies, tanning leather, or removing garbage, became "outcastes"; their position was so low that any contact with people from the four other castes was forbidden. The Aryans succeeded in pushing the Dravidians south of the Vindhya mountains.

As the Aryans became more settled, society became organized into various occupations. The word for these occupational groups is *jati*, which has been translated as "subcaste" or "guild." Weavers, oil merchants, fishermen, physicians, barbers—each belonged to their own *jati* and sometimes lived in their own villages. At some point these professions became hereditary. Marriage outside one's caste or subcaste was forbidden, as was eating with people from other groups (commensality). The evolution of this complex system has been described in the following way:

Occupation alone [cannot] explain the origins of a caste system, whose reflexive ritual roots of totem and taboo were surely at least as important as the type of work performed or the nature of tools employed. Primitive fears of losing power... naturally dictated marriage only within the limits of a trusted group, whose *jati* was close enough to one's own family to assure friendship and support. Tribal fears of losing "identity" or racial fears of losing "purity" further complicated the casual pattern of a *jati* system that was eventually to subdivide each *varna* into hundreds, and in some cases thousands, of "castes" within India's subcontinent. The actual pattern or patchwork quilt of social hierarchy that emerged varied greatly from region to region since it was, in fact, a synthesis of Aryan and pre-Aryan interaction.[7]

The priests took advantage of the division to consolidate their own position. They claimed that only they could bestow divinity on the king and also gave religious sanction to caste divisions, with themselves at the pinnacle. They were believed to have magical powers and were the vehicle by which the Aryans performed sacrifices to their gods—forces of nature that had parallels in Roman and Greek mythology. The head god Indra, the counterpart of Zeus and Jupiter, was the rain god who hurled thunderbolts against his enemies. Other major deities were Surya, the Sun;

Soma, the god of the intoxicating drink *soma*; Yama, the god of death; and Agni, the god of fire. A central feature of Aryan religion was the sacrifice of animals to propitiate the gods. Sacrifices were conducted in the home or in the open air around a fire, which was considered the purest of elements. Although Hindus no longer worship these ancient deities, remnants of Aryan rites can be found in religious rituals, such as a wedding when the bride and groom walk around a fire, or funerals, when the purifying *homa* (fire) ceremony is performed.

Over the centuries of migrations, the Aryans also borrowed many religious customs and deities from the local inhabitants and incorporated them into the system of beliefs that evolved into Hinduism, which is a syncretic religion; that is, it absorbs and combines beliefs and deities from different traditions. The major deities Shiva and Vishnu may have had their origin in the gods of the indigenous people, including the Indus Valley dwellers, while their consorts Parvati and Lakshmi and other female deities may have been adaptations of indigenous mother goddesses.

The use of the iron plough, land fallowing, crop rotation, seasonal sowing, and irrigation expanded the Aryans' food supply and led to a rapid growth in population that continued to expand south and east into the rice-growing regions. The Aryans' first staple was barley, the world's oldest cultivated grain, and a hardy plant that can withstand both drought and frost.[8] It is the only grain mentioned in the *Rig Veda*. One method of preparation was grinding it and forming it into cakes that were fried in butter. Parched barley was eaten whole or ground into a meal that was mixed with yogurt, water, or milk. Barley flour was boiled in water or milk and made into gruel, and fried in butter and dipped in honey to produce sweet cakes, called *apupa*—possibly a forerunner of modern Indian sweets.

Later texts mention wheat, lentils, millet, sugarcane, and rice. The Aryans probably learned the art of rice cultivation from indigenous people. Parching was a common method of preparing rice and other cereals: The grains were soaked in water, roasted in hot sand so that they swelled, and then pounded in a mortar to produce a coarse flour. Parched rice was often used in rituals: The bride at a wedding would throw it in the fire, a forerunner of the custom of throwing rice at a married couple. The Aryans also cooked rice with water, milk, or sesame seeds and milk and ate it by itself or accompanied by yogurt, butter, sesame seeds, beans, lentils, or meat preparations.

An important element in the Aryan diet (and the modern Indian diet) was lentils, a legume originating in the Middle East and cultivated in India as early as 1800 B.C. The most popular lentils (*dal* in Hindi) were *masoor* (red *dal*), *moong* (green *dal*), and *masha* or *urad* (black *dal*). Rice and lentils contain complementary nutritional elements (proteins, amino acids, vitamins, and trace elements), so that when they are eaten with a green vegetable, they provide most of the nutrients needed for good health. Every civilization seems to have discovered this combination; for example, beans and corn in Central America and the Andes, and rice and soybean products in China.[9]

The Aryans also ate peas, chickpeas, and kidney beans, and used mustard and linseed oil as cooking media. Vegetables were grown on riverbanks, near wells, and on the moist beds of lakes. Furrows between the rows of other crops were planted with fragrant plants and medicinal herbs. Although the Aryans cultivated turmeric, fenugreek, ginger, and garlic, and brought pepper and cardamom from the South, the main spices mentioned in the texts are black pepper and asafetida, a pungent spice made from a plant resin.

One of ancient India's most important contributions to the culinary world is sugar. (The English word is a relative of the Sanskrit *sakkhar.*) Sugarcane is a giant grass native to the Ganges Delta. Its stems are filled with a sappy pulp that contains up to 17 percent sucrose. They are crushed to extract the juice, which is boiled down to make a solid piece of dark brown sugar, called *gur* or jaggery. Further refinement produces *khand,* a white crystalline form of sugar. (Some linguists believe this was the origin of the English word *candy.*) In India, sugar gradually replaced honey as a sweetening agent. The Aryans, like modern Indians, had a collective sweet tooth and used sugar in many ways. Sugarcane juice was a popular beverage, sometimes spiced with ginger. *Gur* was cooked with milk and flavored with cardamom, ginger, and other spices or mixed with ground barley, rice, or wheat. Sweets were molded into artistic shapes, such as flowers and fruits (like the modern Bengali sweet *sandesh*). Other sweet dishes included *mandaka,* a large wheat bread stuffed with a sweetened lentil paste baked on an inverted pot, and *payasa,* rice cooked with thickened milk and sugar that is still a popular Indian dessert.

One of the most intriguing foods of the ancient Aryans was an intoxicating, perhaps hallucinogenic, drink called *soma* in India and *hoama* in Iran. *Soma* was offered to the gods and drunk by the priests and worshippers during religious rituals. It was described as "primeval, all-powerful, healing all diseases, bestower of riches, loved by the gods, even the supreme being,"[10] and was said to inspire confidence, courage, faith, and self-trust in those who drank it. *Soma* was collected from the mountains by women, who extracted juice from its stalk, but it became increasingly difficult to obtain and by 800 B.C. is no longer mentioned in the texts. Today, no one is really sure what *soma* was. It has been identified with a leafless shrub called *somalata* in several Indian languages; with the plant ephedra, which carries an adrenalin-like alkaloid; and with *cannabis sativa* (the hemp plant), which yields *bhang* and *ganja,* sometimes taken during modern Indian festivals. Another recent candidate is the fly agaric mushroom (*amanita muscarita*), which produces hallucinogenic effects.

Cattle played an important role in Vedic culture and cuisine, as they do in modern India. Called a "blessing," the cow is regarded as a symbol of bounty. The *Rig Veda* alone contains seven hundred references to the cow. Milk was served fresh, boiled, as cream, churned into butter, or curdled by pieces of green plants to create yogurt, which was eaten with rice or barley or folded into fresh milk. Butter was melted and simmered to boil off the water, leaving a clear oil with a nutty fragrance, called *ghee.* One of the most important ingredients in contemporary Indian cuisine, *ghee* is used as a cooking medium for frying meat or vegetables, an ingredient in sweets, and a flavoring for bread and rice. *Ghee* also plays an important role in Hindu rituals because it is considered extremely pure.

Nonetheless, the Aryans were not vegetarians. Goats, sheep, even cows were sacrificed as part of religious ceremonies and the meat was eaten. The Aryans even ate beef—something anathema to many modern Hindus.[11] According to ancient texts, it was customary to kill a big ox to feed guests, and barren cows were killed at wedding feasts.

Still, the slaughter of cows appears to have been a subject of concern from the earliest days. Starting around 1000 B.C., religious texts began to display a sense of revulsion against eating meat, especially beef, and killing cows became increasingly taboo, a sinful practice associated with the outcastes. This may have coincided with the extension of agriculture. Because of cows' strength (for plowing), their dung that is used for fuel (dried cow patties are still a common cooking fuel in India), and their production of milk and its products, cows were simply too valuable to slaughter. The taboo may also have reflected changes in religious thought, especially the emergence of the belief in reincarnation—the idea that life gradually evolves through many rebirths as animals and humans—and the doctrine of nonviolence (*ahimsa*) that came from two religious sects: the Jains and the Buddhists.

Conquest and Unification of India: The Emergence of Buddhism, Jainism, and Brahmanism, 1000–450 B.C.

The old Aryan religion with its sacrifices gave way to more sophisticated doctrines that were expressed in series of texts called the *Upan-*

ishads, written down around 800 B.C. Their messages were originally transmitted by gurus (teachers) to students in forest schools and became fundamental concepts of Hinduism, or, as it is still called by its adherents, *Dharma,* the sacred law or way. The basic idea is that the individual self is identical with Brahman, the Divine Being or Supreme Spirit that pervades all reality and manifests itself in every soul. There is an endless cycle of births, deaths, and rebirths that arise from our actions in this world. Under the law of *karma,* every action, good or evil, has its effects on the future; the sum of our past karma determines our present existence and our future lives. If a person leads an evil existence, he or she might be reborn as an insect; a more virtuous life allows one to be reborn as a human and into one of the higher castes.

The goal of existence is not worldly comforts or wealth but to realize this basic truth and attain release from the endless suffering of existence and rebirths. People began to withdraw from society and wander in the forests as hermits, meditating, studying with gurus, and practicing yoga, a series of mental and physical exercises that are supposed not only to make those who practice it healthier but to facilitate clarity of thought and spirituality.

As the Aryans moved east, they founded small kingdoms and republics that replaced the old tribes. By the sixth century B.C., there were sixteen political entities and more than two thousand cities in north India. Towns expanded, agriculture flourished, trade developed by land, sea, and river, and learning flourished at famous universities like that at Taxila, now in Afghanistan, which drew students from all over India and from as far abroad as China. Art and science flourished, including medicine and astronomy. Indian interest in herbal medication dates back to the Atharveda (1000 B.C.).

In the sixth century B.C., two important religious leaders were born into the ruling families of two of these kingdoms. The son of the king of the Sakya tribe, Siddartha Gautama, later known as the Buddha ("enlightened one"), preached the doctrine of the Middle Path, or avoidance of extremes. He advocated nonviolence, nonhatred, love for all creatures, continence, and the ideal of reaching nirvana. Gautama opposed the hierarchical caste structure of Hinduism and preached equality, which gave his religion a universal appeal. He founded monasteries for men and women. Over the centuries, Indian missionaries spread Buddhism to Southeast Asia, China, and Japan. Today, there are only around 6.4 million Buddhists in India, less than 1 percent of the population.

Gautama Buddha preached moderation in all things, especially food, and enjoined against both overindulgence and austerity. He opposed ritual sacrifices as a means of personal salvation. The food served at Buddhist monasteries was vegetarian. Outside of the monasteries, Buddhist monks were expected to beg for alms and food but they had to accept anything that was given, even meat or fish, provided that the recipient did not see or hear the killing of the animal, this being the responsibility of the person who gave the food as alms.

Vardhaman Mahavira (540–468 B.C.), also of royal birth, was a wandering ascetic who founded the religion Jainism. The word Jain means "follower of *jina* (conqueror)," which was the name bestowed upon Mahavira because of his self-control. The central doctrine of Jainism is that all nature is alive. Everything from rocks and plants to gods has an eternal soul, called *jiva*, although some souls are more powerful and complex than others. Related to this is the concept of nonviolence, *ahimsa*. Mahavira's "pure unchanging eternal law" was that "all things breathing, all things existing, all things living, all things whatever, should not be slain, or treated with violence, or tortured, or driven away."[12] Even today, some devout Jains wear masks to avoid breathing insects and carry brooms to sweep the ground in front of them as they walk, lest they trod on something living. The prohibition against taking life was so extreme that Jains were forbidden from being farmers, which could involve destroying insects in the soil. As a result, many turned to commerce, business, and banking, and migrated to other parts of India and later the British Empire. They are sometimes called Marwaris from a region in Rajasthan where many lived.

For Jains, the question of eating meat did not even arise. In fact, it may have been the teachings of the Jains and Buddhists that forced Brahmins to end animal sacrifices and led to the spread of vegetarianism among Hindus. The political and religious leader Mohandas K. Gandhi (1869–1948), a strict vegetarian, was very heavily influenced by Jainism. Jains represent less than 0.5 percent of the Indian population (3.4 million people) and are concentrated in Gujarat, Rajasthan, and Karnatka, which have a higher proportion of vegetarians than other states.

The Mauryan Empire and the Unification of India, 300 B.C. – A.D. 300

Around 500 B.C. the Persian emperor Darius annexed the western part of the Indus Valley and the region that is today Punjab became a province of the Persian Empire. For the first time this region was called *India*—literally, "the land beyond the Indus River." When Alexander the Great conquered Persia two centuries later, he moved his armies across the Indus and defeated the armies of Porus, the ruler of a large Aryan kingdom. However, as Alexander advanced farther into India, his troops rebelled and he withdrew. Another tribal leader, Chandragupta, who helped drive out the Greek invaders, marched into Afghanistan, and proclaimed himself emperor. He was the founder of the Mauryan dynasty, the first Indian empire to encompass the entire subcontinent except the far South. The Mauryan capital was at Pataliputra (modern Patna in the state of Bihar), a rich and thriving metropolis that was the largest city in the world.

In 269 B.C. Chandragupta's grandson Ashoka came to the throne. After an early period of warfare and conquest, he became appalled by the carnage and suffering caused by war and renounced violence, declaring that the only conquest worth making was the conquest of oneself. Ashoka converted to Buddhism, sometimes wore a monk's habit, and sent missionaries and scholars throughout the world to propagate the faith. From India, Buddhism spread to Central Asia, Southeast Asia, China, and Japan.

Ashoka erected pillars all over the subcontinent with inscriptions that encouraged tolerance and nonviolence. He became a practicing vegetarian, and during his reign many Indians followed his example. An inscription on a stone in Gujarat states: "No living being may be slaughtered for sacrifice; no festive gatherings may be held. Formerly slaughter in the king's kitchen was great; now it has almost been stopped."

Greek writers who accompanied Alexander on his excursions wrote extensively about the ways of the country and attributed Indians' good health to the simplicity of their food and their abstinence from wine. Rice and barley remained the main staples, but the consumption of wheat was becoming more widespread. Indians ate meat, but there was a growing conviction that it should be avoided, if possible. The ideal was that people who wanted to lead a virtuous life should avoid meat as well as garlic and onions, which were thought to inflame passions. Drinking is also frequently condemned in the literature, although taverns were everywhere. Great importance was attached to hospitality: Many stories tell of the sacrifices hosts made to feed their guests.

In the early years of our era, India may have been the wealthiest land in the world, thanks to the growth of overseas trade. Indian merchants exported ivory, silks, cotton goods, pepper and other spices, and jewels to the Roman Empire in exchange for copper, tin, lead, wine, and gold. The importation of luxuries from India was such a drain on the Roman treasury that it has been cited as one of the causes of the decline of the Roman Empire. Caravans carried Indian goods overland along the Silk Road that linked the Persian Gulf, Central Asia, and China.

Increased wealth stimulated the development of philosophy and religion. In Hinduism, the emphasis shifted from ritual to a more personal relationship with God. The old Aryan gods Varun, Indra, Agni, and the like
were replaced by two main gods, Shiva and Vishnu, their consorts Lakshmi
and Parvati, and a host of minor deities, many borrowed from local cults.
Statues depicting these gods were installed in temples and at home altars.

South India

By the fourth century B.C., much of South India, including the state of
Tamil Nadu, was ruled by three dynasties: the Cholas, whose capital was
in Tanjore; the Pandiyas, with their capital in Madurai, whose rule lasted
in various forms until the thirteenth century A.D.; and the Cheras, whose
kingdom included much of what is today Kerala. South Indian ports were
important trading centers with China, the Roman Empire, and South
East Asia. Although continually at war, these kingdoms had considerable
cultural and commercial interaction with each other and the kingdoms of
North India. This was a time of great cultural achievements under the patronage of the monarchs, including the creation of a rich literature in the
Tamil language; the development of a distinct style of music (called Car-
natic music); and some of India's greatest religious art and architecture.
Around the sixth century A.D. the Brahmins emerged as a powerful class
and were granted land and villages by the kings for their upkeep. Many famous Hindu, Jain, and Buddhist temples were built and served as cultural
and social centers for the community, as they do today in South India.

In the first century A.D. Christianity reached India. According to legend, St. Thomas came to the Malabar Coast, where he converted Hindus,
founded churches belonging to the Syrian Orthodox communion, and
was martyred near Madras. Today a large minority of people in the state of
Kerala are Christians. In the first century A.D., a group of Jews fled to the
West Coast after the Romans destroyed their second temple in Palestine
and later established a settlement at Cochin, still the site of a lovely little
synagogue. In the nineteenth century, a group of Iraqi Jews from Baghdad
settled in Bombay, Pune, and Calcutta. The Jewish community has almost
disappeared from India, depleted by death and immigration to Israel.

The Classical Age, A.D. 300–700

Following Ashoka's death, the Mauryan Empire fragmented and was invaded by Syrians, Greeks, and Scythians from the North. The rise of the

Gupta Empire in the fourth century A.D. marked the revival of the imperial tradition and is sometimes regarded as India's golden age. At its height the Gupta kingdom, with its capital in Magadha in Bihar, stretched across northern India from Bengal to the Arabian Sea. The country was well administered by civil servants, irrigation projects and roads were built, and rich merchants endowed famous universities. This was a period of great achievement in mathematics, medicine, technology, painting and sculpture, and philosophy. One of the major Indian contributions to science was the invention of the numerical system consisting of nine digits and a zero. This system was adopted by the Arabs who transmitted it to Europe during the Renaissance; hence its name *Arabic numerals*. Indian medicine and surgery flourished; medical texts describe operations, such as complex skin grafts, the removal of fistulas, and eye operations. This knowledge contributed to the development of Greek and Western medicine.

Medical treatises codified practices and concepts for a healthy spiritual, mental, and physical life. This holistic view of the body, mind, and spirit in relation to the cosmic moral cycle became known as *ayurveda*. These works contained detailed descriptions of dishes and their effects on physical and mental health. They provided guidance on such matters as appropriate seasonal foods, the relationship between food and temperament, the order in which dishes should be served, the suitability of food at different life stages, and rules of etiquette.

The Emergence of Islam in India: Eighth to Twelfth Centuries

Founded by the prophet Muhammad in the year 622 in Saudi Arabia, Islam is a monotheistic religion whose basic principle is submission to the will of God (Allah). This message was revealed to Allah's prophet, Muhammad, through the archangel Gabriel and recorded in the sacred text, the Quran. All Muslims are considered equal and united in a brotherhood that is a powerful social force.

Within a century, Islam had spread across North Africa, Spain, the Middle East, and Central Asia to Persia and the northern part of the subcontinent. One important consequence of the Arab conquest of Persia was the emigration of Zoroastrians to western India, where they became known as Parsis and played an important role in Indian trade and commerce. Zoroastrians are followers of the teachings of Zoroaster (also known as Zarathrustra), who lived and preached in Central Asia around 1500 B.C. Zoroastrianism was the official religion of the Persian empire from the third to the seventh centuries A.D. Although Arab warriors had

attacked India's West Coast in the seventh century, they never succeeded in conquering it. Between the eighth and the twelfth centuries,
however, various Islamic powers from Central Asia invaded Northwest
India, initially to plunder temples and cities. A Turkic chieftain called
Mahmud seized the fortress of Ghazni in Afghanistan and used it as a
base from which to invade India, which was called Hindustan, "land of
the Hindus."

By 1225 the entire Gangetic Valley was part of an Islamic sultanate
with its capital in Delhi. This Sultanate lasted more than three hundred
years under different Turkish, Afghan, and Central Asian dynasties,
among them the Tughluqs, the Sayyids, and the Lodis. In 1398 the famous
warrior Tamerlane occupied Delhi, massacred its inhabitants, and returned to his capital in Samarkhand with his plunder. Elsewhere on the
subcontinent, dynasties of Turkic and Afghan descent established independent kingdoms in Rajasthan, Gujarat, Bengal, and Kashmir. The administrative system and land systems were left more or less the same, so
that the common people probably did not notice much difference.

The Islamic rulers of the subcontinent built magnificent tombs,
mosques, and palaces that followed the architectural traditions of Central
Asia. Another important legacy was culinary. The rulers had no prohibitions about food other than pork and alcohol. As the leading historian of
Indian food writes: "To the somewhat austere Hindu dining ambience, the
Muslims brought a refined and courtly etiquette of both group and individual dining. The Muslims influenced both the style and substance of Indian food."[13] They enriched native Indian dishes with nuts, spices, and
raisins and brought dishes and ingredients from Central Asia and the
Middle East, including meat and grain dishes, such as *halim*, a porridge of
grains and meat; sweetened drinks; elaborate dishes of rice and cooked
meat called *pulao* and *biryani* (originally both Persian words); *samosa*, a
stuffed pastry; various kinds of grilled and roasted meats called kabobs;
and many sweet dishes, including frozen *kulfi*, a kind of ice cream, and
halwa, a soft or hard dessert made from different flours. These dishes,
today part of Indian cuisine, would be brought to new heights of sophistication at the Mughal court.

In the fifteenth century, a new religion, called Sikhism, developed in
the Punjab. Its founder was Guru Nanak (1469–1538), who was born a
Hindu but rejected caste and preached the doctrine of "one God, the Creator, whose name was truth." Under the leadership of his successors, the
Sikhs became a distinct community who adopted five distinguishing symbols: the beard, the dagger, an iron bracelet, special underwear, and the

turban. A Sikh scripture, the *Adi Granth* or the *Granth Sahib*, was compiled based on the writings of twenty authors over a period of six centuries. It is considered the real guru that provides leadership to the community and is the focal point of Sikh places of worship, the *gurdwaras*. There are more than 16 million Sikhs in India today.

Hinduism saw the emergence of the egalitarian *Bhakti* movement, which was influenced by a mystical strain of Islam called Sufism. It stressed the need to unite with God through devotion rather than ritual, disregarded caste, stressed the equality of women, and conducted teachings in the local languages rather than the Sanskrit of the priests. Followers of this movement tended to be vegetarian. Lord Krishna, an incarnation of Vishnu, was a focus of devotion. The modern Hare Krishna movement is an offshoot of this sect.

The Chola dynasty ruled much of South India from the ninth to the thirteenth century. The only Indian dynasty to become a major maritime power, they conquered Ceylon, the Maldive Islands, and parts of the Malaysian peninsula. South Indian food was well documented in court chronicles and other writings as early as the tenth century. By the twelfth century, wheat had staged a comeback after being nearly replaced by rice during the Vedic period. Rice was eaten either plain or mixed with vegetables, cooked greens, tamarind, and yogurt. Wheat flour was made into many kinds of breads and snacks. Some dishes sound very similar to those eaten in the South today: *idlis,* a spongy steamed bread, and *dosas,* crispy crepes (although they were made from lentils, not lentils and rice); *vadas,* a deep-fried lentil snack; *dahi vadas,* soaked in yogurt; crispy lentil wafers, called *papadums;* *dal* (lentils) cooked with vegetables; and many kinds of pickle and yogurt-based relishes. Standard spices were turmeric, salt, pepper, fenugreek, and asafetida.[14]

North India was ruled by several powerful kingdoms, including the Palas and Senas in the Northeast and the Pratihars in the West, but they eventually broke up into small kingdoms, some of which came under the rule of Rajput princes. According to legend, the Rajput clans were the descendants of the warriors of Vedic India. They later founded kingdoms in Rajasthan, including Mewar, Jaipur, Marwar, and Jaisalmer. Their palaces and fortresses are today popular tourist attractions.

The Mughal Dynasty, 1526–1857

By the fifteenth century, India was fragmented politically. Fierce resistance to the invaders came from the Rajput rulers of Rajasthan, whose kingdoms ranged from small principalities to large states. By the middle of the fifteenth century the Rajputs had become a major political force in northern India. In the South, a great Hindu kingdom stretching from Orissa in the north to Goa on the west arose with its capital in Vijayanagar, then the largest city in the world. The economy prospered and architecture and culture reached their pinnacle.

In the North, the power vacuum was filled by Babar, a prince of the tiny kingdom of Farghana in Central Asia, whose ancestors included both Tamerlane and the Mongol leader Genghis Khan. In 1526 Babar entered the Punjab with a small army at the invitation of a local ruler, defeated the opposing armies, and proclaimed himself emperor of all Hindustan. He founded what came to be called the Mughal dynasty, from the Persian word for Mongol. By 1560 Babar's grandson Akbar had established his authority over the Gangetic Valley.

Akbar was a ruler of outstanding ability, wisdom, and tolerance, and a brilliant administrator. He divided the empire and its 100 million inhabitants into twelve provinces and smaller subdistricts. Each province was ruled by a governor, known as a *subadar* or *nawab* (a word that came to mean a person of great wealth and importance). Their courts were miniature reflections of that of the emperor in Delhi. Because the wealth of Mughal grandees reverted to the emperor on their death, lavish spending and high living became the order of the day. Poetry, painting, music, and cuisine flourished.

During his long reign (1556–1605), Akbar won the support of his Hindu subjects by abolishing discriminatory taxes, appointing them to high posts in his administration, encouraging and patronizing Hindu culture, and marrying the daughters of the Hindu Rajput kings. Akbar banned the eating of beef at his court and avoided eating other foods that would offend orthodox Hindus. Hindu, Muslim, Jain, and Parsee scholars as well as the Jesuits who were active in Goa were all invited to his court to explain their religions to him. Akbar even tried to found his own religion, *Din-I-Illai* (Divine Faith), that combined features of them all.

Thanks to his military strength and prowess Akbar extended his kingdom to encompass all of northern and western India, including Bengal, Kashmir, Gujarat, and Baluchistan as well as part of the Deccan Plateau. His son Jahangir (1605–1627) and grandson Shah Jahan (1627–1658) preserved and slightly extended Akbar's empire. Shah Jahan built the world's most famous monument to love, the Taj Mahal in Agra, as the mausoleum of his beloved wife Mumtaz. Shah Jahan was deposed by his son Aurangzeb (1658–1707), who reversed the prevailing policy of religious tolerance and cooperation. The Rajputs and Punjabis in the North and the Marathas in the West rose up in rebellion. Persecution of the Sikhs ended their pacifism and by the early eighteenth century they had become a potent military and political organization.

In 1738 the Persians invaded India, defeated the Mughal army, and sacked Delhi, slaughtering tens of thousands of people and looting a treasure of gold and jewels. Meanwhile, other foreign powers were starting to make inroads into the subcontinent. The Portuguese, the Dutch, the French, and the British filled the power vacuum left by the declining central power. By the early eighteenth century, the Mughal Empire had ceased to exist as an effective political organization, although it existed in name until 1857.

Although the Mughal emperors were the descendants of Central Asian nomads, the main cultural influence on their court came from Persia. The dress, décor, manners, morals, and cuisine of the Persian court at Isfahan were considered the last word in refinement and sophistication. Persian became the official language of the Mughal administration and law courts (and remained so in parts of India until well into the nineteenth century.) But Persian culture was not swallowed whole; rather, it was modified by local elements to create an entirely new culture—and cuisine. An important role in transmitting these local influences may have been played by the wives and concubines whom the emperors took for political reasons from the diverse communities of the subcontinent and Central Asia.

This cosmopolitanism is apparent in the Mughals' food, which is now regarded as one of the subcontinent's haute cuisines and served in upscale Indian restaurants around the world. The meticulous records of Akbar's Prime Minister Abul Fazl, an Indian-born Muslim who was a great gourmet, and the accounts of European visitors provide a complete picture of the food eaten by the Mughal emperors and their courts.

The royal kitchen was a department of state that reported directly to the prime minister. Its enormous staff included a head cook, a treasurer, a storekeeper, clerks, tasters, and more than four hundred cooks who came from Persia and various regions of India. The cooks were all men and had to be of good character. The kitchen commanded the finest ingredients from every part of the empire: Special varieties of rice came from different regions, depending on the season; butter from a certain town; ducks and water fowls from Kashmir. The birds and animals were fattened and slaughtered outside the city. Special breeds of chicken were raised for banquets or for particular dishes. The palace chickens were hand-fed with pellets flavored with saffron and rosewater and massaged daily with musk oil and sandalwood. Only when they were deemed plump and fragrant enough were they ready for the emperors' tables. Beef was rarely eaten, in deference to the many Hindu officials at the court. Pork was forbidden to Muslims, but wild boar was allowed.

A kitchen garden provided a continual supply of fresh vegetables. The Mughals were connoisseurs and lovers of fruit. Abul Fazl writes, "His Majesty looks upon fruits as one of the greatest gifts of the Creator, and pays much attention to them."[15] Akbar brought horticulturists from Central Asia and Iran to India to supervise his orchards. They cultivated many varieties of melons, peaches, apricots, walnuts, pistachios, pomegranates, almonds, plums, apples, pears, cherries, chestnuts, and grapes. Before being presented to the emperor, the fruits were marked according to their quality.

Akbar himself led an austere existence. He ate only once in 24 hours and frequently fasted. Apparently he cared very little for meat and would have been a total vegetarian, had he not been under so much pressure. As it is, over his lifetime he gradually increased the number of days on which he fasted so that he was fasting more days than not. One of his favorite dishes was *khichri*, a simple dish of rice and lentils.[16]

This austerity did not apply to the rest of his court. There was no fixed time for eating, so the kitchen staff had to be on constant alert, and within an hour could produce a hundred dishes. The food was served in dishes of gold, silver, stoneware, and earthenware, tied up in cloths, inspected and approved by the head cook, and tasted several times before being served as precautions against poisoning. Ice was brought daily from the Himalayas by an elaborate system of couriers for cooling drinks and making frozen desserts. Water was dripped through saltpeter to cool it.

A typical meal at the court consisted of dozens of dishes of vegetables, grains, rice, and meat, including lamb, goat, chicken, waterfowl, and venison. A popular way of preparing meat was to put it on skewers and roast it over a fire or in an oven. This dish, known as *kabobs* (which means "without water" in Persian), probably originated with the Mughals' Mongol and Turkic nomadic ancestors, since it was easy to make over a campfire. Bread was an essential component of every meal, as were side dishes of pickles, fresh ginger, limes, and yogurt. Sweet dishes made from sugar, thickened milk, spices, and sometimes meat were served throughout the meal. A meal ended with servings of *paan*—betel leaves smeared with camphor, lime, and musk and rolled up with spices and betel nuts—an ancient Indian custom enthusiastically adopted by the Mughals.

Many ingredients had their origins in the Persian court: aromatic flavorings such as rosewater; saffron, the stamen of a flower grown in the mountains of Kashmir; almonds, pistachios, raisins, and dried fruit; and thinly beaten gold and silver leaf for decoration. But whereas Persian dishes are subtly flavored with tarragon, parsley, mint, dill, marjoram, and perhaps a little garlic and onion, the flavoring of Indian cuisine became much bolder: cloves, cumin seeds, cinnamon, cardamom seeds, black and long pepper, chilies, ginger, and lots of garlic and onion.

Cooking techniques could be very complex. *Murgh mussalam*, for example, was made by removing the bones of a chicken so that it remained whole, marinating the chicken in yogurt and spices; stuffing the chicken with rice, nuts, minced meat, and boiled eggs; and baking it coated with clarified butter and spices. To make *biryani*, rice was parboiled, sometimes in meat broth; pieces of lamb or chicken were cooked in a mixture of onions, ginger, crushed almonds, spiced yogurt, and clarified butter; the meat and rice were layered in a pot, sprinkled with saffron threads and baked slowly in an oven; and the final dish was decorated with nuts, raisins, and gold foil.

The diet of the common people was much like it is today: rice, lentils, and diary products were the main foods, with meat served on rare occasions. Agriculture was primitive and at the mercy of the weather, so that a late monsoon meant devastating famines.

As the Mughal Empire disintegrated, the viceroys, generals, and nawabs who ruled the provinces became in fact, if not in name, independent of the imperial court in Delhi and set up their own courts. The main centers were Hyderabad in South India; Lucknow (then called Oudh) in the modern state of Uttar Pradesh; Murshidabad in West Bengal; Lahore, now in Pakistan; and Kashmir. The traditions of Mughal cuisine were preserved, even enhanced at these courts and are still evident in their cuisines.

The Arrival of the Europeans

For centuries Europeans had sought a sea route to the Indian subcontinent. Spices were a great luxury in Europe, valued not only for their taste and reputed medicinal properties but also as a way of showing off wealth. Until the fifteenth century, the trade in spices had been controlled by Arab traders who shipped them across the Persian Gulf to Alexandria, where Italian merchants transported them across the Mediterranean. The enormous profits from the spice trade helped to make Venice, Genoa, and other cities rich and powerful and were an engine of the Renaissance.

The fall of Constantinople to the Turks in 1453 interrupted this trade and drove pepper prices sky high. As a result, the maritime European powers sought a direct sea passage to the Indies. In 1498 the Portuguese explorer Vasco da Gama rounded the Cape of Good Hope to reach Calicut (today called Kozhikode) on India's Malabar Coast, a thriving port where Arabs, Hindus, and Chinese merchants came to buy spices, cloth, and luxury goods. The Portuguese established a fortress on the island of Goa, which became Europe's first base on the Indian subcontinent (and the last to be relinquished in 1961.) The Portuguese subsequently established trading posts along the Malabar Coast, on the island of Ceylon (now Sri Lanka), and near the mouth of the Hooghly River in Bengal.

Goa was a key link in a chain of Portuguese forts and factories extending from Brazil to Japan, including outposts on the Persian Gulf, the Malacca Straits, Indonesia, the East and West Coasts of India, and South Africa. The products traded included gold from Africa and Sumatra; pepper from India; mace, nutmeg, and cloves from the Spice Islands; cinnamon from Ceylon; gold, silks, and porcelain from China; silver from Japan; horses from Persia and Arabia; and cotton textiles from Gujarat, the Malabar Coast, and Bengal. So great was Portuguese influence that, at one point, it was rumored that Portuguese King Sebastian (1557–1578) might occupy the throne of the Great Mughals.

Never in history has a single country—and such a tiny one at that—so profoundly affected the eating habits of the entire world. In what is today called the *Columbian exchange*, the far-flung trading posts of the Portuguese and Spanish Empires (Portugal united with Spain in 1580) became the hubs of a global exchange of fruits, vegetables, nuts, and other plants between the Western Hemisphere, Africa, Oceania, and the Indian subcontinent. In India, the Portuguese introduced potatoes, tomatoes, chilies, okra, papayas, pineapples, cashews, peanuts, guavas, and tobacco (see Table 1.1). All these products were thoroughly assimilated into the regional cuisines. In Bengal, the Portuguese may have introduced the technique of curdling milk that became the basis of the sweet industry.

The glory days of the Portuguese Empire lasted little more than a century. The task of maintaining such an extensive empire was too great for a small nation of around a million people. The Portuguese system of administering the spice trade was inefficient, if not obstructive. The Viceroy in Goa and his advisors had an aristocratic disdain for merchants, many of whom were converted Jews, and even turned some over to the Inquisition in India. The real blow came when Portuguese ports were closed against the Dutch, who revolted against their Spanish rulers in the late sixteenth and early seventeenth century. Forced to get an empire of their own, the Dutch wrested much of the trade in Southeast Asia, Ceylon, and India from the Portuguese. The Dutch had settlements in Bengal and Ceylon

Table 1.1
Sampling of Plants Introduced by the Portuguese into India

English name (Botanical Name)	Comments
Cashew (Anacardium occidentale)	Native of Southeast Brazil, introduced on West Coast of India to check erosion. *Kaju*, the Hindi word, is Portuguese corruption of Brazilian *acajau*.
Pineapple (Ananas Sativa)	Introduced in 1594 from Brazil. Tupi Indian name is nana.
Peanut (Arachis Hypogaea)	Introduced from America, perhaps via Africa.
Papaya (Carica Papaya)	Originated in C. America. Came to India via Philippines and Malaysia.
Mangosteen (Garcinia Mangostana)	Brought from Malacca.
Sweet Potato (Impoaoea Batatas)	Introduced from Africa or Brazil.
Potato (Solanum tuberosum)	Spanish took first potatoes to Europe in 1570. Grown in the foothills of the Himalayas in 1830. By 1860, potatoes had become popular on the East and West Coasts.
Tomato (Lycopersicon Lycoperiscum)	Orig. in Mexico or Peru. Came via England in late 18th century.
Chilies (Capsicum Frutescens)	Originating in C. America, chili spread rapidly in India as a substitute for long or black pepper. By the mid-16th century, Europeans were calling it "Calcutta pepper."
Custard Apple (Anona Squamosa)	Native to S. America, came to India from West Indies via Cape of Good Hope or the Philippines.
Tobacco (Nicotiana Tabacum)	Introduced into South India by Portuguese in the early 16th century.
Guava (Psidium Guyava)	May have originated in Peru. Known in Eastern India as early as 1550.
Corn or Maize (Zea Maya)	Originated in Central America.
Sapodilla (Manilkara Achras)	The bark of the tree yields chicle used by Aztecs for chewing; hence Hindi *chikoo*. Brought from Mozambique to Goa or Phillipines to Malaysia, and then to East Coast.
Litchi (Niphelium Litcvhi)	Native to southern China.
Okra, Lady's Fingers (Abnelmoschus Esculentus)	Probably from Africa.

Source: Adapted from Colleen Taylor Sen, "The Portuguese Influence on Bengali Cuisine," *Proceedings of the Oxford Symposium on Food and Cookery 1996*, ed. Harlan Walker (Oxford: Prospect Books, 1997), 295–296.

but focused their efforts on the Spice Islands (Indonesia). The French, English, and other European powers followed.

On December 31, 1600, Queen Elizabeth I of England granted a royal charter to a group of English merchants, the East India Company (popularly known as the Company), which gave them a 15-year monopoly on all trade with the "Indies," defined as all lands between the Cape of Good Hope and the Strait of Magellan. In 1618 a British ship landed on the West Coast of India at Surat, the principal port of the Mughal Empire. The following year Surat became the site of England's first "factory"—the term for a trading establishment at a foreign port. By 1647 the British had established 28 factories in India and gained access to the Mughal emperor. In 1665 the Portuguese viceroy handed over Bombay with its excellent harbor to the English as part of the marriage settlement of King Charles II with a Portuguese princess. In 1696 the Mughal Emperor let the Company establish a new settlement in Bengal, called Fort William, which later became Calcutta.

In 1664, King Louis XIV of France founded the French East India Company to give France a seat at the spice table. Its headquarters were at Pondicherry, 85 miles south of Madras. France and England went to war over control of South India, and while the French were temporarily victorious, in the long run the British prevailed. By 1761 the French presence had been reduced to a few small settlements, which did not become part of India until 1954. (Even today Pondicherry has a French flavor: Older residents speak French, the policemen's uniforms resemble those of French gendarmes, and streets are named after French admirals and political figures. But virtually no trace of French cuisine remains.)

As long as the Mughal emperors were able to enforce their authority, the activities of the foreigners were limited to trade. They exported cotton goods from Madras and Gujarat; silk, sugar, and saltpeter from Bengal; spices from the Malabar Coast; and opium, which the Company forced upon the Chinese in exchange for tea. Profit margins of 25 percent were regarded as moderate; as a result, some of the English merchants became fabulously wealthy.

In 1757 the Company's English troops and their Indian allies defeated the forces of the Mughal viceroy at the battle of Plassey and secured permission to collect the Mughals' taxes in return for an annual tribute and for maintaining order. They subsequently installed puppet rulers in Bengal, Bihar, and Orissa. In the late eighteenth century, the English government established a separate administration and civil service to run India. They appointed governors in Madras (name changed to Chennai in 1996) and Bombay (called Mumbai since 1995), and a governor-general in Calcutta (name changed to Kolkata in 2000), which remained the capital of British India until 1905. This vast land of 200 million people was defended by 232,000 Indian soldiers, called sepoys, and 40,000 British troops. In the second half of the nineteenth century, the British defeated and annexed the Punjab, Nepal, and Burma.

Until the early nineteenth century, the Company men in India lived much like the native population:[17] They spoke Indian languages, took Indian mistresses and wives (very few Englishwomen then lived in India), wore Indian clothes, smoked hookahs, and ate Indian food prepared by local cooks. The prodigal meals eaten at the British settlements were similar to those eaten by the Mughals and their local representatives, featuring spicy rice *pulaos* and *biryanis, dumpokhed* chicken (baked in a seal of dough), *kedgeree,* chutneys, and relishes, washed down with Persian shiraz wine, English beer, or *arrack,* a liquor made from aniseed.

According to a chronicler of the food during British rule (sometimes referred to as "the Raj"), the first British settlers may not have considered the highly spiced cuisine of India very strange. "In 1612, English cooking had itself barely emerged from the Middle Ages and was still heavy with cumin, caraway, ginger, pepper, cinnamon, cloves, and nutmeg."[18] The Indian *dumpokhed* chicken, stewed in butter, stuffed with spices, almonds, and raisins, and baked with a dough crust, was very similar to an English chicken pie described in a contemporary cookbook. Forks were still relatively uncommon in England, and the English scooped food into their mouths with pieces of bread—just as the Indians did. Even the custom of eating spices *(paan)* after a meal as an aid to digestion had its counterpart in the old English custom of voidee: offering departing guests assorted spices and wine at the end of a banquet.

During this period, the British made what are generally recognized as important contributions to Indian society. They include the founding of schools and universities with English as the language of instruction, the promulgation of laws that became the basis of a uniform legal system, construction of a good system of railroads and roads, implementation of a unified postal and telegraph system, and the creation of a civil service entered by open competition and a competent administrative machinery.

The Raj: British Rule, 1857–1919

In 1857 North India went up in flames. Starting with a mutiny of Indian regiments in Meerut, other Indian troops rebelled and slaughtered their British commanders and local British residents. The initial spark was lit by the introduction of a new rifle with cartridges that were smeared with animal fat and lard that the soldiers had to bite before firing. The idea that the fat could come from pork or beef was anathema to Muslims and Hindus. A more recent explanation is that the rebellion was due to a pay discrepancy.

The mutineers headed for Delhi with the goal of restoring the Mughal emperor Bahadur Shah II to power. But ultimately the revolt failed, in part because of lack of communication among the rebels, and the British reprisals were savage. This event—called the Indian Mutiny by British commentators, the First War of Independence by Indians—had important consequences. Emperor Bahadur Shah II was exiled to Burma and the reign of the Mughals came to an end. The Company was disbanded, and in 1858, the British Parliament transferred all its rights to the British Crown. In 1877 Queen Victoria was named Empress of India. Until India gained its independence in 1947, around 60 percent of India's land area would be under direct British rule. The rest of the subcontinent, called the Princely States, retained their rulers, who pledged obedience to the Empress and were under the indirect control of the British authorities. The administration was reorganized and a trickle of Indians began to enter the civil service, the railways, public works, and other government agencies.

The events of 1857 had a profound impact on the social and gastronomical life of the British: "Virtually all the bridges so painstakingly enacted between the British and Indian cultures were destroyed by fear and hatred."[19] The British became increasingly isolated from Indians, as they moved to new neighborhoods and towns reserved only for them. The opening of the Suez Canal in 1869 made it easier and faster to ship both goods and people to India, among them young unmarried English women who came here in search of husbands. These women were known, collectively, as the "fishing fleet."

By the early nineteenth century, Indianized habits among the British had become much more rare. British wives replaced Indian mistresses, and these women had no interest in exploring local cultures or cuisine. Curries were no longer acceptable dishes at parties; as one contemporary writes, "The delicacies of an entertainment consist of hermetically sealed salmon, red herrings, cheese, smoked sprats, raspberry jam, and dried fruits; these articles coming from Europe, and being sometimes very difficult to procure, are prized accordingly."[20]

Nonetheless, Queen Victoria had two Indian cooks on her staff who prepared curry every day at lunch in case one of her imperial subjects should visit, while her grandson, King George V, a great lover of Indian food, ate curry every day.

Among the British in India, dinner parties were an important part of so-cial and official life. They consisted of multiple courses of bland English food with an emphasis on meat: joints, legs of lamb, great saddles of mut-ton, and boiled chicken. However, Indianized dishes such as curries, *kedgeree*, and mulligatawny soup (a spicy chicken lentil soup) were served at breakfast and lunch, which was sometimes called tiffin (from an English slang word "to tiff," meaning to eat small amounts of food). Until the late nineteenth century, most Indians had little social contact with the British. The exceptions were at the very top of the social structure: the ruling princes, the great landowners, and wealthy merchants in cities like Calcutta and Bombay, who made their fortunes by acting as go-betweens.

Despite this separation, the two civilizations had a great impact on each other's cuisine. A famous food historian has noted that

No source of influence in cookery...has exceeded imperialism.... The tides of empire run in two directions: first, the flow outward from an imperial center cre-ates metropolitan diversity and "frontier" cultures—cuisines of miscegenation—at the edges of empires. Then the ebb of imperial retreat carries home colonists with exotically acclimatized palates and releases the forces of "countercoloniza-tion", dappling the former imperial heartlands with enclaves of sometimes sub-ject peoples, who carry their cuisine with them.[21]

This two-way flow seems to have grown stronger with time. There are now officially more Indian restaurants in England than fish and chip shops, and some people have proposed making curry the national British dish. Meanwhile, Indians have incorporated such dishes as chops, cutlets, and omelets into their daily cuisine, albeit in a modified form, while roast beef with Yorkshire pudding still appears on Pakistani army canteen menus.

This cultural interface gave rise to hybrid foodstuffs that are now an in-trinsic part of world cuisine, foremost of which are curry and curry pow-der. For most non-Indians *curry* is a convenient catchphrase for every Indian dish, even though a dish by that name never existed. As one In-dian food writer states, "To me, the word 'curry' is as degrading to India's great cuisine as 'chop suey' was to China's."[22] The word comes from the Tamil *kari*, which means a soupy sauce served with rice. The earliest ref-erence to a *karil*, referring to a spicy South Indian dish, appeared in 1502 in a Portuguese cookbook. In England, the first mention of curry appears in Hannah Glasse's *Art of Cookery* (1747), where she describes a curry as a chicken stew spiced with turmeric, ginger, and pepper "beat very fine."

To the colonial Englishman in India, a curry denoted a dish of vegeta-bles, meat, or fish in a spicy broth or gravy that was generally served with rice. The spice mixture was ground to order by the Indian cook using a mortar and pestle. A typical mixture would include coriander, cumin, red and black pepper, fenugreek, turmeric, even curry leaves. (The latter come from a small fragrant bush that grows wild in India but is not an essential ingredient in curry.) When British officials retired and returned home, they no longer had cooks who could produce such mixtures. Enterprising returnees began to manufacture commercial curry powder mixtures. (The idea of such a powder was not new: In medieval times British cooks prepared powders that often contained ginger and pepper for use in the kitchen.)

Today curry powder is a universal flavoring, used in the West Indies, Europe, Africa, China, and even Japan, where curry and rice dishes are a staple of family meals. Other hybrid dishes are *kedgeree*, a favorite British breakfast dish that is a variation of *khichri* (rice and lentils); mulligatawny soup, a modification of a thin broth eaten in South India; and Worcestershire sauce, a popular condiment said to be based on an Indian recipe brought back to England by a governor of Bengal in the early nineteenth century.

Another item of mutual exchange was tea. In the seventeenth century, green tea imported from China to England by the Company was a popular drink among the wealthy. However, the cost of these imports was becoming a drain on the British treasury. To break the Chinese monopoly, the British began looking for another source of tea and discovered tea bushes growing wild in Assam. Using Chinese seeds, plus Chinese planting and cultivation techniques, the government launched a tea industry by offering land in Assam to any European who agreed to cultivate tea for export. Tea cultivation spread to the Darjeeling area in the Himalayas, to the Nilgiri hills in the south, and to Ceylon. The price dropped dramatically, and by the end of the century tea had become a mass drink in Britain.

Ironically, it was the British who introduced tea drinking to India, initially to anglicized Indians. Afternoon tea with snacks, cakes, and sandwiches became an important meal, especially in Calcutta. Tea did not become a mass drink in India until the 1950s when the India Tea Board, faced with a surplus of low-grade tea, launched an advertising campaign to popularize tea in the North, where the drink of choice was milk. In this form, tea is typically boiled with milk and spices and is called *chai*.

In South India, coffee is the traditional drink, especially at breakfast. The Arabs introduced coffee to India in the seventeenth century, and the first European plantations were started in Mysore in the 1830s. By the end of the nineteenth century, more than 250,000 acres in South India were planted with coffee.

The Birth of Modern India: 1919–1947

As Indians learned about British ideals of democracy and justice, they wanted to see them applied in their own country, and tensions grew. In 1885, a group of Indians and British liberals formed the Indian National Congress to seek a greater share in political power for Indians. Calls for Home Rule became more insistent after World War I, in which a million Indian troops fought in defense of Britain.

The massacre of four hundred unarmed citizens in Amritsar in 1919 by an English general brought the situation to a crisis and saw the emergence of Mohandas K. Gandhi as a national leader. He later became known as the Mahatma, Sanskrit for "great soul." Gandhi's policy was based on *satyagraha* ("holding fast to the truth"). He advocated a policy of peaceful noncooperation with the government in all spheres, and political action based on *ahimsa,* or nonviolence, a concept taken from Jainism. He was also a strict vegetarian and something of a food faddist, who took his own goat along when he traveled so he could always have fresh milk. Gandhi called for a boycott of British goods and institutions, including schools and colleges, and advocated self-reliance (*swadeshi*).

Gandhi was both a great spiritual leader and a shrewd politician. Although born a Hindu, his beliefs and actions transcended those of any religion. He advocated a secular state where all religions would be equal and India's 50 million outcastes, who lived isolated from society and subjected to subhuman living conditions, would be treated as equals. Gandhi did not aspire to political office and his choice to lead the struggle for freedom was Jawaharlal Nehru, a handsome aristocrat from a politically active Kashmiri family. The outbreak of World War II interrupted the struggle for independence. The Japanese attack on Singapore and Southeast Asia and China made India a critical base for the Allies in the war effort and it became incumbent on the British government to reach an agreement with India. British Prime Minister Winston Churchill (who once declared that he found it "nauseating" to see a "half-naked fakir [Indian mendicant monk regarded as a holy man]" striding to "parley [talk] on equal terms" with the king-emperor's viceroy) met with Gandhi in London. When negotiations broke down, Gandhi launched his last great campaign, the Quit India movement, now calling for total independence.

In 1907, a group of Muslim leaders formed the Muslim League to represent the political rights and interests of the subcontinent's estimated 60 million Muslims. They eventually demanded their own state encompassing provinces that had Muslim majorities: Punjab, Sind, Baluchistan, the Northwest Frontier, and part of Bengal. The name of the country was to be Pakistan, an Urdu word meaning "Land of the Pure." In 1947, the British government sent the war hero Lord Louis Mountbatten to India as viceroy and governor-general to bring about a final settlement. Despite Gandhi's opposition to the "vivisection of India," Mountbatten concluded that the creation of Pakistan would be a lesser evil than continued discord. The princely rulers of the two-fifths of India that were not under direct British control were persuaded to accede to the new India. On August 15 and 16, 1947, India and Pakistan emerged as two independent countries. Originally they were dominions within the British Commonwealth with the Queen as head of state but later they became republics, though remaining within the Commonwealth. Ceylon (now Sri Lanka) became an independent dominion in 1948.

The transfer of millions of Hindus and Sikhs from what became Pakistan to India and millions of Muslims from India to Pakistan was accompanied by terrible violence and bloodshed. The problem of Kashmir, which has a Muslim majority but whose Hindu ruler opted to join India, remains a source of discord and has been the cause of three wars since independence. The Nizam (king) of Hyderabad in the South held out for special status, since his was a Muslim enclave in the midst of the Hindu South, so the Indian government sent troops to force his allegiance. Negotiation secured the eventual transfer to Indian control of the small French enclaves of Pondicherry and Chandernagar. Portugal, which still held Goa, resisted until 1961. In 1971, the province of East Pakistan rebelled against the Pakistan government, which was dominated by West Pakistan, and became the independent republic of Bangladesh.

In January 1948, Mahatma Gandhi was murdered by a Hindu extremist. In 1950 India became a sovereign republic and the following year Jawaharlal Nehru was elected India's first prime minister, a position he held for 17 years. He launched a program of social reforms that included the modernization of Hindu law, the abolition of the practice of untouchability, and a guarantee of public and political power for women. In 1966, twenty months after his death, his daughter Indira Gandhi (no relation to Mahatma) was elected prime minister. She was voted out of office in 1977 and assassinated in 1984. The current (March 2004) government is a coalition lead by the BJP, a Hindu nationalist party.

ATTITUDES TOWARD FOOD

Cuisine, like language, is never static and Indian cuisine continues to evolve. Indians are becoming increasingly exposed to other cuisines—those from other parts of India and from abroad—thanks to the availability of processed and frozen foods, the publication of cookbooks, the popularity of television cooking shows, and a profusion of restaurants and fast food chains. Eating out is becoming a part of middle-class Indian life, especially in cities. However, these developments represent a departure from traditional attitudes toward food.

In traditional India, what and how people ate was inseparable from their religion, life-cycle stage, town and region, caste and/or social status, family traditions, health concerns, and spiritual beliefs. The subcontinent's many religions have their own rules and preferences about what is and what is not acceptable to eat, and within each religion there are a myriad of sects and subgroups with their own culinary attitudes. The avoidance of certain foods has been prevalent in all communities and is especially marked in Hinduism, Jainism, and Islam. Fasting is also a part of most religions.

An important dimension of Indian food attitudes is the hot/cold dichotomy, not in the sense of a food's temperature but of its physiological action. This medical theory, which may have originated in India, traveled to the Middle East, China, and Europe, although how foods are classed as "hot" and "cold" varies in different countries and even within India. This topic is discussed in chapter 7, "Diet and Health," together with a summary of the dietary prescriptions of *Ayurveda*, the Hindu system of medicine, and the Muslim system called *Unani*.

Hinduism

In Hinduism, food has from time immemorial been inextricably linked to spiritual and physical health. According to the ancient texts, of all things created, food is the most important since it enables people to use all their faculties and frees them from ignorance and bondage. "Purity of thought depends on the purity of food," said the ancient sages, or, as we would say today, "You are what you eat." Medical texts provide detailed commentaries on the properties of food and their effects.

Hinduism is not a single faith but a vast complex of beliefs and practices with infinite nuances and variations. Middle-class Westernized Hindus living in cities behave quite differently from villagers. But everywhere in

India, there is great attention to cleanliness in connection with food, which among orthodox Hindus—those who follow traditional ways most closely—takes the form of concern about purity and its opposite, pollution. As a noted anthropologist writes:

The Hindu... ideally considers procuring, cooking, and eating to be an integral part of his composite moral order. Foods for him are a moral category and food handling an equally thorough moral imperative and a moral activity... Food... is a moral cosmographic principle which stands synonymous with the universal moral order (*Brahma*).[23]

What was eaten was often less important than who served the food and how it was handled and prepared. For orthodox people, caste would play the major role in determining with whom people could eat and what foods they could take from the servers. These restrictions were parallel to those governing marriage: Just as people could not marry outside their caste, so too they could accept most foods only from members of their own or a higher caste. All lower castes could receive cooked food or water from a Brahmin, for example, but a Brahmin could not accept food from them. As a consequence, many cooks were and still are Brahmins. (Although caste systems are associated with Hinduism, they exist to a certain degree among other religious groups and reflect a family's caste status before it converted to, say, Christianity or Sikhism.)

The following story by an anthropologist visiting western India shows how this social principle works:

On my first evening in Nandol, a number of people came to greet us, including the elderly scholar, Kalidas.... On his arrival I fetched some water to offer him, as I would have done in Africa and elsewhere. When I handed him a glass, he set it aside, firmly but politely, saying that he only ate in his own house, by which he meant in his own caste. All other food he considered polluting, not because of the nature of the constituents but because of the status of the person who had prepared or offered it.[24]

In South India, a Brahmin could not eat food if even the shadow of a person from a scheduled caste (formerly called an untouchable) fell upon it. Even today, in rural regions of Bihar and Orissa, people from scheduled castes have been murdered because they drank water from a well reserved for upper castes. Some of these taboos may have been inspired by sanitary and hygienic concerns that developed when the nomad Aryans settled in agricultural and urban communities—the Vedas mention diseases that were the results of careless collective living—but over time they became calcified and a means of social demarcation.

Generally, members of the priestly castes, the Brahmins, are vegetarians, although there are many regional and individual exceptions. People who belong to the Kshatriya, or warrior, castes, eat meat. Farmers (*vaishya*) may or may not eat meat, depending on their local tradition. People who belong to groups associated with waste, dead bodies, and other polluting substances, such as sweepers, leather workers, and butchers, eat meat when they can afford it.

In addition, the higher Hindu castes were not supposed to eat certain items under any circumstances, such as items that have stood overnight or turned sour, leftovers, food that has been touched by an unclean substance or an insect, or food touched by another person's lips. In North India, foods traditionally were divided into two categories: *kaccha* and *pukka*.[25] *Kaccha* foods are prepared in the family kitchen by boiling or roasting, such as rice, *dal, khichri*, some breads, and vegetables, and served to the family. This food is what everyone rich or poor, modern or orthodox, eats every day in some form; it is the basic core meal of India. Meat and fish can be added for family members who are nonvegetarian.

The second category, *pukka* foods, are prepared by frying in or basting with *ghee* (clarified butter), an ingredient that is considered ritually pure. This quality gives it a certain protection from pollution. *Pukka* foods include fried breads and many sweets, provided that the first contact in cooking is made with *ghee*. These foods can be taken out of the kitchen for consumption and shared with people outside the family. *Pukka* foods are served at temples and during festivals and feasts, so that everyone can eat them.

However, all these taboos and prescriptions, while interesting to the anthropologist, are gradually disappearing in India, especially in cities and large towns. Even in the same household, the orthodox and the modern, the young and the old may go their separate ways at mealtimes.

Among Hindus, fasting is encouraged for spiritual and health reasons but the frequency and timing of fasts vary considerably. Food is also supposed to be appropriate to a person's age and stage in life. Students and widows are advised to avoid meat and any other dishes that might inflame their emotions. While not forbidden, alcohol is frowned on in many sectors of Hindu society. Hospitality has always been highly valued in Hindu society. The Vedas say that giving food was more blessed than to receiving it, and the act of feeding a guest is equivalent to serving God. The act of cooking food by using fire is considered equivalent to a sacrifice.

A basic distinction is between vegetarian and nonvegetarian, although these terms have a wide gradation of meanings. Despite the widespread belief that most Indians are vegetarians, in fact only 25–30 percent of all Indians avoid meat entirely, and this varies widely depending on region, as shown in Table 1.2. In North and Central India, some women will not eat meat, fish, or eggs, although men in the same family will do so. Indians may be vegetarians for many reasons:

- Economics: Meat is expensive, so that even most nonvegetarians eat it only on special occasions.
- Religion and Caste: All Jains are strict vegetarian, as are some Hindus who belong to the higher castes, especially Brahmins. Exceptions include Brahmins in Kashmir, who eat meat, and those in West Bengal, who eat fish.
- Groups trying to rise in the social pecking order may adopt vegetarian habits.
- Worshippers of the god Vishnu tend to be vegetarian.
- Because a vegetarian diet is associated with spiritual serenity, meat is avoided by swamis (holy men), yogis (serious practioners of yoga), and their followers.
- Some vegetarians are driven by concern over the suffering of animals and the immorality of killing them.
- Health concerns have come to the fore in recent years.

Table 1.2
Vegetarians by Indian State, 1994

State	Population who are Vegetarians (%)
Gujarat	69
Rajasthan	60
Punjab and Haryana	54
Uttar Pradesh	50
Madhya Pradesh	45
Karnataka	34
Maharashtra	30
Tamil Nadu	21
Andhra Pradesh	16
Assam	15
Kerala	5
West Bengal	5
Orissa	5
All India	Approx. 25

Source: K. S. Achaya, *Indian Food: A Historical Companion* (New Delhi: Oxford University Press, 1994), p. 57.

Cow slaughter is outlawed in all states except Kerala and West Bengal, and legislation has been proposed to make it a criminal offense nationwide. Some Hindus add chicken to the list of taboo meats, perhaps because the fowl is a scavenger and not considered clean. The same prohibition applies to pigs. Garlic and onions have many medicinal virtues but are considered be inferior foods, perhaps because they emit strong smells that overpower the subtle flavors of vegetables.

Muslims

India has the second largest Muslim population in the world. Islam has few restrictions about food and diet, derived from the Quran and the *Sunnah*, the recorded words of the prophet Mohammed, but they must be strictly observed.[26] Pork, as well as alcohol and other intoxicants, called *haram*, are forbidden to believers. Animals must be slaughtered according to the Islamic method by a person appointed to the task. They must be handled with mercy and kindness and killed swiftly with a sharp cut across the neck, severing the windpipe and the jugular veins, while saying the name of Allah (God). The blood should be drained thoroughly before the meat is eaten. This meat is called *halal*. During the ninth month of the Islamic lunar calendar, Ramadan, every Muslim observes a total fast from dawn to sunset. There are also a number of voluntary fasts that may be observed for atonement or to observe certain religious events.

Christians

Christians have few food taboos, although, like other groups, they may be sensitive to local customs. In Kerala and Goa, Catholics fast during lent.

Sikhism

Sikhism is a monotheistic religion born in the Punjab in the late fifteenth century. Between 1469 and 1708, ten spiritual leaders, called gurus, preached a message of devotion to God and universal equality. They rejected the caste system, ritualism, asceticism, and idol worship associated with Hinduism, and recognized the equality of the sexes and all religions. Sikhs have their own holy book, the *Guru Granth Sahib*, written by the gurus, which is their ultimate source of spiritual guidance and has a place of prominence in Sikh temples, called *gurdwaras*.

Sikhs are not vegetarian, but they do not advocate meat-eating either. Their sacred writings contain passages that indicate concern over the morality of killing animals for food, but say that the decision about whether to eat meat should be left to the individual. Like Hindus, Sikhs believe there is a close connection between body and mind. Guru Nanak, the founder of Sikhism, wrote "Do not take that food which affects health, causes pain or suffering to the body, or produces evil thoughts in the mind."[27] Sikhs are not supposed to smoke tobacco.

Sikh temples have a community kitchen, called a *langar*, that provides free meals to all worshippers and visitors, even those from other religions. Everyone is served the same food and no distinction is made between rich and poor. The work involved in preparing and serving the food is called *seva*, voluntary selfless service. The food served here is always vegetarian, which makes it accessible to people of all religions. Sikhs are not allowed to eat *halal* meat.

Jainism

Not surprisingly, in view of their belief about the omnipresence of life, the Jains developed extremely rigid food prescriptions—probably the most rigid in the world. The question of eating flesh does not even arise; only "absolutely innocent" foods are permitted. Prohibited foods include not only meat, fish, and eggs but thirty-two things that are believed to contain the germs of infinite life. This includes the potential for life to manifest itself, such as putrid and rotting foods; underground bulbs, roots, and tubers; and pickles more than three days old. Pulses that split into two parts (such as the chickpea) are not allowed, nor are eggplants, figs, and other fruits with many small seeds; ginger; carrots; or the tender green leaves of any vegetable. Honey is banned on the grounds that its removal from the comb means the death of bees. All water has to be boiled and reboiled every six hours and all liquids strained before drinking. Jain monks are not allowed to eat even permitted food if it has fallen from the tree or been sold at a roadside stand. Not only are Jain monks not allowed to drink liquor; they are not permitted to stay in a place where liquor is stored.

Parsis

Parsis, a very small minority centered in Bombay, have few food restrictions, but have adopted voluntarily some Hindu customs, including the prohibition on beef. They also observe certain fasts.

Jews

On the West Coast, especially in Cochin and Bombay, and in Calcutta, India once had significant Jewish communities, now depleted by immigration to Israel. Jews follow the dietary laws established in the Talmud and the rabbinical regulations called *Kashrut*, which forbid the eating of pork and require that animals be slaughtered by cutting the jugular vein and draining the blood. Orthodox Jews, and observant Jews of other denominations, do not eat meat and dairy products at the same meal and prepare them using separate dishes and pots.

NOTES

1. For an excellent discussion of prehistory, see K. T. Achaya, *Indian Food: A Historical Companion* (New Delhi: Oxford University Press, 1994), pp. 5–10, and K. T. Achaya, *A Historical Dictionary of Indian Food* (New Delhi: Oxford University Press, 1998), pp. 166–167.

2. Achaya, *Indian Food: A Historical Companion*, pp. 41–44.

3. Stanley Wolpert, *A New History of India*, 6th ed. (New York: Oxford University Press, 2000), p. 11.

4. Romila Thapar, *Early India: From the Origins to AD 1300* (Berkeley: University of California Press, 2002), pp. 106–7.

5. The word *Aryan* has negative connotations because of its association with Nazism and Adolf Hitler, who modified the swastika, an ancient Hindu symbol, to serve as the Nazi party symbol. A prominent Indian historian writes, "Aryan is in fact a linguistic term indicating a speech-group of Indo-European origin, and is not an ethnic term. To refer to the coming of the Aryans is therefore inaccurate. However, this inaccuracy has become so current in historical studies of early India that it would sound unduly pedantic to refer to the Aryans by their ethnic name." Romila Thapar, *A History of India*, vol. 1 (Baltimore: Penguin Books, 1966), p. 27.

6. Thapar, *History of India*, p. 37.

7. Wolpert, *New History of India*, pp. 42–43.

8. Om Prakash, *Food and Drinks in Ancient India* (New Delhi: Munshiram Manoharlal, 1961), p. 34. This dissertation is a thorough study of Indian foods from prehistoric times to A.D. 1200 based on archaeological evidence and Sanskrit texts.

9. Sidney W. Mintz and Daniela Schlettwein-Gsell, "Food Patterns in Agrarian Societies: The Core-Fringe-Legume Hypothesis," *Gastronomica* 1, no. 3 (Summer 2001): 40–53.

10. Achaya, *Indian Food*, p. 38. In his novel *Brave New World*, Aldous Huxley used the term *soma* to describe a narcotic that people used to control and mellow their feelings.

11. See, for example, Dwijendra Narayan Jha, *Holy Cow: Beef in Indian Dietary Traditions* (New Delhi: Verso Books, 2002). The publication of this scholarly book by a leading historian set off a storm of protest among religious Hindus for whom cow protection and avoidance of beef are fundamental marks of Hindu identity. A spokesman for the World Hindu Council called it "sheer blasphemy," and the book was banned by one Indian court. For an account of this controversy, see Emily Eakin, "Holy Cow a Myth? An Indian Finds the Kick Is Real," *New York Times,* 17 August, 2002, A13, A15.

12. Wolpert, *New History,* p. 54.

13. Achaya, *Indian Food,* p. 154.

14. Ibid., pp. 118–122, 125–127.

15. Abul Fazl Allami, *The A'In-I Akbari,* vol. 1, trans. H. Blochmann (New Delhi: Atlantic Publishers, 1989), p. 68.

16. The recipe for *khichri* given by Abul Fazl (p. 63) calls for equal parts of rice, lentils, and *ghee*—not exactly an austere dish. The emperors Jahangir and Aurangzeb also liked *khichri,* and the cooks of the court outdid each other to improve the dish by adding meat, spices, butter, cream, nuts, and other flavorings. *Khichri* was prepared in vast quantities for the Mughal armies on the move.

17. For an account of this period, see William Dalrymple, *White Mughals* (London: Flamingo, 2002).

18. David Burton, *The Raj at Table* (London: Faber and Faber, 1993), pp. 3–4.

19. Wolpert, *New History,* p. 237.

20. Emma Roberts, *Scenes and Characteristics of Hindoostan, with sketches of Anglo-Indian Society,* 2 vols., 2nd ed. (London, 1837), 1:75, quoted in Dalrymple, *White Mughals,* 52.

21. Felipe Fernandez-Armesto, *Near a Thousand Tables: A History of Food* (New York: The Free Press, 2002), p. 140.

22. Madhur Jaffrey, quoted in Burton, *Raj at Table,* p. 73.

23. R.S. Khare, *The Hindu Hearth and Home* (New Delhi: Vikas Publishing House, 1976), p. 116.

24. Jack Goody, *Cooking, Cuisine and Class: A Study in Comparative Sociology* (Cambridge: Cambridge University Press, 1996), p. 124.

25. See Khare, *Hindu Hearth and Home,* pp. 61–65, and Achaya, *Indian Food,* pp. 62–63, for a discussion of these concepts.

26. For a survey of Islamic food practices and beliefs, see Mohammad Mazahar Hussaini, *Islamic Dietary Concepts and Practice* (Bedford Park, Ill.: The Islamic Food and Nutrition Council of America, 1993).

27. Quoted on the Web site http://allaboutsikhs.com/mansukh/076/htm.

2

Major Foods and Ingredients

India is a predominantly agricultural country, and the ingredients used in Indian cooking were produced and consumed locally, giving rise to distinctive regional cuisines. Prior to the construction of railways in the nineteenth century, goods were moved from village to village by bullock carts. Even today, most fruits and vegetables are produced in farms surrounding a city or town and sold in open-air markets. However, in India, as in the rest of the world, the advent of modern methods of refrigeration and transportation, and the development of large-scale agriculture, are promoting greater homogeneity. A few decades ago many regions of India had their own varieties of rice; today only a few varieties are available on the marketplace. The consumption of processed and frozen food is also on the rise in cities.

CEREALS

Cereals, the seeds of plants, have played a crucial role in human nutrition. Around ten thousand years ago people began to selectively propagate food crops, beginning with grains and legumes found growing wild. Cereals have been described as "compact, desiccated packages that contain a plant's embryonic offspring, together with enough food for them to develop their roots and leaves and become self-sufficient."[1] They are a concentrated source of protein as well as carbohydrates or fats that, unlike other foods, can be easily stored for long periods of time.

Cereals are still the essential food of most of humanity. In India and China they provide around 70 percent of the population's caloric intake,

Spice and vegetable market, Kolkata. Photo © TRIP/H. Rogers.

considerably more than in the developed Western countries, where meat and dairy consumption is much higher. However, whereas meat, milk, and other animal products provide all the amino acids essential for life, cereals per se do not. People also need vitamins, iron, and calcium to thrive and survive. Over the millennia, societies learned to combine different grains, legumes, and green vegetables in such a way as to provide all the nutrients necessary for health and life.[2]

Traditionally, the Indian subcontinent has been divided into two regions on the basis of whether the inhabitants' basic dietary staple was wheat or rice. Rice is the mainstay in the South and East, whereas wheat is the staple in the North. In western India, so-called coarse grains, such as barley, millet, and sorghum, were eaten, but are gradually being supplanted by wheat. Indian wheat production rose more than tenfold between 1950 and 2000, thanks to an increase in the area under cultivation, expanded irrigation, greater use of fertilizer, and the development of high-yielding varieties.[3]

Rice

Rice (*chawal*), a staple food for around half the world's population, was a wild grass first cultivated in the foothills of the eastern Himalayas and in Southeast Asia. As rice cultivation spread across the subcontinent, it became the dominant cereal, displacing barley in the North and millet elsewhere.

Of the 100,000 or so varieties of rice, only around 8,000 are grown for food. Four kinds are grown in India: dry or upland rice, cultivated mainly on hillsides; rain-fed rice, which grows in shallow water; irrigated rice grown in shallow water fed from storage and drainage systems; and deepwater rice planted in areas that are flooded. Around one-third of India's rice crop is rain-fed and half is irrigated. Indian rice production has increased fourfold over the 1950–2000 period, and today the country is a net exporter of both rice and wheat.

The leading rice-producing states are West Bengal and Assam in the East, Punjab and Uttar Pradesh in the North, and Andhra Pradesh in the South. Two or three main crops are grown a year, depending on the region. Many festivals are associated with the sowing, transplanting, and harvesting of rice, including Pongal in Tamil Nadu and Onam in Kerala. Milling, either by pounding at home or in rice mills, removes the coarse outer layer of bran and germ. About half of India's rice crop is parboiled by soaking the unmilled rice in water, then steaming and drying it. Parboiling gives greater resistance to insects and fungus, and enhances the retention of nutrients, especially B vitamins.

Indians prefer varieties of rice (called *indica*) that have long slender grains; when cooked, each grain should be rather dry and separate. This contrasts with the short-grained, moist, sticky variety (*japonica*) favored by Chinese and Japanese. Ancient Indian texts refer to hundreds of varieties of rice, but today only a few are available commercially. In North India and Pakistan, the most popular rice is *basmati*, which has a slightly nutty fragrance and is aged six months to a year to enhance its flavor. The finest Indian *basmati* comes from Dehra Dun in the state of Uttar Pradesh. *Patna* rice is a slightly lower-grade rice grown in Bihar. *Gobindavog*, a rice grown in the Northeast, is darker in color and has smaller grains than *basmati*. In rural areas, people eat a red rice that is coarser in texture but richer in nutrients. Residents of Tamil Nadu and Kerala eat a parboiled red rice called *rosematta*, which has a slightly smoky flavor.

Plain, boiled rice is the dietary staple in West Bengal, Assam, Kashmir, South India, and coastal regions. Puffed rice, called *moori* or *poha*, is made by drying rice grains, then roasting them over a hot fire. It is eaten with sugar as a breakfast dish in Bengal or mixed with spices and vegetables to make a popular Bombay snack called *bhelpuri*. In South India, *dosas*, *idlis*, *appams*, and other distinctive breads are made from a batter of ground, lightly fermented rice and lentils. *Pulaos* and *biryanis* are richly spiced blends of rice with meat, vegetables, or seafood, served on special occasions in North India, Pakistan, and Hyderabad. Pudding-like desserts made from rice, boiled milk, sugar, and spices include *kheer* in North India, *payesh* in Bengal, and *payasam* in the South.

Wheat

Wheat (in Hindi *genhu*) is a grass that was the staple of the Indus Valley civilization, where it was ground into flour and made into bread. The Aryans probably learned the cultivation of wheat after they arrived in India. Wheat is planted in October–December and harvested in the spring. The states of Uttar Pradesh, Punjab, and Haryana produce more than half of the country's wheat.

Wheat contains more protein than rice or other cereals (although it is low in lysine, which is abundant in beans and pulses) and it also contains more gluten, which gives bread its elastic texture. The wheat kernel contains three parts: the endosperm, the germ, and the bran. The object of milling is to separate the endosperm, which is the source of white flour. Wholemeal flour *(atta)*, light-brown in color, contains the entire seed except part of the bran, and has more fiber. This is the most common flour used to make Indian bread.

Table 2.1 lists some of the breads eaten on the subcontinent. Traditionally bread is made fresh for every meal. In North India the most popular

Winnowing wheat, Rajasthan. Photo © TRIP/H. Rogers.

Table 2.1
Typical Indian Breads

Name of Bread	Region	Ingredients in dough	Method of cooking	Comments
Wheat Breads				
Chapati or Roti	Everywhere	Atta [1]	Dry roasted, may be held with tongs over an open flame	Saucer-shaped; puffs up to round ball, then deflates and flattens.
Phulka	North India	Atta	Dry roasted, may be held with tongs over an open flame	Slightly smaller chapati
Paratha	North India	Atta, ghee	Fried in a little ghee on a griddle	May be round, square or triangular. Ghee is added during rolling to create layered, flaky texture.
Puri	North and Central India	Atta or atta/white flour mixed	Deep-fried (preferably in ghee)	Round, 4–5" in diameter, puffs up, then flattens.
Dal puri	North and Central India	White flour, moong dal	Fried on tawa	Dough is stuffed with moong dal.
Bhatura, Batora	Punjab, North India	White flour, semolina, sugar, yogurt, baking powder	Deep-fried	Semi-leavened. Round, slightly puffy. Usually served with chickpeas.
Khameeri	North India	Atta and white flour, milk, ghee, yeast, sugar, aniseed, yogurt	Roasted in tandoor or deep-fried	Leavened, sweetened bread.
Lucchi	West Bengal, Assam	White flour, ghee	Deep-fried	Puffs up, then deflates.
Naan or Tandoori roti	North India	Atta or white flour, ghee, sometimes baking powder, eggs, yogurt, milk, sugar	Baked on the wall of tandoor	Slightly leavened. Round or cylindrical-shaped. Rather thick, slightly puffy in places. Served sprinkled with poppy seeds and nigella.

(Continued)

Table 2.1
Typical Indian Breads (Continued)

Name of Bread	Region	Ingredients in dough	Method of cooking	Comments
Bakarkhani	Hyderabad, Bengal	White flour, milk, sugar, yeast, *ghee*	Baked	Small, layered, crispy bread.
Missi roti	Punjab, North India, Rajasthan	*Atta* and chickpea flour, onion, *ghee*, spices, fenugreek leaves	Cooked on hot *tawa*, then roasted over fire	Served with fresh butter and yogurt.
Rumali roti ("Handkerchief bread")	North India	White flour, *ghee*	Cooked on griddle in *ghee*	Many-layered bread. In the past, used to wipe hands and then discarded.
Kulcha	Hyderabad	*Atta*, yeast, milk, yogurt, *ghee*	Baked in *tandoor*	Semi-fermented, circular or square shape.
Sheermal	North India, Hyderabad	White flour, *ghee*, milk, sugar, egg	Baked	After baking, bread is moistened with milk flavored with cardamom and saffron.
Double roti	Everywhere	White flour	Oven	Name for Western-style bread.
Bhakri/ Dhebra	Gujarat	Wheat flour, *ghee* roasted cumin or carom seeds	Roasted or sautéed on tawa	Thicker than *chapati*, biscuit-like texture.
Thepla	Gujarat	Wheat flour, yogurt, spices	Dry roasted or sautéed in a little *ghee*	Dough can be made with fenugreek leaves or grated white pumpkin.
Pao	Goa	White flour	Oven	Elastic bun.
Rava idlis	South India	Semolina (*rawa*), yogurt, bicarbonate of soda	Steamed	Carrots, peas, onions, and cashew nuts can be added to the batter.

Other Grains

Makki ki roti	**Punjab, Haryana**	Corn flour	Dry roasted or sautéed in a little *ghee*	Eaten with mustard greens and spinach.
Phevras	Rajasthan	Millet	Dry roasted, then placed on live coals	Served with *ghee*.
Vedhami	**Gujarat**	Chickpea flour, sugar	Dry roasted	Rolled in *atta*.
Batti	Rajasthan	*Atta*, baking powder	Roasted in oven, then in live coals	Round, hard ball, broken open and served with melted *ghee*.
Rotla	**Western India**	Millet or milo flour	Slowly roasted on *tawa*, then in coal fire	A thick bread eaten in rural areas.

Rice and Lentils

Idli	**South India**	Fermented *urad dal* and ground rice	Steamed	Disk-shaped, spongy texture. May be made with other grains (e.g., semolina) and with spices.
Dosas	**South India**	Fermented *urad dal* and ground rice	Lightly fried, like a crepe	Very thin and crisp. May be stuffed with vegetables (*masala dosa*).
Amboli	**South India**	Rice flour, coconut milk, oil, spices	Poured from a height onto a hot griddle	Softer than a *dosa* with a lacy texture.
Appam	**Kerala and Tamil Nadu**	Rice flour and yeast or palm liquor	Cooked in special concave pan	Spongy center, crispy edges. Eaten as breakfast food in Tamil Nadu; with meat or vegetable stews in Kerala.

(Continued)

43

Table 2.1
Typical Indian Breads (Continued)

Name of Bread	Region	Ingredients in dough	Method of cooking	Comments
Adai	Tamil Nadu	Rice, *moong*, *urad*, and *tur dals*, fenugreek seeds, chilies, ginger	Cooked in oil on concave griddle; oil is sprinkled on top during cooking	Crispy and golden brown on both sides; hole in middle.
Chokna ni rotli	Western India, Parsees	Fine rice flour, salt	Dry roasted	Made be made with milk or toddy instead of water.
Moong dal idlis	South India	*Moong dal*, carrots, cashew nuts, coconut, soda bicarb	Steamed	
Kanchipuram idlis	South India	Rice and *urad dal*, yogurt, *chana dal*, turmeric, *ghee*, fenugreek leaves	Steamed in *idli* maker lined with banana or turmeric leaves	
Mysore idlis	Karnataka	Boiled rice, *urad dal*, fenugreek seeds	Steamed in baskets	
Sanna	Goa	Rice, yeast or toddy, grated coconut	Steamed in small plates stacked on each other	Easter specialty.
Apa de Arroz (Rice chapati)	Goa	Rice, wheat flour, coconut, chilies, coriander leaves	Sautéed in a little oil	
Papads/papars or pappadams	Originally from South India but eaten all over India	Lentils, esp. *urad dal*. May be plain or seasoned with peppers, chilis, garlic, etc.	Deep fried or baked	Become crisp and hard in seconds. Popular snack or accompaniment to meals.

[1]*Atta* is a soft whole wheat flour that has much of the bran and husk left in.

Preparing *poori*, Kolkata. Photo © TRIP/H. Rogers.

breads are *chapatis*, sometimes called *roti* (which is also used as a generic word for "bread"), made from a dough of wheat flour and water. These are thin soft disks, about six inches in diameter, that puff up slightly when cooked on a hot cast-iron pan using little or no fat. A more upscale bread, *paratha*, is made by rolling and oiling the dough several times and then making a flat circle that is fried in a little oil or *ghee*. *Parathas* may be filled with potatoes, onions, and other vegetables. If the disks are deep-fried, they puff up into round spheres called *puris*. The version preferred by Bengalis, called *lucchis*, are made from white refined flour.

In North India and Pakistan, bread is also baked in large clay ovens called *tandoors*, used for roasting meat. A large round or oblong-shaped bread made from leavened white flour, called *naan*, has a soft center and crisp exterior. A leavened dough that includes rosewater, milk, and *ghee* is made into a bread called *sheermal* that is associated with Muslim cuisine. After baking, the bread is soaked in milk and saffron. Western-style breads leavened with yeast are sometimes called "double breads." They are bought from commercial bakeries and toasted for breakfast.

Halim (*harissa* in some Arab countries) is a thick porridge-like stew of whole and cracked wheat, barley, several other grains, lentils, spices, and meat. The inside of the wheat kernel is processed into small grains to make semolina, which is used in *uppuma*, a breakfast porridge eaten in the

South. Wheat flour is also made into vermicelli (a pasta) that are added to North Indian rice puddings.

Other Grains

The world's oldest cultivated cereal, barley (in Hindi *jaun*) was a wild grass domesticated and cultivated in the Middle East, Asia Minor, and Central Asia as early as the sixth millennium B.C. The second staple of the Indus Valley Civilization, it is the only cereal mentioned in the oldest Indian texts. Today, barley is a minor cereal crop, grown and consumed mainly in the western part of India.

Other coarse grains grown in India, mainly by small farmers in areas of low rainfall, are sorghum (*bajra*) and millet (*ragi*). Flour from these grains is used by people living in the desert areas of Rajasthan and Gujarat to make *rotla, bhakri, thepla,* and other distinctive breads.

The production and consumption of corn, originally brought from the New World, is increasing in northern and western India, where it has been thoroughly assimilated into the cuisine. In the Punjab, corn flour is used to make a tortilla-like bread called *makkai roti*. In Rajasthan, a thick bread is made from whole wheat flour and corn mixed with onions, garlic, chilies, and coriander leaves. Corn kernels are used regularly in western India stews. Corn-on-the-cob roasted over hot coals and slathered with butter is a popular streetside snack.

Legumes

Legumes comprise lentils, peas, chickpeas, and beans. Their seeds contain twice as much protein as grains and are rich in iron and B vitamins. The oldest cultivated legume is the lentil. In northern India, lentils are grown as a winter crop, along with wheat and barley, and are often planted in the same fields. Much of the acreage is devoted to the chickpea or garbanzo bean, also called Bengal gram or *chole* in Hindi, the country's most important legume.

In both Hindi and English, the word *dal* is used to describe all dried peas, beans, and lentils, as well as the boiled dish that is made from them. Most Indians (as well as Pakistanis, Bengalis, and Nepalis) eat *dal* every day, although they vary widely in flavor, ingredients, and consistency. In fact, *dal* and *roti*—dal and bread—is a metaphor for a person's daily fare, like meat and potatoes in the Anglo-Saxon world.

More than fifty kinds of *dals* are on the market, and they are sold skinned and unskinned, split and whole. Most varieties must be soaked in water for several hours to soften, and then they are cooked for an hour or two, the exact time depending on the variety. After boiling, salt is added plus a flavoring, or tempering, which is made by lightly frying spices, garlic, onions, green chilies, and other ingredients in *ghee*, then folding them into the boiled *dal*.

Masur dal, also called red or Egyptian lentils, are small, salmon-colored disks that cook very quickly and are mainly used by Bengalis. *Channa dal* is bright yellow and is often cooked with meat or vegetables. It is also used to make sweet dishes. *Toor dal*, also called yellow lentils, *toovar dal*, or *arhar dal*, is pale yellow and sometimes rubbed with oil to preserve it. *Urad dal*, black gram or black lentil, is either sold whole with a gray-black skin or split and skinless, in which case it is white. Ground, lightly fermented *urad dal* and rice are combined to make the batter for many South Indian breads. *Mung* or *moong*, a round green lentil, is used whole to make thick *dals* and split to prepare *khichri*. Sprouted *moong* beans may be used in salads.

Channa, also called *kabuli channa*, Bengal gram, chickpea, or garbanzo, is a large, spherical, tan-colored pea that is soaked overnight to remove the skin and then boiled whole for use in stews, salads, and pulaos. A dough made from water and chickpea flour *(besan)* is standard for fried snacks. Other legumes eaten in India, especially in the Punjab, are green peas *(mattar dal)*, kidney beans *(rajma)*, pink beans *(choti rajma)*, and black-eyed peas *(lobhia)*.

Nuts

Rich in fats, protein, and B vitamins, nuts are one of the most concentrated foods available and an important part of a vegetarian diet. With the exception of the betel nut and *charoli (chironji)*, most of the nuts cultivated in India were originally brought from elsewhere: cashews and peanuts from the New World and almonds, pistachios, and walnuts from neighboring Iran and Central Asia. Almonds *(badam)*, grown mainly in Kashmir, may be ground to a paste for stews or fried whole or sliced as a garnish for rice and meat dishes and desserts.

Betel nuts *(supari)*, the fruit of the areca palm, are hard, round, brown nuts that are dried in the sun. They contain a stimulating alkaloid and tannins, which give them a slightly astringent flavor. They are thinly sliced and mixed with sugar and spices to make *supari*, which is chewed after meals as a breath freshener and aid to digestion. Betel nuts and the leaves of a climbing vine also called betel (although botanically they are not related) are used to make the quintessential Indian snack *paan*. It is usually purchased from a professional, whose stand is a familiar sight along Indian streets and roads. First he trims a betel leaf to a three-by-five-inch rectangle, then adds a filling made of sliced or ground betel nut plus spices such as cloves and cardamoms; *chuna,* a paste of slaked lime (calcium oxide); a sweet, red paste from the sap of a tree; dried fruits; and sometimes tobacco. He folds all this into a neat little package that the customer places in the side of his mouth and chews until it disappears. *Paan* has a mildly stimulating effect that some people believe is addictive.

Another indigenous Indian nut is the *charoli,* also called *chironji,* the seed of a bush that grows in the Northwest. It looks like a pine nut and has a rich flavor and slightly oily texture. Charolis are added whole to sweet dishes and ground into powders for use in sauces and kormas.

Grown in Goa and Kerala, whole or chopped cashews (*kaju*) are an ingredient in many South Indian vegetable dishes. In North India, they may be fried until golden and added as a garnish to rice. Salted and spiced cashews are a common component of snacks. Goans make a strong liquor called *fenni* from cashew nuts. Peanuts (*moongphal*) are a legume that often is used in Gujarati and Maharastrian dishes. Pistachio nuts (*pista*) are a garnish for North Indian rice and meat dishes and add color and flavor to North Indian sweets. Walnuts (*akhrot*) are grown and eaten mainly in Kashmir.

DAIRY PRODUCTS

There is probably no other country in the world where milk and its products are more important than India. Unlike the majority of people in the world, 75 percent of North Indians produce an enzyme (lactase) that enables them to digest lactose, the main sugar in milk. (Perhaps they inherited this trait from their cow-raising Aryan ancestors, since people of northern European origin are the only other major ethnic group to have this enzyme). In South India, by contrast, 70 percent of people are lactose-intolerant. They consume dairy products in the form of yogurt, which loses most of its lactose in the fermentation process. In Bengal, Bihar, and Uttar Pradesh, some people drink goat milk, since is it more easily digested. In high mountainous regions, such as Ladakh and Tibet, people drink goat, sheep, and yak milk and make cheese and butter from it.

Dairy products provide an important source of protein, especially when meat is absent from a diet. Milk is the main drink in Punjab and Haryana, drunk by itself or as a major component of the tea-based hot drink called chai. Slowly boiling down cow or buffalo milk produces *khoa,* a thick paste that is mixed with sugar, *ghee,* and flavorings to make sweet dishes, especially in northern India. Boiling milk can also be separated with a souring agent to produce curds, or *chhana,* the basic ingredient in many Bengali sweets. This procedure may have been learned from the Portuguese, who manufactured cheese at their settlements in Bengal in the seventeenth century. Another Portuguese legacy are India's only indigenous Western-style cheeses, Dacca, Bandal, and Surti, still produced only in West Bengal and Bangladesh.

Milk solids are pressed under a weight and cut into cubes called *paneer,* an important ingredient in vegetarian cuisine. Yogurt (called curd in Indian English; *dahi* in Hindi) is produced by seeding boiled fresh milk with a starter (either a small amount from a previous batch or the twig of certain plants) and putting it in a warm place to set overnight. Yogurt is a frequent accompaniment to a North Indian meal, served either plain or as part of a salad. South Indians always end a meal with yogurt, sometimes mixed with rice. A blend of yogurt and spices is a common North Indian marinade for meat dishes, such as tandoori chicken and korma. *Lassi* is a popular drink made from yogurt, water, and fruit. Buttermilk, the liquid formed after yogurt is churned and butter removed, is another popular Indian beverage, especially in the summer.

Cream is churned to produce butter. Because butter is perishable, it is usually transformed into clarified butter, called *ghee* or *ulsi ghee,* by cooking it over low heat until all the water has evaporated, and filtering the product to remove sediment. Clarified butter can last a year or longer without refrigeration, provided it does not come into contact with air. Another advantage is that it does not burn easily when used for cooking. *Ghee* is the preferred cooking medium in India for those who can afford it (and are not overly concerned about cholesterol). It is added to the dough of some breads, sprinkled on vegetables and baked bread, and stirred into *dals. Vanaspati ghee* is a vegetable shortening made from highly saturated oils such as coconut and rapeseed that are hydrogenized and processed to look, smell, and taste like natural *ghee. Ghee* used to be made at home but today most people buy it ready-made.

Milk and *ghee* are considered very pure and play a role in Hindu religious rituals; for example, statues of the deities are anointed with milk and *ghee.* In ayurveda, the traditional Hindu system of medicine, milk is classified as a *sattvic* food, strengthening and calming and especially beneficial to children, the elderly, and the convalescent. For Muslims, it is one of the foods taken to break the Ramadan fast.

COOKING OILS

Peanut oil *(moongfalli ka tel)* is widely used in central and northern India. In Bengal, mustard oil *(sarson ka tel)*, which has a very pungent aroma, is used for cooking and pickling. (In western India, mustard oil is rubbed into the scalp to promote hair growth.) Sesame or gingelly oil *(til ka tel)* was once a popular medium, but today it is used mainly in South-west India. The Indian version is made from raw seeds, unlike the Chinese version where the seeds are roasted.

Coconut oil *(nariyal ka tel)*, made from the dried meat of coconuts, used to be the dominant cooking medium in Kerala. Because it is very high in saturated fats and triglycerides, health-conscious people are substituting other oils. It too is massaged into hair to encourage shine and growth. Sunflower seed oil and corn oil are becoming increasingly popular in India as a substitute for traditional oils.

SPICES, HERBS, AND OTHER SEASONINGS

The intensive use of spices and seasonings is the most distinctive feature of Indian cuisine. *Spice* is a broad term covering many different parts of a plant: dried berries (mace), bark (cinnamon), seeds (cumin, cardamom, coriander), roots, underground roots or stems called rhizomes (ginger), leaves (bay leaves), and flower buds (cloves). The words *spicy* and *hot* are sometimes used interchangeably, although incorrectly. Hotness, that is, a burning sensation in the mouth, is produced by black pepper and chilies. The pungency of pepper is due to the volatile oil piperine and resin, which increase the flow of saliva and gastric juices. Chilies' hotness is produced by capsaicin, an alkaloid found mainly in the membranes lining the pod. In India, the degree of hotness of a dish is largely a matter of individual and regional preference. Generally speaking, food in South India tends to be hotter than that in the North, although Pakistani food can also be quite mouth-searing.

The purpose of spices is to add flavor, texture, and body to a dish. They also provide flavor at low cost for poor people whose diet is otherwise bland and unvarying. Over the years many nongastronomical explanations have been offered for the intensive use of spices in India, Mexico, and other hot countries—and most them are myths. Hot spices do not, for example, induce enough perspiration to cool people down, as some people claim. Nor do they mask the flavor of tainted meat, since those who eat such food would probably fall ill and die. Spices do provide nutrients such as vitamins A and C, but in very small amounts.

The latest theory, backed by scientific evidence, is that spices contain powerful antibiotic chemicals that can kill or suppress the dozens of kinds of bacteria and fungi that spoil foods, including E. coli. The most potent are garlic, onion, allspice, cinnamon, cumin, cloves, and chilies. The antibiotic effects are even more potent when spices such as chilies, onions, garlic, and cumin are combined with each other.[4]

In preparing simple dishes, cooks may use just two or three spices, whereas more complex meat dishes can be prepared with twenty or more. Spices may be added once, twice, even three times during the cooking process. They may be ground into a powder, sometimes called a *masala*, which means mixture. Spices can also be used whole, or ground with water, chilies and onions, yogurt, or tomatoes to make a paste. They are generally dry-roasted or slightly fried first to intensify their flavor.

What spices are used depends on the kind of dish, the region, and a household's or even an individual eater's preferences. Generally, spices are simplest for South Indian vegetarian dishes and more complex for North Indian meat preparations. Table 2.2 lists some examples of spice mixtures by regional cuisine.

Garam masala, which means "warm mixture," is a highly aromatic, powdered mixture that in North India is sprinkled on top of dishes that have almost finished cooking. While there are many different variations, a typical *garam masala* includes coriander seeds, cumin seeds, cardamom, cloves, and cinnamon.

In ayurvedic medicine, spices have many medicinal uses, some of which are being confirmed by modern science. Ginger, for example, is a nearly universal remedy used to treat such conditions as respiratory congestion, cough, and loss of appetite. Ginger compounds have been shown to have anti-inflammatory properties. Turmeric paste is a household antiseptic for minor burns and wounds and has high concentrations of a potent antioxidant. Cumin is prescribed for indigestion.

The following are the most common spices used in Indian cuisine:

Ajowain (sometimes called carom seed or lovage; Hindi *ajwain*) is a tiny gray seed related to dill and cumin that has a slightly bitter flavor. It is popular in Gujarat.

Aniseed (*saunf*) are small oval seeds that impart a licorice flavor to vegetables, lentils, and meat curries. Either alone or mixed with nuts and spices, it is part of after-dinner mouth fresheners.

Table 2.2
Sampling of Typical Spice and Flavorings by Region and Dish

Region	Kind of dish	Cooking medium	Commonly used spices
North India, Pakistan, Hyderabad	Meat, rice dishes	Ghee, vegetable oil	Ginger, garlic, onions, red chilies, coriander seeds and leaves, saffron, black pepper, asafetida, black cumin, cumin, cardamom, cloves, cinnamon, poppy seeds, turmeric powder, chili powder, paprika, nutmeg, mace
Punjab	Tandoor	Roasted	Cumin, coriander, cinnamon, cloves, chili powder, ginger, turmeric, garlic, mace, red dye
Bengal	Fish, vegetables	Vegetable oil, mustard oil	Cumin, black mustard seeds, nigella, fennel, fenugreek, green and red chilies
Kerala	Fish, vegetables, meat	Coconut oil, gingelly oil	Grated coconut, curry leaves, green and red chilies, turmeric, cumin, garlic, onions, mustard seed, coriander, fenugreek, urad dal, tamarind
Tamil Nadu, Karnataka	Vegetable dishes, dals	Vegetable oil, sesame oil	Coriander, cumin, black peppercorn, mustard seeds, fenugreek, urad dal, tamarind, red chilies, asafetida
Gujarat	Vegetable, dals, snacks	Vegetable oil	Turmeric, cumin, black pepper, green and red chilies, black mustard seeds, asafetida, sesame seeds, coriander, ajowain, ginger, jaggery, khokum
Goa	Meat, fish, vegetables	Vegetable oil, coconut oil	Vinegar, black peppercorns, green cardamom, cloves, green and red chilies, cumin, garlic, ginger, turmeric, coconut
Rajasthan	Vegetables, dals	Vegetable oil, sesame oil	Mango powder, turmeric, cumin, asafetida, curry leaves, ginger, green and red chilies, cardamom, cloves

Kashmir	Meat, rice dishes	Mustard oil, vegetable oil	Kashmiri chilies, saffron, green and brown cardamom, ginger, fennel, cumin, garlic or asafetida, cinnamon, cloves, nutmeg, mace, aniseed, black pepper, pomegranate seeds
Parsi	Meat, rice, vegetables	Any	Cinnamon, cloves, white cardamom, black pepper, cumin seed
Maharashtra	Vegetables, meat, fish	Peanut oil	Coriander seeds, poppy seeds, coconut, cumin, sesame, red chilies, turmeric, cloves, black pepper, cardamom

Asafetida (hing) is the dried resin of the rhizomes of giant fennels. The Latin name means "stinking gum" because of its rather offensive odor. It is valued for its digestive properties and truffle-like flavor. *Hing* is sold as a powder or in lumps, which are crushed or ground at home. A pinch is added to dals and vegetable dishes, especially in South India. Orthodox Hindus and Jains use *hing* as a substitute for garlic.

Basil or **holy basil (tulsi),** although often grown in pots in Indian homes, is rarely used in cooking. Considered one of the most sacred plants, it is associated with the Hindu god Vishnu and used in ceremonies and rituals.

Bay leaf (tej patta) comes from an evergreen tree that grows in the mountains. Bay leaves are generally sold dry and have a sweet, woody aroma. They are fried in oil and added to North Indian meat and rice dishes.

Caraway (siya jeera) seeds have a warm, slightly bitter flavor and are used either whole or ground as a powder, mainly in North Indian meat dishes or to flavor bread.

Cardamoms (illiachi), called the queen of spices, are the dried fruit of a member of the ginger family. A spice catalog gives an evocative description of its flavor: "It defies the boundaries of normal sensory comparisons. It is compellingly strong, yet delicate; sweet, yet powerful; with an almost eucalyptus freshness."[5]

There are two kinds of cardamom: green and black. Green cardamoms, which are picked just before ripe and then dried, are small, light-green pods containing little black seeds. Black cardamoms are large, dark-brown, wrinkled pods with a somewhat stronger flavor. The whole or slightly crushed pods of either green or black cardamoms are added to *biryanis* and other North Indian meat and rice dishes. (The cardamoms should be removed before eating.) When ground, skin and all, cardamoms are a component of *garam masala*. Green cardamoms are also added to Indian sweets and rice puddings, breads, and tea and coffee.

Cardamom pods.

Cassia *(jungli dalchini)*, also called Chinese cinnamon, is the bark of a laurel tree that grows in China, Burma, and Northeast India. It looks and smells like cinnamon (and is sometimes sold as cinnamon) but is much harder and has a woody flavor.

Chilies *(mirch)* or **chili peppers** originated in South and Central America and were brought to India by the Portuguese in the early sixteenth century. They were rapidly assimilated into Indian cuisine as a substitute for a local spice, long pepper. Chilies are such an integral part of Indian cuisine that it is hard to imagine that they are a transplant. As one noted food writer puts it, "Indian food without chilies is like summer without sunshine."[6]

Today India is the world's largest producer of chilies, a fruit belonging to the capsaicin family. There are many varieties (e.g., Kashmiri, Tinnevelly, Goan) that vary in size, shape, color, flavor, and piquancy, ranging from relatively mild to extremely hot. Local varieties impart quite different flavors to regional dishes; the hottest varieties tend to be South Indian.

In India, chilies are used both in their green fresh form and in dried form (*sabat lal mirch*), which concentrates their flavor. Broken, dried, red chilies are frequently used in South Indian dishes. Before using, they may be soaked, which softens the skin and reduces their hotness, and then ground into a paste or powder.

Cinnamon *(dalchini)* is the inner bark of an evergreen that grows in Kerala and Sri Lanka. The bark is rolled, dried, and sold in dark brown sticks. Cinnamon has a warm, sweet, exotic flavor. Whole or ground, it is an essential ingredient in *garam masala* and used to flavor North Indian meat and rice dishes and desserts.

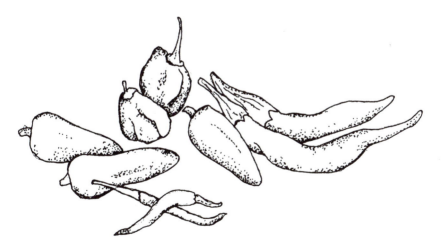

Chilies.

Cumin.

Cloves *(laung)* are the dried flower buds of an evergreen native to Indonesia. They have a sharp warm flavor that can numb one's mouth. Whole cloves are added to North Indian rice and meat dishes and sweets.

Coriander seeds *(dhania)* are the small round gray-brown seeds of an aromatic herb known in the United States as cilantro or Chinese parsley, and one of the most widely used spices in India. They have a sweet, heady aroma and are usually roasted, then crushed or powdered before using. The lacy leaves and stems add a fresh, gingery taste to curries, dals, and salads.

Cumin seeds *(zeera, jeera)* are the little grayish-brown seeds of a herb belonging to the coriander family. They have a slightly bitter flavor and are widely used for cooking and medicinal purposes. Black cumin *(kala jeera)* are darker in color and have a more refined, complex flavor.

Curry leaves *(kari patta)* are the small, dark-green leaves of a shrub that grows wild throughout India and is cultivated in Tamil Nadu and Karnataka. They are important in South Indian cuisine, where they may be fried with spices and added at the end of the cooking process or ground with coconut and spices to make a chutney.

Fennel *(saunf)* is the dried seed of a dill-like plant that grows in North India. Fennel seeds look and taste like anise seeds and add a slight pungency to meat dishes. Roasted fennel seeds are a popular after-dinner mouth freshener.

Fenugreek *(methi)* are very hard, rectangular, dark yellow seeds with a slightly bitter flavor. The seeds are sold whole, crushed, or powdered. The dried stalks and leaves *(kasuri methi)* are used as a flavoring or are eaten as a vegetable. Whole fenugreek seeds are a common ingredient in South Indian dishes.

Garlic *(lahsun)* is the bulb of an ancient herb belonging to the onion family. It is extensively used in North Indian cooking, especially meat dishes, and in pickles and chutneys. Garlic, onions, and sometimes ginger are ground to form a pungent paste that is a common gravy base. However, because garlic and onions are believed to have aphrodisiac properties, they are forbidden to Hindu students, widows, and people seeking to lead a spiritual life. Jains and orthodox Hindus also avoid onions and garlic.

Ginger *(adrak)* is the rhizome of a tropical plant. Kerala is the main producer. Ginger has a beige, potato-like skin, a smooth pale fibrous interior, and a warm fresh aroma that adds flavor and hotness to all kinds of dishes.

Gongura, the leaf of the hibiscus plant, is an essential element in the cuisine of Andhra Pradesh, where it is used as a spice, an herb, and a vegetable.

Kababchini (cubeb berries) are pungent, bitter berries slightly larger than a peppercorn that add flavor and texture to meat kabobs. It is sometimes mistakenly called allspice.

Kokum, **also called fish tamarind or *kodampoli*,** is the dried rind of the fruit of an evergreen tree that imparts a sour, smoky flavor to fish dishes in Kerala and vegetable dishes in Gujarat and Maharashtra.

Long pepper *(pippali)* is a form of pepper grown in India from prehistoric times. The name comes from its long pods that look like little bulrushes. Today it is mainly grown wild for local use and is rarely found in stores. Long pepper was widely exported to Europe until the sixteenth century, when it was replaced by chilies. It has a more pungent, warmer flavor than pepper, and is used as a spice and in pickles and preserves.

Mango powder *(amchur)* is made from raw, sour, green mangoes that are dried in the sun and powdered. It is used as a souring agent in North Indian *dals*, vegetable dishes, chutneys, and pickles, and sprinkled on meats to tenderize them.

Mint *(podina)* was probably introduced to India by the Mughals. Mixed with yogurt and spices, it can serve as a meat marinade. Chopped fresh mint leaves are added to chutneys and salads or sprinkled on bread.

Mustard seeds *(rai)* are the tiny dark seeds of the mustard plant. There are three varieties: white, brown, and black, and all are more pungent than the yellow seeds used in the West. South Indians fry whole seeds in oil until they pop and add them to cooked *dal* and vegetable dishes and to yogurt salads. In Bengal, they are ground with water, ginger, and chilies to make a paste for fish and vegetable dishes. The seeds are also ground to make mustard oil, which, along with mustard seeds, is a key component of many Indian pickles.

Nigella seeds *(kalonji)*, sometimes called onion or celery seeds, are tiny, pointy, black seeds with a fresh onion-like flavor. They are used for pickling and can be sprinkled over breads. Nigella seeds are a component of the Bengali spice mixture *panchphoran*.

Nutmeg *(jaiphal)* is a fragrant nut that grows in the center of an apricot-like fruit of a tropical evergreen originally brought from Indonesia in the late eighteenth century and now grown in South India. It has a brown wrinkled exterior and an intense piquant flavor. Whole nutmegs are cut into slivers or ground into a powder to flavor North Indian rice and meat dishes, and are also used in making jams, jellies, and pickles. Mace *(javitri)* is the lacy red membrane that encloses the nutmeg. Its also adds perfume to North Indian meat and rice dishes and desserts.

Onion *(piach)* is an ancient plant believed to be native to Afghanistan. India is the world's second largest producer. Onions are widely used in North Indian meat and vegetables dishes. They can be sliced or ground into a paste with water before frying. Like garlic, onions are believed to stimulate the passions, so they are avoided by strict vegetarians and people who want to attain spiritual perfection.

Paprika *(deghi mirch)*, a powder made from red sweet peppers that grow in Kashmir, adds flavor and color to dals and gravies in North India.

Peppers *(mirch)*, called the king of spices, are the dried berries of a tropical vine native to Kerala, which is India's major producer. Good pepper has a heady, pungent aroma. Green peppercorns *(badi mirch)* are the immature berries picked from the vine, used mainly to make pickles. Black peppercorns *(kali mirch)* are dried in the sun until they become hard and shriveled. The most expensive are the large Tellicherry and Malabar varieties. White peppercorns *(safed mirch)* are berries that have nearly ripened on the vine and are soaked in water to remove the skins. They are hotter than black pepper but less aromatic.

Peppers, whole or ground, are one of the most popular spices in India. In North India, whole peppers are cooked with rice and meat dishes; in South India pepper is roasted and ground with coconut and spices and applied to meat as a marinade or cooked with *dals* and vegetable dishes. Black pepper is a key ingredient in *garam masala*.

Pomegranate seeds *(anardana)*, which originated in Persia and Central Asia, have a dry, astringent flavor that perks up *dals*, vegetable dishes, lamb dishes, and yogurt salads in North Indian cooking.

Poppy seeds *(khus khus)* are small pale seeds from the pods of the opium poppy. Indian poppy seeds are ivory-colored and have a distinct nutty aroma when cooked. Their graininess adds texture to dishes. They can be lightly roasted and then ground with other spices to form a paste for thickening sauces and meat dishes. Poppy seeds are an important element in Bengali vegetarian cuisine. In Goa the seeds are roasted and mixed with coconut, chilies, and spices to make a gravy.

Saffron (kesari) is made from the dark-red stigmas from the flowers of a crocus that grows in the mountains of Kashmir, Iran, and Spain. The flower blooms for only two weeks each year. Each flower has three stigmas that are carefully picked by hand and dried. It takes 75,000 flowers to make one pound, making saffron the world's most expensive spice. Saffron imparts a sweet, slightly bitter flavor and a bright-yellow color to meat and rice dishes, especially *biryanis*, and to milk-based desserts. A few strands soaked in water or milk are added to a dish at the very end of cooking. Widely used in Persian cuisine, saffron was introduced by the Mughals to India. It also plays a role in Hindu rites and is used to dye the robes of Hindu and Buddhist priests. Saffron is one of the three colors (with green and white) on the Indian flag.

Sesame seeds (til) are the small cream-colored seeds of the sesame plant. (The black variety used in Chinese cooking is not found in India.) The whole seeds are generally roasted before sprinkling over yogurt raitas, vegetable dishes, and breads. Sesame seeds are native to India and from ancient times were used in religious rituals. Even today, they are considered especially auspicious.

Tamarind (imli) refers to the brown seeds and pulp found in the pods of an evergreen that has been cultivated in India since prehistoric times. The pulp is processed into pressed cakes that are soaked in water and made into a paste. Tamarind is one of the main souring agents in Indian cuisine, especially in the South and West, and an essential component of South Indian *sambars*.

Turmeric (haldi) is the rhizome of a plant belonging to the ginger family that is probably native to India. Its brilliant golden-orange color makes it a nearly permanent dye. It is usually purchased as a ready-made powder, although whole dried roots are also sold. Turmeric is an essential ingredient in curry powder and in Indian cuisine in general, where it imparts a bright-yellow color and a slightly pungent flavor to virtually every meat, vegetable, lentil, and rice dish (except greens). It can be rubbed on meat and fish as a marinade and added to batters for

Turmeric root.

snacks. It is a preservative agent in pickles. In Hinduism, turmeric is a highly auspicious material that is applied to the face and hands of brides. It is also a natural antiseptic with many medicinal uses.

VEGETABLES

An Indian meal essentially consists of grain and vegetables (sabzi). Even among nonvegetarians, meat or fish is never the centerpiece of a meal, but a supplement. Vegetables are part of main dishes, side dishes, appetizers, snacks, relishes, pickles, desserts, and breads. As a main dish, they may be sautéed or deep fried, roasted, mashed, stuffed, prepared dry or in a gravy, and in general cooked, as one leading cookbook writer puts it, "in just about every way conceivable to man."[7]

Many popular Indian vegetables were brought to India by the Portuguese from the Western Hemisphere and Africa, including potatoes, tomatoes, green peppers, winter squash, corn, and okra, also called ladies fingers. (In return, India sent the mango and sugarcane to the Caribbean and South America.) The British introduced temperate European vegetables such as the cabbage, cauliflower, lettuce, long orange carrots (which differ from the local variety), green beans, and navy beans. Leafy greens, called saag, may include the leaves of fenugreek, mustard, radish, and chickpea plants, and spinach. Eggplant (brinjal or baingun) is native to the subcontinent and one of the most popular vegetables. One of its virtues is that it absorbs the flavors of whatever sauce it is cooked in. The Indian version may be dark and round like a ball, or long, thin, and curved.

Other vegetables indigenous to the subcontinent but not so well known elsewhere include:

Arvi or patra (taro) is a tuber with a rough, brown skin. Colocasia leaves (arbi ki patra) are the large, dark-green leaves of the taro plant used in Gujarati cuisine. They have a strong, chard-like flavor and must be cooked for at least 45 minutes to destroy a poisonous substance.

Bitter melon or bitter gourd (karela) looks like a warty cucumber and has a very bitter flavor due to the presence of quinine.

Bottle gourd (louki, lau) is a long smooth squash with translucent flesh.

Drumsticks (sahjan, saragova) are the long, slender pods of an Indian tree that look like drumsticks. The only edible part is the soft interior pulp. They have very little flavor in themselves and absorb the flavor of the liquid they are cooked in.

Green beans (seema). Many varieties are grown in India, including tuvar, which are short plump pods filled with several peas, and sem or papri, which have curvy, bulging pods holding the seeds. Snake bean (payaru or lobhia) is a long bean sold in coils or knots.

Gourds are trailing or climbing plants whose fruits have a hard skin, soft body and many seeds. Some common varieties include the following:

Ash gourd or winter melon (*petha kaddu*) is a pumpkin-shaped gourd with a pale-green skin and soft flesh with a sweet flavor. Cubes soaked in sugar and crystallized produce a famous sweet called *petha*.

Parwal, a small, plump, light-green gourd that is fried, cooked in stews and curries, and prepared in a spicy yogurt sauce.

Ridged gourd (*toray* or *sinqua*) is 8 to 12 inches long with long spiny ridges. The flesh tastes like a cross between zucchini and cucumber.

Snake gourd (*chicinda*) is a long, slender, curved gourd that can range from pale to dark green in color and be as long as six feet.

Tinda, a plump, round, pale-green squash with the texture of cucumber.

Tindora, a short, stubby, bright-green squash with pale stripes.

Lotus roots (nedar or kamal) are the rhizomes of flowers that grow in the lakes of Kashmir and are cooked as vegetables there. Their cream-colored, crispy flesh has a sweetish taste like that of artichokes.

Neem (Azadirachta indica), a tree native to India, has been called a "wonder plant" and the "village pharmacy."[8] For centuries, its leaves, twigs, and seeds have been used in various forms to clean teeth, cure skin disorders, drive away insects, and treat fevers, infections, and other diseases. The bitter leaves are edible and used in Bengali dishes. On New Year's Day, a couple of leaves may be chewed with sugar to symbolize acceptance of the bitter and the sweet during the coming year. Today scientists are studying its potential as a natural pesticide, birth control measure, and pharmaceutical.

White radish or daikon (mooli) is popular in North India and Bengal.

Yams (jamikand or suran) that are native to India are different genetically from those in Africa and the New World and come in many different shapes and colors, including white, purple, and red.

FRUITS

India is a fruit-lover's paradise. Virtually all the fruits and berries cultivated in temperate climates grow in the cool mountains, as do those that thrive only in the tropics and semi-tropics, creating an incomparable variety and abundance. In most parts of the country, one need only step outside to pluck a mango or banana from a tree.

Like vegetables, fruits grown in India originated in many parts of the world. Some are native to India and Southeast Asia, such as bananas, mangoes, Indian gooseberry (*amla*), citrus fruits, and coconuts. It is a matter of debate whether melons are native to India or arrived from Africa (perhaps by water) in prehistoric times. Grapes probably came to India thousands of years ago from the Middle East, where vines were cultivated in the fourth millennium B.C. Today they are grown in Kashmir and in Maharashtra. From the fifteenth century onward, the invaders from the North introduced peaches, plums, apricots, mulberries, and perhaps apples from Afghanistan, Persia, and Central Asia. The Mughals, who were great connoisseurs of fruit, planted orchards and improved fruit quality by grafting and other horticultural methods.

In the sixteenth century, a wave of fruits began to arrive from the New World, including papayas, guavas, sapotilla, custard apples, and pineapples. The British introduced strawberries, raspberries, and apples, which today are grown in the foothills of the Himalayas, Kashmir, and Maharashtra.

Fresh fruit is a favorite dessert in India. It may be peeled, sliced, and served on platters, or served in a fruit salad. Milk desserts are often flavored with fruits. Mangoes, papayas, and other fruits are made into drinks. A mixture of mango pulp and yogurt called *lassi* is a summertime favorite. Dried apricots, raisins, and plums are used in North Indian rice and meat dishes, reflecting a Persian influence.

The following fruits are very popular in the subcontinent:

Amla, sometimes called the Indian gooseberry, is the berry-like fruit of a deciduous tree. It has a very acidic taste and is used in chutneys and preserves. It is considered very healthy and an all-purpose cure for liver disorders, indigestion, constipation, and colds.

Bananas (kela), native to Southeast Asia, have been grown in India for thousands of years. They come in many varieties, ranging from tiny, finger-shaped fruits to large red fruits. Plantain (*kacha kela*) are unripe green bananas eaten as a starchy vegetable, especially in South India and Bengal. Banana leaves—large, waterproof, and disposable—are the traditional serving plate in India and are still used in South Indian restaurants, in temples, and at wedding banquets. Banana flower (*kere kafool*), the large reddish-purple flower of the banana plant, is prepared as a vegetable.

Bilimbi is a waxy, light-green fruit that looks like a miniature cucumber and has a very sour flavor. It is used to add sourness to meat and vegetable dishes, and it is made into jams and chutneys.

Citrus fruits originated in northern India or Southeast Asia and were first cultivated in India and China. The appearance and variety of Indian citrus fruits sometimes bewilder foreign visitors, since they do not always fall into recognizable categories, such as orange, lime, or lemon. The English word *orange* is related to the Hindi *narangi*, a type of sweet orange. *Nimbu* is the name of a round, yellow-colored, thin-skinned lime, which Indians sometimes call a lemon. Freshly squeezed lime juice and a little salt is added to make *nimbu pani*, a popular drink in hot weather. The thick-skinned lemons found in the United States are not grown in India. Tangerines, which have loose orange skins, are also called mandarins, *santhra* in Hindi.

Coconut (*nariyal*) is the nut inside the fruit of the coconut palm tree that grows along India's coastline. An auspicious symbol in Hindu rituals, coconuts are called *shriphala*, the fruit of the gods. Pieces of coconut are offered to the deities during religious ceremonies. A coconut's interior consists of a white "meat" filled with a clear, sweetish liquid that is a refreshing drink. Grating the meat and mixing it with water yields coconut milk, a popular gravy for curry-like dishes in Kerala and Goa. Grated coconut meat and the milk are key components of sweets, chutneys, and snacks, especially during festivals.

Guavas (*amrood*), native to Central America, vary in size, shape, and color (pale-green, yellow, or red) and have a ring of small seeds. Their taste is acidic but sweet. In India, ripe guavas are eaten raw and made into jellies and jams or prepared as a paste.

Jackfruit (*kathal* or *chakka*), native to South India, is the world's largest fruit. It can be one to three feet in length and weigh as much as a hundred pounds, although most are between 15 and 30 pounds. They have a hard outer skin and an interior divided into a number of sections with a light-orange flesh. Each section contains hundreds of edible seeds that are roasted and eaten as a snack or added to curries. Raw jackfruit is used as a vegetable in curries.

Mango (*aam*), called the king of fruits, is native to India or Southeast Asia. (The English word comes from the Tamil *manga*.) Revered by Hindus and Buddhists, the mango has an important place in Indian art, culture, and religion. The distinctive curving shape is a popular motif in Hindu art and textiles and was the origin of the paisley design.

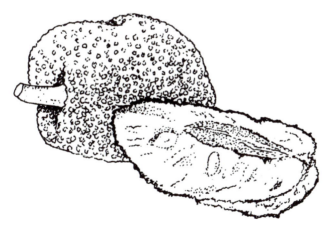

Jackfruit.

The Portuguese were the first to scientifically cultivate mango trees. The Mughal emperors gave tax incentives to nobles who planted orchards and even employed experts who indicated the precise moment at which each mango should be picked and eaten. Today more than a thousand varieties are grown. They fall into two categories: firm-fleshed mangoes for eating and juicy mangoes for sucking. Each region has its own varieties, which the local residents consider far superior to those produced elsewhere. Famous varieties include *dussehra, langra, chowsa, ratnal,* and *safeda,* all from Uttar Pradesh in North India; *neelam, banganapalli, benishan,* and *mulgoa* from South India; and, in Western India, the famous *alfonso,* named after a Portuguese noble.

The taste of the mango is exquisite: sweet, slightly tangy, and perfumed. Fresh fruit are always eaten in season and the arrival of a new variety to the market is celebrated at special parties. Mango juice is a popular drink. Tart, green mangoes are used as a vegetable in curries. Green mango is the most popular ingredient in pickles.

Papayas *(pappali)* probably reached India from South America via the Philippines or Brazil. They look like large, light-green pears with a soft, orange-red–colored flesh and a mass of black seeds. Unripe papaya is pickled and used as a vegetable. Papaya powder, which contains the enzyme papain, is used as a meat tenderizer.

Sapodilla *(chikoo)* is an import from the New World that reached India in the nineteenth century. It looks like a kiwi and has a granular, sweet, juicy flesh that has been compared with brown sugar. *Chickoos* must be eaten very ripe.

Star fruit *(caramabola)* is a waxy, yellow fruit with five lobes; when it is sliced, the slices resemble stars. The flesh is very juicy and crisp. It is added to salads and soups and curries as a souring agent and made into chutney.

Sugarcane, a giant grass that needs rich moist soil and tropical heat, is the main source of sugar in India, which is the world's largest consumer and second largest producer. Sugarcane cultivation and the process of sugar refining are native to India. The stems are filled with a sappy pulp that contains sucrose. They are crushed to extract the juice, which is boiled down to make a solid piece of dark brown sugar, called *gur* or jaggery, which has a caramel-like taste and is sold in large lumps or slabs. Jaggery is also made from the sap of coconut and Palmyra palms. Many Indian desserts and sweets are made with jaggery. Small amounts are added to *dals* and vegetable dishes in Gujarat and West Bengal. White crystalline sugar, called *chini,* is used as a sweetener for tea, especially in eastern India. Sugarcane juice, extracted and sold on the roadside, is a popular drink.

Fruits may be preserved in several ways:

Chutneys (from a word that means "lick") were originally freshly ground relishes of coconuts, nuts, vegetables, and other ingredients. In South India, chutneys are still generally uncooked and often made with yogurt, but in North and East India the word denotes a sweet and sour relish usually cooked ahead of time. They can

Pouring melted sugar juice and solidifying it in the field, Rajasthan. Photo ©
TRIP/H. Rogers.

be made from tomatoes, mangoes, papayas, mint leaves, and grated coconut,
which are blended with spices, yogurt, vinegar or lime juice, and a little sugar.

Morabbas are preserves of boiled fruit in a spiced, thick, sugar syrup. They are
more commonly eaten in Muslim households.

Pickles *(achar)*, an essential part of Indian meals as a condiment, are believed to
enhance appetite. Unlike Western pickles, Indian pickles are not necessarily sour
and can be very hot. Pickles can be made from raw mangoes, limes, lemons,
onions, garlic, eggplants, chilies, fish, meat, and other ingredients. They are preserved in spices, such as mustard seed, fenugreek, and turmeric; lemon juice or
vinegar; salt; and oil. Mustard oil is generally used in northern and eastern India,
sesame oil in the South and West.

Meat and Fish

Indian meat consumption is very low compared with that in the rest of
the world: an average 5.2 kilograms a year in 2001 compared with 51 kilograms in China and 121 kilograms in the United States.[9] According to
United Nations statistics, the most widely consumed kinds of meat are
beef, a term which refers to the meat both of cows and water buffaloes,
and mutton, a word that denotes the flesh of goats and sheep. Goats are

easy to raise, since they are foragers that can graze in open fields and wastelands, especially in arid regions.

Chicken has more of an upmarket image in India than in the West because it has been relatively expensive and only recently have large-scale breeding programs been put in place. Although a wild Indian fowl is the progenitor of the world's domestic fowls, there is evidence that originally it was not bred for food or eggs but for cock fighting. Because chickens are scavengers and therefore considered unclean, some Hindus will not eat them. Chicken is a popular ingredient in North Indian haute cuisine.

India was once covered with forests filled with wild boar, quail, deer, and other game. The Mughal and Rajput rulers were avid hunters and prepared many special dishes from their kill. Venison features in Rajasthani cuisine as a main dish and is made into a pickle.

The meat of pigs is forbidden to Muslims and is avoided by non-Muslims for practical and social reasons. An exception are Christian Goans who prepare a number of distinctive pork-based dishes.

Indians eat an average 4.4 kilograms of fish per year, about half of it freshwater varieties. Fish is a staple of people who live along India's very long coastline, especially in West Bengal, Kerala, Orissa, and Goa. Famous for their love of fish, Bengalis prefer freshwater fish from rivers and ponds over sea fish. *Hilsa,* a kind of shad with a myriad of tiny bones, is the Bengali national dish. Other popular fish are carp, catfish, the perch-like *bekti,* pomfret, kingfish, catfish *(magur);* and *pabda.* Shrimp (called prawns in Indian English) are considered a delicacy, but crabs and other crustaceans are not generally eaten by middle-class people in eastern India. India and Bangladesh are major exporters of shrimp and prawns. In Kerala, which has an important fishing industry, sea fish are widely eaten, including varieties of sardines, mackerel, pomfret, seer, squid, and prawns. Goa is famous for its seafood delicacies.

BEVERAGES

Water is served with all meals. Milk and buttermilk are popular drinks in northern and western India. Yogurt, water, and flavorings are mixed to make a popular summertime drink called *lassi.* Sweet *lassi* is made with mango pulp, salty *lassi* with salt and lime juice. Bottled soft drinks are popular among young urbanites. Sugarcane juice, sometimes spiced with ginger and coconut water, is sold at roadside stands. Also popular are fruit sherbets, made with the essence of fruits, especially mangos.

Although contemporary India is the world's largest exporter of tea, it was not grown commercially until the middle of the nineteenth century.

Crushing cane, Kolkata. Photo © TRIP/H. Rogers.

Today it is grown on plantations in Darjeeling, Assam, the Nilgiri Hills in Tamil Nadu, and Sri Lanka. In West Bengal and Assam, tea is prepared and drunk in the British style (i.e., the leaves are infused with water in a pot, the tea is poured into a cup, and milk and sugar may be added). In these areas tea is served before and during breakfast and in the late afternoon, when it is accompanied by a lavish spread of sweets and snacks, a meal that in Bengal is also called *tea*. In Punjab, Haryana, and elsewhere in North India, people drink *chai*—a mixture of inferior-grade tea leaves, milk, water, and spices all boiled together. This drink was popularized by the Indian Tea Board during World War II as a way of disposing of surplus stocks.

The British started planting coffee around the same time as tea, and today coffee is mainly grown and consumed in South India, especially at breakfast. Homeowners often buy their own beans and roast and grind them at home. In restaurants, coffee is prepared by mixing a thick extract with boiled milk and sugar to make a drink that resembles cappuccino.

Islam forbids its followers from drinking alcohol. While Hinduism does not ban liquor, it has a strong puritanical strain manifested in a disdain for liquor and those who drink it. Gandhi was strongly opposed to drinking alcohol, and even today several Indian states are dry. Per capita consumption of alcohol in India is roughly one-seventh that in China. Still, ancient texts describe the manufacture and consumption of alcohol made from fermented grains, fruits, sugarcane, the sap of coconut and date trees, and flowers. Today rural people drink home-brewed liquors, such as rice wine and rum distilled from molasses. In Central India, tribal peoples make an alcoholic beverage out of the flowers of the mahua tree and other plants. *Toddy*, a fiery beverage made from the sap of the date palm, is brewed in Kerala. It is consumed as a beverage and added to bread dough as a fermenting agent. In Goa, the Portuguese left behind a distinctive liquor from cashews called *feni*.

The British introduced scotch whiskey, gin and tonic (which contains quinine, a preventive of malaria), sherry, beer, and wine to India, and scotch remains the preferred drink of middle-class Indian men. In recent years there have been attempts to develop a commercial wine industry using grapes grown in Maharashtra, which is said to have a climate similar to Bordeaux, France. The result has been some so far undistinguished red and white wines and a champagne called Marquise de Pompadour that has received favorable reviews from Western wine writers. Commercial distilleries produce domestic whiskey, rum, gin, and beer.

NOTES

1. Harold McGee, *On Food and Cooking: The Science and Lore of the Kitchen* (New York: Collier, 1984), p. 226.

2. Sidney W. Mintz and Daniela Schlettwein-Gsell, "Food Patterns in Agrarian Societies: The Core-Fringe-Legume Hypothesis." *Gastronomica, The Journal of Food and Culture* 1, no. 3 (Summer 2001): 40–53.

3. Indian Agricultural Statistics Research Institute, *On-line Agriculture Data Book, 2002.* Available at http://www.iasri.res.in/agridata.

4. Jane E. Brody, "Adding Cumin to the Curry: A Matter of Life and Death," *New York Times*, 3 March 1998, B11, B14.

5. The Spice House, *Catalog* (Chicago: Illinois Seasoning Merchants, Inc., 2001), p. 5.

6. Monisha Bharadwaj, *The Indian Pantry* (London: Kyle Cathie Ltd. 1988), p. 24.

7. Julie Sahni, *Classic Indian Cooking* (New York: William Morrow & Company, Inc., 1980), p. 293.

8. National Research Council. *Neem: A Tree for Solving Global Problems.* (Washington, D.C.: National Academy Press, 1992), p. v.

9. Food and Agriculture Organization of the United Nations, FAOSTAT: *FAO Statistics Databases.* Available at http:apps.fao.org.

3

Cooking

WHO DOES THE COOKING?

In India, as in the rest of the world, cooking is usually done by the women of a household. In rural areas, women spend half their waking hours preparing meals. In a joint family, where several generations live in one household, the mother-in-law is in charge of the food preparation, aided by her daughters and daughters-in-law, all under her strict supervision. Middle-class families hire professional cooks and other domestic help. In orthodox Hindu homes, the cook is usually a Brahmin, since everyone could accept food from his hands. (In the old days, being a professional cook was the second most common profession of Brahmins after the priesthood.) For special occasions, such as weddings, families hire professional chefs who bring their own cooking equipment and staff.

Until modern times, recipes were rarely written down. The writing and use of cookbooks was much less developed in India than in, say, medieval Europe or China, where cookbooks with detailed recipes appeared as early as the eleventh century. Hindu writing about food focused on its spiritual and religious aspects, not the aesthetic and gastronomical character of foods, and Hindu culinary traditions "stayed oral in their model of transmission, domestic in their locus, and regional in their scope."[1] Nor did the cooks of the Mughal Court leave behind recipes with detailed descriptions of ingredients and procedures. As a result, Indian dishes never became as standardized as French or Chinese cuisine.

The oldest Indian cookbooks in the modern sense—those that provide exact information about ingredients and instructions—date back to the middle of the nineteenth century and were written in English for the wives of Englishmen stationed in India. Some have quaint titles, such as *Dainty Dishes for Indian Tables*, and *The Madras Cookery Book, Specially Compiled for the Requirements of Europeans and Anglo Indians in India by an Old Lady-Resident*. In addition to recipes, these books often contain advice on household management, hiring servants, and home remedies. Sometimes a version was published in local languages for the benefit of the local domestics who actually did the cooking, such *as What to Tell the Cook, or the Native Cook's Assistant*, published in English and Tamil in 1875.

Starting in the 1920s and 1930s, an increasing number of cookbooks were published in Indian languages. The breakup of joint families meant that young housewives found themselves without the benefit of an elder's culinary example and advice. Since the 1980s, there has been a rapid increase in the publication of cookbooks in English and Indian languages as well as women's and lifestyle magazines. Popular television cooking shows help to spread awareness of Indian regional dishes and non-Indian cuisines.

INDIAN APPROACH TO COOKING

In the typical Indian kitchen, the cook does not measure ingredients; instead, she estimates the amount needed during the cooking process and adds it as she goes along. As an Indian chef puts it:

Mood and intuition also play a very critical part in the taste of Indian food. Western chefs are trained in the process of cooking before they're allowed to cook. But process means little to Indian chefs; the mutability of the moment is the guiding light. Western-trained chefs rely on codified rules and formulations—a monolithic prescription for a béchamel sauce, for instance—and strive for consistent results over a long period of time. In India, a dish of chicken curry will vary, depending on when it's cooked, by whom, that person's mood, and where it's being cooked.[2]

Also, Indian ingredients are not as standardized as those in the West, so their flavor and intensity varies considerably. Thus, while there may be a general concept of what, say, constitutes a *korma* or a *sambar* in terms of main ingredients and basic methods (frying, steaming, etc.), the proportion of different ingredients and actual cooking times are left up to the individual cook.

Presentation and appearance are not very important in Indian cuisine. Although sweet dishes and desserts are sometimes decorated with edible silver foil, generally food is presented without embellishment.

COOKING EQUIPMENT AND UTENSILS

Stoves and Ovens

Even in affluent homes, Indian kitchens are simple, even austere, by Western standards.[3] Almost all cooking is done on top of a stove or a burner. Traditional fuels included dried cow patties (dung), charcoal, coke, twigs, or wood shavings. The use of cow patties is an ancient form of recycling that also provides a source of income for the people who collect, dry, and sell them. They provide a gentle heat, ideal for slow-cooking dishes with gravies and liquids, which are sometimes left overnight on hot coals. In middle-class urban households, the standard cooking device is a small cooktop with two burners fueled by bottled gas (propane). It is astonishing what elaborate feasts can be prepared on this simple piece of equipment. Pressure cookers, invented in France in the seventeenth century, are popular in India and owned by three-quarters of all urban house-

Woman and boy by a mud oven, near Jodhpur. Photo © Art Directors/TRIP.

holds. A sealed lid increases the air pressure, lowering the temperature at which water boils and significantly reducing cooking times.

A *tandoor* is a large clay oven with a small opening in the top that is either built into the ground or freestanding. In North India, it is used for baking many kinds of bread and roasting meat, which is plastered on the sides or strung on skewers. The *tandoor* originated in Iran or Central Asia and did not enter mainstream North Indian cooking until the early 1950s. Most Indian households do not have *tandoors* because they are expensive and difficult to use, but some North Indian villages have a communal *tandoor* for baking bread and roasting meat. People may also take meat to local bakeries for roasting.

Utensils

The Indian *batterie de cuisine* is restricted to relatively few pieces of equipment. In ancient times, pots and cooking utensils were made of earthenware and cleaned with ashes, earth, and acidic or alkaline natural substances. Today they are made of metal. One of the most frequently used receptacles is a deep pot (*karahi*) with two handles and a flat or slightly concave bottom made of stainless steel or cast iron that is used for sautéing and deep frying. Rice and curry-like dishes with a liquid gravy are prepared in a straight-sided pan with a lid. The lid is saucer-shaped, so that live charcoal can be placed on it as needed for certain dishes. A flat, heavy, iron griddle eight or nine inches in diameter with a long handle, called a *tawa*, is used for roasting spices and preparing breads that require little or no oil. A perforated metal spoon is used for frying and draining and a ladle for used for stirring.

Grinding and Cutting Equipment

In some parts of India, the cook crushes spices, onions, garlic, and herbs by pressing and rolling them with a small stone rolling pin without handles on a large stone slab. In South India, a mortar and pestle is more often used for this purpose. Modern cooks use electric grinders and blenders. Very large kitchens, such as those in a wealthy home or a restaurant, may employ a person whose sole job is to grind spices. Spices and flavorings are often ground early in the morning for the day's meals. Spices are kept in a spice box next to the stove.

Certain dishes or ingredients may require specialized equipment. A large knife mounted on a wooden board is used to cut fish and large veg-

Mortar and pestle.

etables, which is done by the highest-ranked person in the kitchen. In Kashmir, some utensils resemble those used in Central Asia, such as a samovar for brewing tea. In South India, the soaked rice and lentils used to make breads are ground in a special device consisting of a stone base with a hole in the center and an egg-shaped stone that fits into the stone. Because they are so heavy, they are permanently fixed in kitchens and pantries, but today they are being replaced by electric wet grinders. South Indian and Gujarati kitchens have a variety of unusually shaped devices for steaming breads and snacks.

THE PREPARATION AND USE OF SPICES

Spices and other flavorings (e.g., garlic, onions, ginger, chilies) are the heart and soul of Indian cooking. No other cuisine uses so many spices in so many ways; indeed, the range of possibilities is almost infinite. Contrary to popular myth, Indian food need not be searingly hot. The doyenne of Indian cooking writes:

The excessive use of spices has probably been fostered by various restaurants and eating houses both inside and outside India who camouflage with the help of spices the flavor of a dish which they are unable to produce properly. The art of Indian cookery lies not in high spicing, but in the delicacy of spicing. It is the use of selected spices in a particular manner to bring out the dormant flavors of a dish or to drown the undesirable ones which is the real art.[4]

From a gastronomical (not a medical) standpoint, spices and flavorings have three purposes:

- They add flavor to a dish. Flavor is a combination of taste and aroma: Taste is what we detect with taste buds, special receptors in our mouth and tongue, while aroma is discerned with special cells at the back of our throat and in our nose. There are four basic tastes—sweet, bitter, sour, and salty—plus two others that affect the entire mouth area: astringency (making the mouth pucker) and pungency or hotness, created by chilies.
- They create body. Grinding onions and garlic or poppy seeds, for example, makes a paste that thickens a gravy.
- They enhance texture: Small crunchy seeds or even lentils are fried and added to cooked vegetables and *dals*.

The kind and amount of spices used depends on the dish, the geographical region, and the preferences of a household and its cook. Table 2.2 shows the spices most commonly used in regional cuisines. The greatest number of spices are used in North Indian meat and rice dishes. For example, a recipe for *rogan josh*, an aromatic meat curry with a creamy gravy, calls for ginger, garlic, onions, red chilies, coriander leaves, saffron, black pepper, asafetida, black cumin seeds, cumin powder, cardamom seeds, cloves, cinnamon sticks, poppy seeds, turmeric powder, chili powder, paprika, nutmeg powder, mace powder, and a final sprinkling of powdered white and black cumin seeds, cardamom seeds, black peppercorns, cloves, fennel seeds, cinnamon sticks, and mace.[5] South Indian vegetarian dishes typically are made with far fewer spices. A rather elaborate recipe for South Indian *sambar*, for example, uses turmeric, chilies, onions, asafetida, coriander, cumin seeds, fenugreek, black peppercorns, mustard seeds, and curry leaves.[6]

Spices may be added in several forms—whole, crushed, ground, or mixed with water as a paste—and at different stages in the cooking process. Sometimes the same spice is used both whole and powdered in the same dish, especially cumin and coriander. Whole peppercorns, cloves, cardamom seeds in their pods, and cinnamon sticks are essential ingredients in North Indian meat and rice dishes. At the start of many meat and vegetable dishes, whole spices are sautéed in *ghee* or oil in order to release their essential oils into the cooking medium and impart their flavor to the other ingredients. Whole spices may also be boiled with water, vegetables, or meat and bones to make a stock called *yakhni* in which rice is cooked to make *biryanis* and *pulaos*. Crushed cardamom seeds (removed from their pods) are an ingredient in *payesh* and other milk-based desserts. For some reason cinnamon, a popular flavoring in Western rice pudding, is never used in Indian sweet dishes.

Another way of using spices is to grind them into a powder, which in North India is called *garam masala*, which means "warm seasonings." Usually the spices are dry-roasted before grinding to bring out their aroma, and they can be stored in air-tight bottles for a couple of weeks. A few pinches are added to a dish just before serving in order to add bouquet. A standard North Indian *garam masala* contains cumin seeds, coriander seeds, cinnamon, cloves, and cardamoms. In South India, *dals* are flavored with *sambar* powder that typically includes *urad dal*, coriander seeds, white cumin seeds, fenugreek seeds, and black pepper. Powdered turmeric and chili powder may be used as a dry marinade for fish and chicken.

Curry powders are ready-made spice mixtures that are sold commercially in India, the United Kingdom, and throughout the world. They were first produced in England in the late eighteenth century for English colonials who returned home after living in India and missed Indian food and flavorings. Most commercial curry powders contain coriander, cumin, black pepper, fenugreek, and turmeric. They are usually a poor substitute for freshly ground spices, although they are extremely appropriate for an English-style curry. One of their drawbacks is that most curry powders contain turmeric, which must be cooked to a fairly high temperature to bring out its flavor. Coriander and cumin powders, by contrast, require less cooking, so either they are burned or the turmeric is undercooked, leaving a raw aroma.

Whole, ground, and powdered spices are often sprinkled near the end of the cooking process to add an extra dimension of flavor. This procedure, unique to Indian cooking, is called *baghar*, *tarkha*, or *chaunk* in Hindi and *tempering* in English (from the Portuguese *temperado*, meaning "to season"). A little *ghee* or oil is heated to the smoking point; then seasonings and spices are added one after the other. Once the spices begin to crackle or change color, they are combined with the main dish—either the seasoned oil is added to the food or vice versa—and cooked for a while to meld their flavors. In North India, tempering ingredients often include fried onions and garlic as well as whole spices and/or *garam masala*. A final garnishing of sliced onions, fried until they are brown and crispy, may be placed over the dish. In South India, a mélange of lightly sautéed mustard seeds, asafoetida, fenugreek seeds, red chilies, and *urad dal*, is a standard finishing touch for *dals*, vegetable dishes, chutneys, and salads.

Another method of adding spices is to grind them into a wet paste with onions, garlic, ginger, yogurt, coconut milk, vinegar, or some other liquid. This mixture becomes the basis of a gravy. Onions and garlic play an important role in North Indian cuisine, but are used less frequently in West and South India. Gujaratis make a paste from green chilies and ginger. Bengalis sometimes use ground poppy seeds to make a paste. In North India, yogurt, cream, and or ground nuts may be used to thicken the gravy. In South India, coconut milk and grated coconut serve the same purpose.

COOKING TECHNIQUES

Indian cooking requires more or less the same techniques as Western cuisine: deep frying, sautéing, boiling, steaming, braising, and grilling. Baking and roasting are done relatively less frequently, since few people have ovens in their homes. Lentils are gently boiled to produce *dals*. Rice is steamed or boiled.

A very common Indian cooking technique that has no exact equivalent in Western cuisine is a combination of sautéing, stir-frying, and stewing. The cook starts by frying spices and a paste made from garlic, onions, ginger, and perhaps tomatoes in a little *ghee* or oil until they soften. Then he adds pieces of meat, fish, or vegetables and sautés it until it is brown. The next step is to add small amounts of water, yogurt, or other liquid a little a time while constantly stirring to keep the ingredients from sticking, which can be a labor-intensive process. The amount of liquid added and the cooking time determine whether the dish will be wet or dry.

Frying is a very popular cooking method: panfrying or sautéing in *ghee* on a griddle and deep frying in a pot using peanut, safflower, or canola oil. Many popular snacks and breads are deep-fried. *Qorma* or *korma*, sometimes translated as "braising," is a technique that involves marinating meat and sometimes vegetables in yogurt, wet spices, and seasonings, then slowly cooking it in the marinade over very low heat, sometimes adding cream and butter at the end. The goal is to produce a thick, rich sauce that coats the meat pieces.

Roasting and grilling are popular in North India. Pieces of lamb, goat, chicken, fish, or *paneer* (Indian cheese) are impaled on a stick and grilled over hot coals or in a *tandoor*. Such dishes are called *kabobs*, a word that means "without water" in Persian. The meat may be marinated in yogurt and spices before cooking. There are many kinds of kabob, including chunks of mutton (*boti kabob*), marinated chicken (*tikka kabob*), flattened pounded meat (*chapli kabob*), and sautéed meat and chickpea patties (*shammi kabob*).

Most regional cuisines feature a few steamed dishes. South Indians steam *idlis*, disk-shaped spongy bread about 3 inches in diameter, using a device that looks like a stack of perforated egg poachers placed over boiling water. In Kerala, a long, round, bamboo tube is attached to the spout of a vessel containing boiling water and filled with a ground rice and coconut mixture to make a popular breakfast dish called *puttu*. The Assamese use a similar device to make a kind of rice-flour sweet. *Dhokla*, a famous Gujarati snack, is made by steaming slabs of fermented flour and yogurt.

In Lucknow, capital of the state of Uttar Pradesh, a school of cooking developed called *Dum Pukht*, which means "steam cooked." It may have originated in Persia, where a prepared dish was sealed and buried in hot sand to mature. Vegetables, potatoes, and or pieces of meat are fried with spices and seasonings in a liberal amount of *ghee* or oil in a large pot until they are lightly browned. The lid is sealed with flour dough and the dish cooked very slowly in the aromatic vapor. In the old days the pot was placed on smoldering coals, with live coals placed on top, sometimes left overnight. The *dum* technique is also used in the final cooking of North Indian rice dishes.

Pickling, a very old Indian technique, is essential in a country where the climate is hot most of the year. Pickling is a way of preserving fruits, vegetables, meat, or fish by impregnating them with acid, which discourages the growth of most microbes. This can be done either by adding an acid, usually vinegar, or by soaking them in a strong salt solution, which encourages acid-producing bacteria to grow.[7] Indian pickles come in countless varieties, and are eaten at most meals to add an accent or a contrasting flavor. They can be sweet, sour, salty, cooling, hot, or very hot indeed. Pickles are considered to have many health benefits: Spices such as ginger, asafetida and turmeric are digestives, while red chilies are antiseptic. Traditionally women made pickles at home, but today about half of all households buy them commercially.

To make pickles, fruits, vegetables, meat, or fish are cut into pieces and placed in a mixture of spices and oil that is heated in the sun. A souring agent is added, such as lime or vinegar, and the pickles are stored in sterilized bottles where they can last for months without refrigeration. In North India and Bengal, common pickling ingredients are mustard oil, vinegar, and such spices such as cumin, ajowain, fennel, and red chilies. South Indian pickles are usually made with sesame, gingelly or peanut oil; mustard seeds, curry leaves, and red chilies; and tamarind, yogurt, or lime juice as the souring agent. In western India sesame oil, mustard oil, and palm vinegar are common ingredients.

Green mango is by far the most popular item for pickling. Other candidates for pickling include limes and lemons, cauliflower, turnips, onions, eggplants, chilies, cashew nuts, berries, wild game, shrimp, and pork. The well-known Goan dish, *vindaloo*, was originally a pickle made by cooking pork in a mixture of mustard oil, ground spices, and palm vinegar.

Chutneys are a sweet and sour relish usually cooked ahead of time. They can be made from tomatoes, mangoes, papayas, mint leaves, and grated coconut, which are blended with spices, yogurt, vinegar or lime juice, and a little sugar. Under the British, the word *chutney* came to mean a preserve of slightly spiced mango slices in sugar syrup that is still manufactured under colonial-sounding names like Major Grey's and Bengal Club.

HINDU EATING AND COOKING TRADITIONS

Orthodox Hindus—those who follow their caste traditions—developed elaborate rules for the handling, preparation, and serving of food based on their concerns about purity and pollution. High status is associated with purity and low status with pollution. In traditional orthodox households, the kitchen is considered an area of sanctity, similar to the inner sanctum of a temple. It is located far from waste disposal areas and near the place of worship. Only a family member (generally the senior woman) is supposed to do the actual cooking, although she may be assisted by outside workers. She must bathe and wear fresh unstitched garments before entering the kitchen. She never tastes the food during preparation, since contact with saliva would pollute the food; she determines flavor by odor and appearance alone. Traditionally the stove and utensils were placed on a raised platform, which are still widely used in southern and western India.

When it comes to what kind of food is served, different standards may apply even within households, which are composed of people of different ages and different degrees of Westernization. Teenagers might ignore some rules entirely—for example, they might eat onions or eggs, whereas their grandparents will avoid these foods—a state of affairs that can place a considerable burden on the overworked cook. Some homes have a secondary cooking area, often located outside the house, where dishes are prepared using onions, garlic, chicken, and other ingredients shunned by orthodox family members but enjoyed by more modern family members and their friends. Very affluent households may have entirely separate kitchens with different sets of pots and pans for preparing Hindu vegetarian food, Hindu nonvegetarian food, and Western-style dishes.

The food is served in an area near the kitchen. In a traditional household, the diners sit on the floor and eat with their right hand only. If bread is part of the meal, small pieces are broken off and wrapped around pieces of food. In the old days, meals were served on neatly trimmed squares of fresh banana leaves sprinkled with water that can be disposed of after eating. This practice is still followed at weddings and temple meals. Today, in some parts of India, meals are served on a flat, round tray with a slightly raised rim called a *thali*. Originally, *thalis* were made of brass or even silver; today they are made of stainless steel or aluminum. The rice or bread is placed on the *thali* and accompanied by small bowls holding *dal*, yogurt, vegetables, and meat dishes. In cities, many middle-class families eat at a table and use ordinary dinnerware with Western-style cutlery, mainly forks and spoons, since the meat is already cut into pieces.

Hospitality is very important among all religious and social groups in India. "A guest is god," says a proverb. Indians often have many guests for meals and as overnight guests. Even in the poorest homes in villages, people will sacrifice to make sure visitors eat and drink well and the choicest portions are offered to them.

NOTES

1. Arjun Appadurai, "How to Make a National Cuisine: Cookbooks in Contemporary India," *Comparative Studies in Sociology and History*, 30, no. 1 (1988): 12.

2. Suvir Saran, "Passage from India," *Food Arts* (July/August 2001): 94.

3. A national survey found that only 59 percent of rural households had a separate kitchen inside the house compared with 76 percent of urban households. Firewood, crop residue, and cow dung patties accounted for 89 percent of the fuel used in rural areas but only 15 percent in cities. These statistics come from the Office of the Registrar General, India, April 17, 2003. The information can be found on the Indian Census Web site, http://www.censusindia.net/2001housing/S00-018.html.

4. Mrs. Balbir Singh, *Indian Cookery* (New York: Weathervane Books, 1973), p. 15.

5. Joyce Westrip, *Moghul Cooking: India's Courtly Cuisine* (London: Serif, 1997), pp. 60–62.

6. Mrs. K.M. Mathew, *Kerala Cookery* (Kottayam, India: Manorama Publishing House, 1964), pp. 84–85.

7. Harold McGee, *On Food and Cooking* (New York: Macmillan, 1984), pp. 172–173.

4

Typical Meals

Defining and describing a typical Indian meal is a daunting task in view of the enormous physical, climatic, ethnic, and religious diversity of a country of 1 billion people. Even within individual households, there are variations in what family members eat. However, some generalizations are valid most of the time. An Indian meal is centered on a starch, either rice or a grain. Nationwide, cereals provide 70 percent of all the calories and protein consumed, although the percentage falls as income rises.[1] Grains are usually accompanied by pulses (beans, peas, and lentils). Together the two foodstuffs provide the full complement of amino acids necessary for good health in the absence of meat in the diet.

In rice-producing regions (the Northeast, South India, Uttar Pradesh), rice is the staple grain, whereas people in the wheat-producing North (Punjab and Haryana) eat bread made from wheat. Both rice and wheat are eaten in Uttar Pradesh, a top producer of both grains. In western India, so-called coarse cereals, such as millet and sorghum that grow on arid land, were traditional staples. However, Indian wheat production has increased fourfold since 1950 and is gradually replacing these grains here and elsewhere.

Relatively small amounts of meat, fish, and vegetables are added to enhance the taste and texture of the main grain. Contrary to popular belief, only a minority of Indians are vegetarian: 25–30 percent nationwide. The proportion varies considerably between states from 6 percent in Kerala, Orissa, and West Bengal to 60 percent or over in Rajasthan and Gujarat.[2]

However, meat is expensive, so most people cannot afford to eat meat or fish every day, and even affluent people eat relatively little meat by Western standards. On average, Indians get 92 percent of their calories from vegetable products and only 8 percent from animal products (meat, dairy products, and eggs), around one-tenth the level in China or the United States.[3]

An Indian meal usually includes small amounts of condiments to complement the other dishes: dairy products, such as yogurt or clarified butter; fruit and vegetable chutneys; and sweet, sour, or pungent pickles. In South India, a meal ends with yogurt or buttermilk, which is believed to aid digestion and counteract the effect of the spices.

In the past, most people traveled no further than their village or local market to obtain ingredients. Even today poor transportation remains a constraint on variety in rural areas where vegetables tend to be seasonal and locally produced. The consumption of milk and dairy products is especially sensitive to local availability: People in Punjab, a major dairy farming area, consume seventeen times as much milk per capita as those in Orissa and twice as much as the national average. Similarly, Gujarat, the largest producer of oil seeds and the largest manufacturer of oils, and Punjab, where butter and *ghee* (clarified butter) are eaten every day, top the list in oil and fat consumption. In the past, local oils were used as the cooking medium—coconut oil in Kerala, mustard oil in West Bengal, sesame oil in the South—but today vegetable oils are becoming more widespread.

Religion also determines the choice of ingredients. Orthodox Hindus and Jains do not eat meat, fish, or eggs, so grain and lentils dominate their diet, regardless of their income. Nonvegetarian Hindus who can afford meat will, in theory, not eat beef. Muslims avoid all pork but eat other kinds of meat. Christians eat all kinds of meat, so it is not surprising that consumption of lentils is lowest in Kerala and Goa, which have the largest Christian populations.

Most middle-class Indians eat two main meals a day, supplemented by one or two smaller meals. In rural areas, the main meals are a hearty breakfast or early lunch to prepare for the day's labor and a light dinner, perhaps supplemented with bread and snacks in the afternoon. In towns and cities in North and Central India, people start the day with a light breakfast, followed by a large lunch, a light afternoon tea or tiffin when family members return from school or the office, and a dinner in the evening. Breakfast often consists of food left over from the previous day's dinner or bread served with vegetables. However, Western-style breakfasts of toast, eggs, or prepared breakfast cereals are becoming standard in middle-class urban households. In South India, breakfast is the main meal of the day. In northern and eastern India, lunch and dinner are very similar, although usually fresh dishes are prepared for each meal.

According to ancient Hindu dietary theory, every meal is supposed to include all six tastes in the following order: sweet, sour, salty, pungent, bitter, and astringent. Today most people are unaware of this theory, and the only meal at which all the tastes are experienced—except perhaps for the distinctly bitter—is a formal wedding banquet. Nonetheless, usually four or five tastes are present in an Indian meal. As in any country, a skilled cook also tries to achieve a harmonious interplay of colors and textures. For example, if a meat dish has a thin gravy, the vegetables will be thick; a thin *dal* (lentil stew) will be served with dried meat dishes, such as kabobs. Theories about hot and cold foods, religious and caste beliefs, household traditions, and ultimately personal likes and dislikes also determine ingredients, dishes, and methods of preparation.

This chapter reviews Indian meals by state and region, a distinction that is admittedly artificial. Like language, food is a continuum that changes gradually, sometimes imperceptibly, over space and time. Crossing a state or national border does not mean that people suddenly start speaking a different language or eating entirely different foods. Within states there are important regional and social differences as well as distinctions between town and country that are rooted in historical and political developments. For example, in the states of Andhra Pradesh and Uttar Pradesh, which have predominantly Hindu populations, the tradition of Mughal Court cuisine prevails in Lucknow and Hyderabad. In Rajasthan the rich, meat-based cuisine of the majarahahs who once ruled independent kingdoms is in striking contrast to the austere vegetarian fare of the common people.

The following section describes the meals eaten by a middle- to upper-middle-class family, headed by, say, a university-educated professional, a mid-level government official or business executive, or an affluent farmer. Around 26 percent of all Indians (250 million people) live below the poverty level, though this is a big drop from 51 percent in 1972. Poor people consider themselves fortunate if they can obtain a simple meal of *chapati* (flat bread) or rice with a little salt and pickles.

NORTH AND CENTRAL INDIA

Jammu and Kashmir

Jammu and Kashmir is India's northernmost state, bordered by Afghanistan, China, Tibet, Pakistan, and the Indian states of Himachal

Pradesh and Punjab. One of the largest princely states of British India, after independence it was claimed by both India and Pakistan and since 1972 has been divided by a Line of Control. Two-thirds of the original territory now comprises the Indian state of Jammu and Kashmir; the rest, called Azad Kashmir, is under Pakistani control. India and Pakistan have fought several wars over the region since the 1950s.

The region was predominantly Buddhist and Hindu until the fourteenth century, when it was conquered by Muslim invaders from Afghanistan and Central Asia. Later the Mughal emperors built their summer residences in Kashmir and left behind splendid buildings and gardens and a sumptuous haute cuisine that some people consider the finest in India. Of the state's 12 million residents, approximately 70 percent are Muslims; the rest are Hindus, Sikhs, and Buddhists.[4] Many Hindus are Brahmins, called Pandits. Unlike most Brahmins, they eat meat, mainly mutton.

The climate is moderate in summer but can be bitterly cold in winter. The state's heartland is a 65-mile-long valley, the legendary Vale of Kashmir, six thousand feet above sea level and surrounded by mountains. Its fertile alluvial soil is ideal for growing rice, wheat, corn, barley, pulses, barley, walnuts, and many tropical and temperate vegetables and fruits. To increase the amount of arable land, farmers created a unique system of floating lake gardens by binding reeds and weeds with mud to make islands on which they raise cucumbers, melons, tomatoes, and other crops. The lakes also supply fish, water chestnuts, and lotus roots, a Kashmiri delicacy. Goats and sheep are supplied by nomadic herdsmen. Game and venison were once plentiful in the valley.

Distinctive Kashmiri ingredients include saffron, a flavoring and coloring agent made from the stamens of crocus flowers; small sweet red shallots called *praan;* morel, a kind of wild mushroom; wild asparagus; and a mild-flavored red pepper called Kashmiri chili that resembles paprika. There are also many varieties of seasonal greens. Mustard oil was the traditional cooking medium.

For breakfast, Kashmiris have tea and bread, bought fresh daily from neighborhood bakeries. Most bread is made from wheat and comes in a profusion of textures, shapes, and sizes and flavors (see Table 2.1). Kashmiri tea is brewed with green tea leaves in metal samovars like those used in Russia and probably shares a common origin in Central Asia. Tea is drunk plain or mixed with milk, salt, ground cardamom, cinnamon, sugar, ground almonds, and saffron to make a distinctive drink called *kahwa.*

Lunch consists of rice or a simple bread, such as *chapati, dal* (lentils), a meat or fish dish, and one or two vegetable dishes, traditionally cooked in

Kashmiri samovar.

mustard oil and yogurt. Around 4:00 P.M., people serve bread, cookies, or a snack with tea. Dinner is served around 9:00 in the evening and is similar to lunch.

On special occasions, such as engagements and weddings, Hindus and Muslims hire professional caterers, called *wazas*, to prepare a lavish, meat-centered banquet called a *wazwan*, which consists of at least seven and as many as forty meat dishes. Dozens of cooks (all men), headed by a master chef, arrive days before the event, bringing their own cooking pots and herds of sheep and goats. The *wazas* believe there are 72 parts to an animal and most of them will be cooked, including the liver, kidneys, and other organs. The guests sit in groups of four on white sheets spread on carpets under canopies and share the meal from a large metal plate. The plate is served heaped with rice and pieces of dry meat, onto which various kinds of meat curries are poured during the meal. The meal is accompanied by yogurt, pickles, and small clay pots of chutney made from fresh walnuts, cashew nuts, sour cherries, pumpkins, radishes, and other vegetables.

Kashmiris add spices with a generous hand. Meat dishes are flavored with highly aromatic spices, such as brown and green cardamoms, cloves, ginger, cinnamon, mace, and nutmeg. Muslims make liberal use of onions and garlic in preparing meat dishes, whereas Hindus use asafetida, fennel seed, ginger, and aniseed instead. Kashmiris have a unique way of preparing and using spices: They grind them, add a little mustard oil, and shape them into disks with a hole in the middle. The disks are dried in the shade until they become hard, then hung on a string and kept in the kitchen. Pieces are broken off as needed.

Kashmir is famous for its rich, aromatic meat dishes. The preferred meat is goat—the younger the better—cut into fairly large pieces. Often the meat is marinated with yogurt and spices; milk and cream may be added during cooking to create a rich, thick gravy. Some famous Kashmiri meat dishes are *gushtaba*, lamb pounded with ginger and garlic or asafetida and spices and then cooked slowly in a gravy made from onions, sliced almonds, cream, milk, yogurt, and spices; *rogan josh*, a curry made by slowly cooking pieces of lamb in yogurt and spices until it is dry and then simmering it in a cream and saffron-flavored gravy; *Kashmiri rann*, roasted leg of lamb marinated in yogurt, spices, nuts, and honey; *alu bokhara korma*, lamb curry with almonds and dried plums; and *zardhalo boti, a* sweet-and-sour stew of lamb or chicken fried in a paste of ginger, garlic, chili, and cumin seed, then simmered in water and flavored with soaked, dried apricots, vinegar, and sugar that give the dish a distinctive sweet and sour flavor.

Kamargah, lamb chops marinated in yogurt and spices, then fried in a batter, is sometimes called the Kashmiri national dish.

Kamargah (Kashmiri Lamb Chops)

- 8 small lamb cutlets
- 1 tb aniseed
- 5 green cardamoms
- 1 small stick cinnamon
- 5 cloves
- 6 whole black peppercorns
- 16 ounces milk

Batter

- 1/3 cup chickpea flour
- 1 tsp coriander powder
- 1/2 tsp chili powder
- 1/2 tsp salt
- 4 ounces *ghee* or oil

Tie the spices in a small piece of cheesecloth. Put the milk, meat, and spice bag into a large pot, bring to a boil, and cook over low heat for twenty-five minutes or until the meat is tender and the liquid has almost dried up. Remove and dry the lamb chops. Combine the flour, chili, coriander powder, and salt with enough water to make a batter and mix thoroughly until it is smooth. Heat the oil or *ghee* in a frying pan. Dip the cutlets into the batter and fry until they are golden brown. They can be fried for a second time just before serving to make them extra crisp.

Kashmiri Hindus tend to eat more vegetables than Muslims, sometimes in unusual combinations. A dish called *soont vaangan* is made by sautéing eggplants and apples in asafetida-flavored mustard oil and then cooking it in a paste of ground fennel seeds and chili powder. Turnips, a popular seasonal vegetable, are eaten raw, pickled, sautéed with spices and simmered in yogurt, or cooked in a creamy gravy with meat. Kashmir is one of the few parts of India where mushrooms, especially morels, are standard fare.

Lotus roots are a versatile vegetable, prepared with fish, lamb, and greens; minced, shaped into balls, and fried; deep-fried as snacks; or cooked with a yogurt gravy. A popular *dal* is made with *urad* or *black dal* and a tarkar of asafetida, cumin seeds, tomato purée, coriander, chili powder, and onions and garlic or asafetida. Yogurt, cream, and raisins may also be added. A famous Kashmiri vegetable dish is *dum aloo*, small potatoes that are boiled, then fried and simmered in a gravy of yogurt and spices.

Dum Aloo (Boiled and Fried Potatoes)
- 2 pounds small potatoes
- 1 cup mustard oil or vegetable oil

The Gravy
- 1 tsp cumin seeds
- 2 cloves
- 2 green cardamom seeds
- 1/4 tsp asafetida
- 1 tsp red chili powder (or to taste)
- 1 tsp turmeric powder
- 1 tsp salt
- 1 cup plain yogurt, beaten until smooth*
- 1 tsp aniseed powder
- 1 tsp ginger powder
- 1 tsp cumin powder

Boil the potatoes in their skins for 10–15 minutes until done, then cool in cold water, and remove the skins. Prick several holes in each potato with a toothpick or fork. Heat the oil in a deep pot over medium heat and fry the potatoes on all sides until they are uniformly golden brown. Remove with a slotted spoon and drain well.

Drain the oil into another pot, heat, and add the cloves, cardamom, cumin seeds, and asafetida. Stir for 30 seconds, then add the chili and turmeric powders with a little water and stir again until the water has evaporated. Add the yogurt, aniseed, salt and ginger powders and mix until well blended. Add the fried potatoes and stir until the potatoes are covered with the mixture. Add enough water to cover the potatoes, cover tightly, and cook over low heat for half an hour. Add a little more water if necessary. Serve hot, sprinkled with the cumin powder.

* In this and other recipes where dishes are cooked, whole-fat or low-fat yogurt should be used, not fat-free yogurt.

Plain boiled rice usually accompanies meals. Banquets feature *pulaos* and *biryanis*; sumptuous preparations of rice fried in *ghee*; onions, spices, and meat or vegetables; and dishes decorated with nuts, raisins, and saffron. In the hands of a master chef, such dishes are the apogee of Muslim haute cuisine. Kashmiris make a dessert called *zarda pulao* from rice, raisins, nuts, and saffron. Another rice-based dessert is *phirni*, a custard made from ground rice paste, sugar, milk, saffron, and rose water that is served chilled with almonds and pistachios.

Uttar Pradesh

With a population of more than 130 million, Uttar Pradesh is India's most populated state and is larger than most countries in the world. Uttar Pradesh, or U.P., as it is called, borders on Nepal and Tibet, the India states Himachal Pradesh and Madhya Pradesh, and India's capital New Delhi. The cuisine of these areas is similar. Situated on a large alluvial plain with a tropical monsoon climate, U.P. is India's top wheat-growing state and a major producer of sugarcane, pulses, potatoes, livestock and dairy products, and fruits and vegetables, including green peas, eggplants, okra, cabbage, raw plantain, black carrot, many kinds of lentils, apples, and mangoes.

From Vedic times U.P. has been the heartland of Hinduism. The great Hindu epics *Ramayana* and *Mahabharata* describe events that took place in the region in prehistory. Vanarasi (formerly Benares), Hardwar, Mathura, Brindaban, and Ayodhya are major sites of Hindu pilgrimage. The region was ruled by Hindu dynasties until the twelfth century, when invaders from Afghanistan and Central Asia conquered northern India and made Delhi their capital. The Mughal emperor Akbar founded his capital in Agra, site of the Taj Mahal that was later built by his grandson Shahjahan, whose son Aurangzeb moved the capital back to Delhi. With the decline of Mughal power, U.P. disintegrated into independent principalities, including the kingdom of Awadh, which today is the state capital Lucknow. In the nineteenth century, the entire area came under British rule.

Around 82 percent of U.P. residents are Hindus; the rest are mainly Muslims. About 60 percent of the Hindus are vegetarians but meat is eaten by a large caste called Kayasthas, the descendants of Hindus who served as administrators for the rulers. A typical vegetarian breakfast consists of bread, a vegetable or sometimes a *halwa*, a sweet dish made from vegetables, nuts, fruits, or grains. Lunch in U.P. and throughout North India consists of *dal*, bread, rice, and one or two seasonal vegetable dishes, such as cauliflower in the winter or bitter gourd in the summer. A meal may end with seasonal fruit. Vegetables can be sautéed in a few spices or cooked in a gravy. In more affluent households, the breads could be fried in *ghee* (*puris, parathas*), whereas less affluent people eat dry-roasted *chapatis* or *rotis*. Nonvegetarians would replace a vegetable dish with a meat curry. Standard spices are turmeric, red chili powder, asafetida, cumin seeds, and mustard seeds.

Dinner is essentially the same, although some households may replace *dal* with a vegetable dish. Although desserts are not a part of meals in many households, sweets are very popular in U.P., served at afternoon tea or eaten as a snack throughout the day. They are usually made with *khoya*, a sticky solid made by boiling down whole milk. Certain cities, neighborhoods, and individual shops are noted for particular items. Varanasi, for example, is famous for its *jalebis*, pretzel-like coils of chickpea batter, deep-fried in oil and soaked in sugar syrup. Agra is known for *pethas*, translucent squares made from ash gourd, alum powder, sugar, and lime juice. Lucknow specialities include *pedhas*, small fudge-like balls shaped from *khoya*, sugar, and nuts, and flavored with rose water or saffron; and *malay gujiyas*, sheets of *khoya* served over mounds of sweetened nuts. The specialty of Benares is *lassi*, a drink of yogurt mixed with mango pulp (called sweet *lassi*) or salt (plain *lassi*). Popular North Indian snacks include *kachoris*, puffy breads stuffed with lentils, corn, or vegetables; and *aloo bhaji*, potatoes spiced with ginger and cumin seeds.

The sumptuous meat-based food of Lucknow, the state's capital, is considered one of India's great cuisines. After the disintegration of the Mughal Empire in the eighteenth century, the governors of this region, called Nawabs, set up an independent court at Awadh. They were famous

for their love of luxury and their court was considered the ultimate in refinement in manners, clothing, arts, and cuisine. Eventually, this lifestyle
trickled down to the local aristocrats and even the middle class.

No expense or effort was spared on food.[5] The Nawabs recruited the
finest cooks from all over the subcontinent and paid them enormous
salaries. These cooks were in demand all over India (like French chefs in
the West today), and took their culinary skills to the courts at Hyderabad,
Bhopal, and elsewhere. They raised Mughal rice and meat dishes to new
heights of refinement and subtlety and created many new dishes. *Ghee*
(clarified butter), a symbol of luxury and the good life, was used in legendary quantities. Some cooks are said to have used as much as ten
pounds of *ghee* to cook a single piece of bread.

Lucknow became famous for the elegance, lightness, and variety of its
pulaos, a rice dish prepared with rice, vegetables or meat, and spices. One
cook was said to have cooked sixty-five pounds of meat to prepare the
broth to cook one serving of rice. Great pains were taken to ensure that
every grain of rice was separate. As many as seventy kinds of *pulao* could be
served at a banquet. Lucknow chefs were valued for their skill in disguising
ingredients: One prepared a meal consisting of hundreds of dishes, including kabobs, bread, *pulaos*, and pickles, that were all made of sugar. Chicken
and wild fowl dishes were another specialty. Wealthy gourmets fed chickens musk and saffron pills until their flesh was scented with the flavor, and
then cooked the chickens to prepare a broth in which rice was cooked.
Murgh Mussalam was a whole chicken stuffed with minced lamb and eggs
and served garnished with silver leaf that took an entire day to cook.

In the eighteenth century, the Nawabs' cooks perfected a cooking technique called *dum pukht*, which means "choking off the steam." It originated in Persia where a cooked dish would be sealed and buried in the
sand to mature. According to a legend, during a terrible famine the
Nawab tried to provide jobs for his people by building a great mosque in
Lucknow. Every day workers labored to build it and every night they tore
it down. The huge amounts of food to feed the workers were cooked in
giant pots sealed with dough and kept warm in huge, double-walled
ovens. One day the Nawab sampled the food and liked it so much that he
adapted the oven for use at court banquets.[6] This style of cooking was re-
vived in the 1980s and today is served in upscale restaurants in Indian
five-star hotels and abroad.

Typical modern Lucknow dishes include *kormas*, meat cooked in a yogurt gravy; *kalias*, meat cooked in a gravy without yogurt; *shami kabobs*,
soft lightly fried patties of boiled mincemeat and ground chickpeas and

spices; *skeekh kabob*, ground meat wrapped around iron skewers; and *kakori kabobs*, meat pounded into a fine paste, wrapped around iron skewers and charred. Popular spices are ginger; garlic and onions; cloves; green chilies; white, green, and black cardamoms; nutmeg and cinnamon; and saffron. Almonds, pistachios, and cashews are used as decoration and as a thickener for gravies. Rose water, *kewra* water, and saffron soaked in milk are added at the end of cooking to impart a characteristic perfume.

Shahi Korma (Lamb Stew with Yogurt)

- 2 pounds boneless lean lamb, cut into 1-inch cubes
- 3 medium onions, sliced
- 2 whole green cardamoms
- 1/2 cup yogurt
- 2–3 cloves garlic
- 1/2 cup oil or *ghee*
- 1-inch piece fresh ginger
- 1 tsp black pepper
- 1 tsp black cardamom seeds
- 1/2–1 tsp red chili powder (to taste)
- 1–2 tsp salt (to taste)
- Several drops of rose water
- 15 roasted almonds

Sauté the onions and the green cardamoms in the oil or *ghee* in a medium pot. When they start to brown, remove them with a slotted spoon and drain as much oil as possible back into the pot. Grind the onions, cardamom seeds, and yogurt in a food processor or blender into a paste and set aside. Grind the garlic, ginger, pepper, and black cardamoms with a little water until smooth. Heat the oil again, add the meat, the garlic mixture, and the chili powder. Cook over medium heat for ten minutes, stirring so the meat is well coated. Add the onion/yogurt mixture, two cups of water, and salt. Simmer, partly covered, for an hour or until the meat is tender. Pour into a bowl and sprinkle with rose water, and garnish with the roasted almonds. Serve with *paratha* or rice.

Madhya Pradesh, Chhattisgarh, and Jharkhand

The states of Madhya Pradesh, Chhattisgarh, and Jharkhand in Central India are among the poorest in India, with 40 percent of the population living below the poverty line. India's largest state in land area, Madhya

Pradesh is an amalgam of former princely states founded by Rajput princes and Mughal and Maratta generals. The state is a major producer of soybeans, rice, millet, wheat, legumes, and peanuts. Hindus constitute 93 percent of the population and their food is very similar to that of Uttar Pradesh. Wheat and *dal* are the dietary staples; 45 percent of the state's population are vegetarian. The tradition of Mughal cuisine, however, flourished at the court in Bhopal, the state capital. Local specialties include meat *korma*; *rizala*, a chili-flavored stew of mutton and yogurt that is often white in color; kabobs; and *biryani*. The cuisine of southern Madhya Pradesh is similar to that of Maharashtra.

Approximately 8 percent of India's total population, or 68 million people, are members of scheduled tribes or *adivasis*, Hindi for "original inhabitants." Racially and linguistically unrelated to most other Indians, they are thought to be the descendants of the original inhabitants of the subcontinent, pushed back into the forests and the mountains by invaders. More than 350 tribal groups speaking 100 languages live in every state except Haryana and Punjab. The vast majority, 87 percent live in central and western India, especially Madhya Pradesh, Orissa, Bihar, Gujarat, Rajasthan, and Andhra Pradesh, notably the Gonds, who number 7.4 million, and the Bhils, whose population totals 5.5 million. In 2001 three new states were created to give the tribals their own states: Uttaranchal, carved out of Uttar Pradesh; Jharkhand, consisting of parts of Bihar; and Chhattisgarh, made from several districts of Madhya Pradesh.

Tribals are the most deprived group in India in terms of their access to education, health care, and income. They survived in the forests by hunting and fishing, gathering wild plants, and practicing shifting cultivation; that is, clearing a piece of land, planting rice or barley, harvesting the crop, and burning the field to let it grow again. With deforestation, the tribals are becoming settled farmers, although their land is often very poor. Sometimes they barter wild cardamoms, resin, honey, and other forest products for oil, rice, salt, and cooking utensils. One source of protein are rats that live in the rice fields, which are smoked out after the harvest and boiled or roasted. Red ants are ground to make a piquant chutney. The tribal people also boil fruits, wild tapiocas, and yams, and fry pumpkins and squash flowers. In Chhattisgarh they make *baris*, sun-dried pellets of *dal* paste, which they combine with vegetable curries.

Many *adivasi* drink some kind of homemade alcohol. In Madhya Pradesh, the Gonds make a drink called *sulfi* from the sap of the sulfi tree. When first tapped, it is mildly alcoholic but after a day or two it ferments and thickens. Another drink, a clear spirit with a heady flavor, has been made from the flowers of the Mahua tree from ancient times and was even commercially produced by the British.

Punjab and Haryana

The region known as the Punjab, which means "five rivers," was where the Aryans made their first incursions in the third millennium B.C. It was ruled in succession by the Greeks, Mauryan and Gupta emperors, the Central Asian Muslim kings, the Mughals, the Sikh maharajahs, who founded a powerful state in the late eighteenth century, and finally the British, who defeated the Sikhs and created the province of Punjab. In 1947, it was divided between Pakistan and India. In 1966, the Indian portion was broken into three states on linguistic and religious grounds: the small mountain state of Himachal Pradesh; Haryana, where the majority of the people are Hindus; and Punjab, which has a large Sikh population. New Delhi, India's capital, is a National Capital Territory, somewhat like Washington, D.C., which was carved out of parts of Punjab, Haryana, and Uttar Pradesh. Once the capital of the Mughal Empire, Delhi was a leading center of Muslim culture and cuisine, but after partition in 1947, many of its residents left for Pakistan. Today its residents include many Punjabis, descendants of people who left Pakistan for India, as well as people from other parts of India who are government employees. The city's cuisine reflects this diversity.

Located on a fertile plain, Punjab and Haryana are both the breadbasket of India and its leading industrial centers. The soil is intensely irrigated and fertilized, almost all villages have electricity, and farming is more mechanized than elsewhere in India. The people have a reputation as hardworking and entrepreneurial, and less than 10 percent of the state's population live in poverty.

Somewhat paradoxically, in view of the area's high income, this region also has a high proportion of vegetarians—54 percent. Most of India's wheat and much of its rice are produced in Punjab and Haryana. Other crops are millet, corn, sugarcane, chickpeas, mustard, and fruits and vegetables, including potatoes, tomatoes, onions, cabbage, cauliflower, and eggplant. Dairy farming (cows and buffalo) is an important industry. Milk, buttermilk, *ghee*, yogurt, and other dairy products are an important part of people's daily fare, and Punjabis are by far India's largest per capita milk consumers.

The cuisine of Hindus and Sikhs is very similar. Haryana is sometimes called the "Land of *Rotis*" because the main staple is bread (*roti*) made

from wheat, millet, or corn flour. The diet of the predominantly Hindu
residents is mainly vegetarian, and although Brahmins here do not eat
meat, they do eat onions and garlic. Seasonal vegetables, such as cauliflower, carrots, turnips, pumpkins, and mustard greens, play a central role
in the daily diet. Most Sikhs are not vegetarian, although they do not eat
beef. People in this part of India have a low rate of lactose intolerance and
drink a lot of milk, flavored yogurt (*lassi*), and buttermilk.

The food of Punjab and Haryana is simple, robust, and closely linked to
the land. Women often work beside men on the farms, so relatively less
time is spent on cooking than in other parts of India. In rural areas, the
day starts with a hearty breakfast consisting of *parathas*, perhaps stuffed
with potatoes, cauliflower, or grated radish, or small thick *rotis* made from
wheat, corn flour, or barley and topped with a large dollop of butter. On
special occasions, breakfast may be supplemented with *halwa*, a dish of
grated vegetables cooked in *ghee* and sugar syrup.

Lunch and dinner consist of bread and butter, *dal*, yogurt, a vegetable
dish, and perhaps meat. Both chicken and mutton are popular in the Punjab. Although tandoori chicken is regarded as the archtypical Punjabi
dish, the vast majority of people do not own their own *tandoor*, though
some villages have communal ovens.

Sikh family meal, Amritsar. Photo © TRIP/H. Rogers.

Paneer—milk solids pressed under a weight and cut into cubes—is used to make curries with peas and other vegetables or grilled as kabobs. A common sauce for curries is based on onion, tomatoes, garlic, and ginger fried in *ghee*. Spicing is straightforward rather than subtle, featuring coriander, cumin seeds, and red chilies.

If meat is part of a meal, it may be accompanied by a yogurt salad, chopped onions and tomatoes, and a plain bread without butter. Typical meat dishes include *keema matar*, a rich, dry stew of minced mutton, beans, tomatoes, onions, garlic, and spices, and *mutton rarha*, cooked with yogurt, tomatoes, and spices until the gravy dries up and the meat is well browned. Rice is served mainly on special occasions, prepared with onions, peas, jaggery, or vegetables.

The region's thick rich *dals* are famous all over the subcontinent. They are made from black lentils, chickpeas, black-eyed peas, or kidney beans, simmered for a long time over a slow fire until they become thick and then flavored with spices and cream. *Dal Makhani* has been called India's favorite lentil dish.

Dal Makhani (Black Lentils)

- 2/3 cup *urad dal* (whole)
- 3 tb dried red kidney beans
- 1-inch piece of ginger or 3 tsp ready made ginger paste
- 4 cloves garlic or 3 tsp garlic paste
- Four tomatoes pureed in a food processor or blender
- 1 tsp chili powder
- 1 tsp salt (or to taste)
- 4 tb *ghee* or oil
- 1/2 cup cream

Wash the lentils (*urad dal*) and kidney beans and soak overnight. If ready-made ginger and garlic paste is not available, grind the ginger and garlic together in a paste with a little water. Drain the water from the lentils and beans and place in a large pot with six cups of water. Add salt, half the garlic and ginger paste, and one tablespoon of *ghee* and simmer until the lentils are cooked. Mash lightly. Heat the remaining *ghee* and cook the tomatoes, chili powder, and the rest of the ginger and garlic paste until the *ghee* separates from the mixture. Add the mixture to the cooked lentils and cook over low heat for 20–25 minutes, mashing occasionally with a spoon against the side of the pot. Add the cream and cook for 15–20 minutes more.

Another well-known Punjabi dish is mustard greens, *sarson ka saag*, served with corn bread *(makki ki roti)* on special occasions. The following is a relatively low-fat version: An authentic version could use as much as a cup of butter!

Sarson Ka Saag (Punjabi-style Greens)

- 2 pounds mustard leaves
- 1 pound spinach
- 2 green chilies
- 2 cloves garlic
- 2-inch piece of ginger
- 1 tsp salt or to taste
- 2 tb corn flour
- 1 tsp chili powder (optional)
- 1 tb butter or *ghee*

The Tempering

- 2 tb *ghee*
- 2 green chilies, finely chopped
- 1-inch piece of ginger, finely chopped.

Wash the mustard and spinach leaves well, peel the leaves from the stems, then chop the stems into one-inch pieces. Tear the leaves into large pieces and put the leaves and stems into a large pot with half a cup of water. Finely chop the garlic, ginger, and chilies and add them to the leaves. Bring the mixture to a boil, turn down the heat, cover and simmer until tender (around 15–20 minutes). Remove, drain, and save any remaining liquid. Make a coarse purée of the vegetables using a food processor or blender. Return to the pot, add the flour and chili powder, mix well, and add the rest of the liquid and the butter. Cover and cook for 15 minutes on low heat, stirring occasionally. When it is done, pour into a bowl. Before serving, melt the *ghee* in a frying pan, add the chilies and ginger, sauté for a few minutes, and pour over the purée. Serve with corn tortillas.

WESTERN INDIA

Rajasthan

The state of Rajasthan was formed by the union of more than twenty princely states, including Jaipur, Udaipur, Jodhpur, Bikaner, and Jaisalmer. The kingdoms were founded in the ninth and tenth centuries by a warrior caste called Rajputs, some of whom later allied with the Mughals and the British. Famous for their chivalry and martial skills, the Rajput rulers built splendid palaces and mountain fortresses, many of which have been converted into hotels.

The Aravalli mountain range divides the state into the hilly southeastern region and the barren Thar Desert, one of the hottest and driest regions of the world. Thanks to irrigation, Rajasthan has become a leader in the production of millet, rapeseed, mustard, barley, corn, cumin, coriander, fenugreek, soybeans, and livestock. Around 90 percent of the population are Hindus and Jains. Some Jains became merchants and traders called Marwaris (from Rajasthan's Marwar district). They migrated all over India and include some of the country's wealthiest industrialists. Approximately 60 percent of Rajasthanis are vegetarians.

There are two Rajasthani cuisines: that of the princes and that of the ordinary people. The Rajput princes adopted the meat and rice dishes of the Mughal Court. A traditional Rajput banquet consisted of many courses, featuring rich, heavily spiced meat dishes, especially wild boar, venison, and other game, since hunting was part of their lifestyle. Some courts developed their own specialties: The rulers of Udaipur, forced to hide in the rocky countryside by the Mughals, developed a form of barbecue called *soola*, while the Jaipur family created a delicacy called *safed maas*, literally "white meat," made only of white ingredients.[7]

Safed Maas (White Meat Curry)

- 2 pounds boneless lamb, cut into 2-inch squares
- 1 cup yogurt
- 2 tsp salt (or to taste)
- 1/2 cup *ghee* or oil
- 1 tsp white pepper
- 2 tb fresh ginger, minced finely
- 2 tb poppy seeds
- 1/4 cup blanched almonds without skins
- 1/4 cup grated unsweetened coconut
- 1/2 tsp white cardamom powder
- 1/4 cup cream
- 2 tsp rose water
- 4 green chilies, sliced lengthwise
- Juice from one lemon or lime

Boil the lamb in water and one teaspoon of salt for five minutes. Drain, and wash
the meat well. Grind the almonds, poppy seeds, and grated coconut in a food
processor or blender with enough water to make a smooth paste. Heat the *ghee* or
oil, and add the meat, the yogurt, one teaspoon of salt, ginger, and three cups of
water. Cover and simmer for one and one-half hours, stirring occasionally, or
until the meat is tender and the water has almost evaporated. Add the almond,
coconut, white pepper, and poppy-seed paste and cook, stirring, for two minutes.
Add the cardamom powder, cream, lemon or lime juice, and rose water, and stir.
Cover the pan tightly and cook for 15 minutes more. Decorate with the green
chilies.

The traditional staples of Rajasthan are millet, barley, and corn, ground
into flour by hand to produce some of the subcontinent's most delicious
breads. (Wheat is increasingly replacing these traditional grains.) Sometimes spiced green peas, fenugreek leaves, or potatoes are added to the
batter. Cooking oil and *ghee* are precious commodities among poor people,
so breads are usually roasted on a heavy pan, with a little *ghee* added before serving. A famous Rajasthani bread called a *batti* is a ball made from
flour and water roasted in the coals of a fire until it is hard, then cracked
open and eaten with *ghee*. Rice is eaten only on special occasions.

Lentils are an important ingredient in Rajasthani cuisine, especially
for Jains, who cannot eat most root vegetables, onions, or garlic. Lentils
are boiled to make *dals* and *kadhis*, spicy curries of yogurt and chickpea
flour, and ground into flour to make breads and snacks. Chickpea flour is
mixed with yogurt, chili powder, and water to make a dough that is rolled
into long, thin strands that are boiled and dried to make an unusual ingredient called *gattas*, which are stored and used like a vegetable in curries.

The varieties of fruits and vegetables is limited by the climate and soil,
so vegetables are sun-dried and stored for future use. Mangoes are abundant and used to make drinks, desserts, and pickles; mango seed is sliced
and cooked with onions and spices. Common Rajasthani spices are cumin
seeds, red chilies, *ajwain*, and asafetida (a pungent-smelling resin sometimes used as a substitute for garlic).

Rural people typically start the day with leftover bread from the night
before and a glass of buttermilk or milk. Lunch and dinner consist of
bread, *dal* or *kadhi*, and a vegetable. For lunch and dinner, an affluent
farmer or town dweller might eat bread, *dal* or *kadhi*, two or three vegetables, a salad, and pickles, to which nonvegetarians would add a meat curry
or kabob. Sweets are generally served only on special occasions, since
sugar is not grown locally. Crushed millet is mixed with buttermilk and

sugar and cooked in the coals overnight to make a sweet dish called *rabri*. Wheat flour, semolina, *ghee*, sugar, almonds, and raisins are shaped into balls, fried, broken into pieces and powdered to make a famous Rajasthani sweet called *churma*. *Churma, dal,* and *batti* is a popular combination. Spicy pickles and sweet chutneys made from chilies, mangoes, garlic, and lemon add an additional dimension.

Gujarat

The state of Gujarat, bordered by the Arabian Sea, Pakistan, and the states of Rajasthan, Madhya Pradesh, and Maharashtra, was created in 1960 when the state of Bombay, a creation of the British, was divided by language into Gujarat and Maharashtra. Two-thirds of Gujaratis are rural, but a large minority are merchants and businessmen who immigrated to other parts of India, East Africa, the United Kingdom, and North America. Ninety percent of the population are Hindus.

The main crops are rice, wheat, millet, lentils, peanuts, and cotton. Seventy percent of the population are vegetarians—the highest proportion in India. Many Hindus do not eat eggs, onions, or garlic; a standard flavoring is a green chili and ginger paste. Spice mixtures include turmeric, mustard seed, fenugreek seeds, asafetida, and cumin seeds. Dishes are made with relatively little oil, by Indian standards, and some are steamed. Sweet-and-sour is a popular flavoring, the sourness provided by *khokum*, the rind of a fruit.

Gujarat grows many distinctive vegetables, including *papri*, a very long, thin, green bean; *arvi*, the leaves of the taro plant; and many kinds of squash and yams. Gujaratis like to add a pinch of sugar to *dals* and vegetables dishes and serve a piece of jaggery (sugarcane) on the side. Milk- or lentil-based sweets are sometimes served as part of the meal.

Gujarat has three regions, each with its own culinary style. Western Gujarat, or Saurashtra, is very dry, so vegetables are hard to grow; this region is famous for its dairy products, dried vegetable dishes, and pickles. Specialties include *chhundo*, a hot and sweet shredded-mango pickle, and *methia masala*, a dry powder made from fenugreek seeds, chili powder, and salt sprinkled over raw vegetables and salads.

Central Gujarat and the state capital Ahmedabad is the granary of Gujarat, known for its breads, snacks, and lentil dishes. Southern Gujarat and its capital Surat is a fertile, well-watered region that produces plenty of green vegetables and fruit, including some of India's finest mangoes. The best-known Surati dish is *undhio* or *oondhiya*, a medley of sweet potatoes, eggplant, green beans, grated coconut, and little dumplings made from chickpea flour and fenugreek leaves. Surat is also home to one of India's oldest Muslim communities, which has its own distinctive cuisine. It is one of the few in India that features soups: hot soups, cold soups, breakfast soups, and soups with lamb and cashew nuts.

Breakfast usually consists of tea with bread left over from the previous night; *papri*, crisp little squares made from chickpea flour; or puffed rice, called *poha*. Many families eat lunch between 10 and 11 A.M., before they go to work. The food is served on a *thali*, a round metal tray, together with a piece of jaggery, pickles, and a crispy snack. Lunch starts with bread, made from wheat flour or, in the winter, millet, served with a vegetable and a bean dish. A standard way of preparing vegetables is to sauté them with cumin seed and asafetida, then add coriander, cumin, red chilies and turmeric, and finally tomatoes. Shredded vegetables are also sautéed with mustard and fenugreek seeds. Yam, cucumber, potatoes, and peanuts are simmered to make a delicious stew that is topped with yogurt, coconut chutney, and fried potato straws. Corn and green pepper slices are cooked in milk that is thickened with flour and tempered with spices.

The second part of a Gujarati meal is plain boiled rice and *dal* or *kadhi*, a spicy yogurt curry thickened with chickpea flour. A more formal meal includes a sweet pudding or dessert. Some Gujarati sweets are milk-based, others are made from lentils, such as a sweet lentil-stuffed bread or a sweet pudding (*halwa*) made from chickpea flour.

Afternoon tea is an occasion for enjoying Gujarat's delicious snacks, called *farsans*. A nuts-and-bolts mixture called *chevda* is made from rice flakes, peanuts, spices, raisins, grated coconut, and sugar. Others are a long cylindrical rice and yogurt cake, steamed in banana leaves; soft, steamed dumplings made of a green *moong dal* batter; puffy wheat bread stuffed with *moong dal*, fried in spices; and mashed potatoes mixed with ginger and chilies and fired in a chickpea flour batter. The equivalent of a national dish is *dhokla*, a savory dish with a spongy texture. Lentils are mixed with water, fermented overnight, then ground and rolled into slabs that are steamed, cut into squares, and garnished with coriander leaves, fried mustard seeds, and coconut. Sometimes chopped carrots, beans, and peas, or yogurt, are added to the batter.

Dinner, served at 8 or 8:30 P.M., is similar to but smaller than lunch. Sometimes it features a thick bread called *bakri* and a vegetable or a one-dish meal, such as a *khichri* made from rice, *moong dal*, and vegetables and nuts or a savory cake, called a *handvo*, made from a batter of fermented ground rice, *dal*, and yogurt baked with grated white pumpkin and spices.

Kadhi (Yogurt Curry)

- 2 cups yogurt, beaten until smooth
- 2 cups water
- 1 1/2 tb chickpea flour
- 2 green chilies
- 1-half inch ginger
- 1 tsp sugar
- 1/2 tsp turmeric
- 1 tsp salt

Tempering

- 1 tb *ghee*
- 1 tsp cumin seeds
- 1/2 tsp mustard seeds
- 1 red chili, broken into pieces
- 7–8 curry leaves
- 1 tb chopped coriander leaves

Grind the chilies and ginger with a little water to make a paste. Mix it with the yogurt, water, chickpea flour, turmeric, salt, and sugar in a heavy-bottom pan and cook over medium heat, stirring constantly, until it comes to a boil. Turn down the heat and simmer on low heat for five minutes. Remove from the flame.

In tempering, heat the *ghee,* fry the cumin seeds, mustard seeds, chili, and curry leaves for a minute, and pour this into the yogurt mixture. Cook for a few minutes and pour into a bowl. Sprinkle the coriander leaves over the top and serve hot with rice.

Maharashtra

The state of Maharashtra, the second largest in India, is India's industrial powerhouse and its capital, Mumbai (formerly Bombay), India's financial center. The state is also a major producer of oil seeds, peanuts, soybeans, sugarcane, turmeric, vegetables, and grapes. Fish and seafood are abundant along the 500-mile coast. Maharashtra, the center of a great empire in the eighteenth century, was created in 1960 for Marathi speakers. Around 80 percent of the population are Hindus, 10 percent Muslims, and the rest Christians and Parsis. The two major Hindu castes are Brahmins, who do not eat meat, and the nonvegetarian Marathas. Around 30 percent of the state's population are vegetarians.

Maharastrian cuisine is very eclectic because of the state's location between North and South—both wheat and rice are dietary staples—and its central role in the transfer of fruits and vegetables between the hemispheres by the Portuguese starting in the sixteenth century. Chilies, tomatoes, potatoes, peanuts, corn, sweet potatoes, green peppers, green beans, cashew nuts, tapioca, and papayas, play a larger role in Maharashtrian cuisine than in other parts of India.

Another distinctive feature is the blending of sweet, salt, hot, and sour flavors in a meal or even a single dish. As they do in Gujarat, cooks often add a pinch of sugar to a vegetable stew and sweets are an integral part of a meal—eaten *during* the meal, not afterward. Foods are placed in a strictly defined order on *thalis* or, at feasts, banana leaves.[8] *Rassa,* the typical spice mixture used in Maharashtrian households, contains coriander seeds, poppy seeds, coconut, cumin seeds, sesame seeds, red chilies, turmeric, and cloves roasted together to produce a characteristic black color. There is little deep-frying or roasting, and dishes are lightly sautéed and steamed to retain their flavors.

A phenomenon unique to Mumbai are the lunch box carriers (*dabba wallahs*). Each day 5,000 of them pick up home-cooked meals in lunch boxes called *dabbas*, or tiffin carriers, from households in the city and suburbs and deliver them to 170,000 office workers. The system relies on multiple relays; a single box can change hands three times during its journey. The margin of error has been estimated at one mistake in 8 million deliveries.

There are two major subregional cuisines. The cuisine of the coast, called Konkani, is based on seafood, coconut, and fruit and vegetables. Popular fish includes bombil, better known as Bombay duck, a small fish that is dried and fried until it is crisp; mackerel curried with chilies and ginger; and pomfret, which is eaten stuffed, grilled, fried, or curried in a coconut gravy. Crabs, prawns, shrimps, shellfish, and lobster are also eaten along the coast.

In the dry, peanut-growing interior region of the Deccan plateau, vegetables are cooked with coconut, corn, and peanuts or prepared in a *pachadi*, a salad-like dish combining green mangos, coconut, and *gur*. Rice is served at every meal either boiled or made into soft bread called *bhakris*. Many meals include *papads*, called *pappadums* in South India—crisp, round disks made from dried lentil flour, sometimes flavored with chilies, pepper, or garlic.

Breakfast may be *idli* (steamed bread made from ground rice and lentils); *sambar* (a spicy lentil stew with vegetables); and coconut chutney, as in

South India, or lightly fried bread with an onion-yogurt salad, a *dal* or curry, and a coconut sweet. Lunch typically starts with *amti*, a lentil and vegetable soup, or *saar*, a thin tomato soup. This is followed by lightly fried vegetables, such as potato with peanuts or a vegetable such as sweet potatoes, cabbage, or eggplant sautéed in a little peanut oil with mustard and cumin seeds served with a plain *dal*, rice, and perhaps a crunchy *papad* or fried vegetables. A nonvegetarian home could include a shrimp or fish curry. The second course would feature wheat chapatis and additional helpings of vegetables, chutneys, pickles and salad, accompanied by plain yogurt.

A more formal meal would include additional vegetables, meat and fish dishes, elaborate rice preparations, and an abundance of sweet dishes such as *puranpoli*, a pancake made with wheat flour, brown sugar, cardamom, and saffron, and eaten with *ghee*; a soft pudding made from strained yogurt flavored with saffron, cardamom, nuts, and candied fruit called *shrikand*; or *chikki*, a peanut-brittle–like sweet made with coconut and sugar. A wedding feast is a lavish affair that follows a time-honored formula: It *must* include three liquid curries, three dry vegetables, three kinds of rice, eight breads and savories, three sweet dishes, a chutney, and a pickle, all laid on carefully prescribed places on a banana leaf, with seasoning, relishes, and savories on the left and vegetables, *dals*, and sweets on the right.

Peanut Potatoes

- 1 1/2 lb potatoes, boiled, peeled, and cut into pieces 1 1/2-inch square
- 2 tb oil
- 1/4 cup roasted unsalted peanuts, ground to a powder
- 1-inch piece of ginger, finely minced
- 1 tsp whole cumin seeds
- 1 tsp cumin powder
- 1 tb coriander powder
- salt and chili powder to taste
- a handful of coriander leaves, finely chopped

Use a nonstick pan or spray the pan before heating the oil. Fry the ginger and cumin seeds until they stop crackling. Add the boiled potato cubes and fry for five to six minutes until they start to turn brown. Add salt; cumin; coriander and chili powders; and the ground peanuts. Toss gently and thoroughly for a couple of minutes and then remove from the fire. Decorate with coriander leaves.

Parsis are the descendants of Zoroastrians who fled the Arab invasion of Persia in the seventh century and settled along the west coast of India. In the nineteenth and early twentieth centuries the Parsi community in Mumbai was instrumental in the development of Indian industry and commerce. However, because they do not allow conversion or recognize the children of mixed marriages as Parsis, their numbers are rapidly declining and were less than 100,000 in the 1991 census.

During their thirteen hundred years in western India, the Parsi community developed a distinctive cuisine that combines Gujarati, Maharashtrian, Iranian, and British influences.[9] Parsis are basically meat and fish eaters, although they may avoid beef and pork out of respect for their Hindu and Muslim neighbors. Meat dishes are cooked Iranian-style with vegetables, such as eggplants, potatoes, spinach, and peas. The Iranian influence is also seen in the use of nuts, dried fruits, and rose water and the popularity of *pulaos* and *biryanis*. The most famous Parsi dish, *dhansakh*, combines meat with as many as seven kinds of beans and lentils, pumpkin, eggplant, fenugreek leaves, onions, ginger, garlic, tamarind, and spices. Spices and chilies are used in moderation.

Eggs are a very popular breakfast dish—in the old days eating three or four a day was not unusual—served over minced meats, fish, potatoes, cooked vegetables, or bananas. Scrambled eggs flavored with onions, garlic, coriander leaves, and tomatoes, and cooked in *ghee* are a popular dish called *akoori*. Other ingredients can be added, including corn, fried potatoes, shrimp, dried fruit, and nuts. Most meals are accompanied by breads made from wheat or millet flour, pickles, and chutneys. The Parsi community adopted many English dishes, including custard, cakes, puddings, and stews. Potato straws are a popular accompaniment to stews.

Some typical Parsi dishes are *patra ni macchim*, fish marinated in salt and lime juice or grated coconut, and steamed with spices in banana leaves; *batero*, chicken or mutton marinated in lightly fermented *toddy* or beer and spices; and hundred-almond curry, chicken simmered in coconut milk, ground spices, and almonds. Parsi cusine features some unusual combinations: chicken with candied sweet potato, gooseberries, papaya, dried apricot, and peaches, or fried eels dipped in sugar syrup.

Goa

The tiny state of Goa 250 miles south of Mumbai was a Portuguese possession from the early sixteenth century until 1961, and even today older Goans speak Portuguese. Its 250 miles of sandy beaches and maze of canals and rivers make it India's favorite tourist spot. The soil is sandy and there is little arable land, but there is plenty of fish, seafood, fruit, cashews, and coconut, and a profusion of the spices that attracted the Europeans five centuries ago. About a third of the population are Roman Catholic; the rest are mainly Hindu but many Brahmins here eat fish, which is a staple of the diet. The state is affluent—less than 5 percent live below the poverty line—and meat plays an important role in Goan cuisine, including pork, chicken, and beef. Goan cooks are famous throughout India and the world for their culinary expertise.

In style and techniques, Goan cuisine is a distinctive amalgam of Portuguese, Indian, and even British influences. There are two styles of cooking. The first are classic Portuguese dishes enlivened by aromatic spices, among them *chorizo*, garlicky pork sausage; *caldo verde*, a chicken and spinach soup flavored with ginger and black pepper; pork pie; pork *assad*, which is pan-roasted meat; pork sausages, sometimes laced with *feni*, a potent liquor made from the fruit of the cashew tree that is the national drink; and *sopa de camrao*, or shrimp soup. Baking is a Goan specialty and the Portuguese tradition lives on in such cakes and pastries as sweet rolls called *pau*; *bibinca*, a cake made stacking layers of pancakes; and *boliho de coco*, little coconut cakes.

The second category of dishes are much hotter and spicier. The most famous Goan dish is *vindaloo* (from the Portuguese *vinha de alhos*, meaning rich in garlic)—a sweet, sour, and fiery-hot pork curry, made with coconut, vinegar, sugar, spices, and red chilies. *Sorpotel* is a savory stew traditionally made with pork, pig's liver, heart, and brain, and fresh pig's blood, flavored with spices, vinegar, ginger, onions, garlic, and chilies. *Arroz reogado* is a kind of *pulao* of rice, piquant Goan sausages, cloves, ginger, onions, and garlic. *Chicken xacuti*, a favorite at Goan restaurants, is made by sautéing pieces of chicken in a paste of roasted coconut, spices, peanuts, and poppy seeds, ginger, garlic, and onions, then simmering it in water, and adding vinegar. A typical Goan lunch starts with a mildly spiced meat or fish dish served with rolls. The second and main course might be a fish curry or fried fish and rice.

Chicken Xacuti (pronounced "shakuti")

- 1 1/2 pounds skinned chicken thighs or legs cut into two
- 4 tb lime juice
- 1/2 tsp salt
- 2 tb coriander seeds
- 1/2 tsp cumin seeds

- 2 to 6 red chilies
- 1/2 tsp fenugreek seeds
- 4 black peppercorns
- 2 tsp peanuts (shelled)
- 1-inch stick of cinnamon
- 2 ounces dried unsweetened coconut
- 4 cloves
- 1/4 tsp turmeric powder
- 3 tb oil
- 2 tb vinegar

Rub the lime juice and salt over the chicken and marinade for 30 minutes. Roast the whole spices, peanuts, and coconut on a dry pan, shaking or stirring frequently, until they start to emit an aroma. Remove from the heat, add the turmeric powder and grind into a powder. Add a little water and grind in a blender or small food processor into a paste. Heat the oil in a heavy pan and fry the paste for several minutes until it starts to release oil. Add the chicken pieces, mix well, and fry for 9 or 10 minutes over medium heat, stirring frequently. Add a cup of water, bring to a boil, and simmer until the chicken is tender, around 40–45 minutes. When done, add the vinegar.

SOUTH INDIA

India's four southern states—Tamil Nadu, Karnataka, Andhra Pradesh, and Kerala—are linguistically and gastronomically distinct from the rest of the country. The languages spoken in these states (called, respectively, Tamil, Kannada, Telugu, and Malayalam) are not Indo-European, like most North Indian languages, but belong to the Dravidian family and have their own scripts and vocabulary (albeit with many Sanskrit words). Some scholars theorize that the Dravidians were the original inhabitants of the subcontinent, but were pushed south by the Aryan invaders thousands of years ago. The region was the center of several great empires and, except for parts of Andhra Pradesh, never fell under Mughal control.

Although the population is predominantly Hindu, there are large Muslim and Christian minorities. Hindus have a reputation of being more devout than people in the rest of the country. There are more than 30,000 Hindu temples in Tamil Nadu alone. The caste system was more rigid in this region than in other places, and South Indian Brahmins were known for their orthodox lifestyles and strict vegetarianism. A very large number of South Indian dishes are made with rice and a wide variety of lentils.

Typical spices include mustard seeds, fenugreek, cumin seed, asafetida, curry leaves, red chilies, and tamarind. Grated coconut is used to flavor dishes or to make a gravy. However, such commonalities should not overshadow differences between the cuisines of these four states as well as some distinctive regional styles of cooking.

Tamil Nadu

Tamil Nadu, India's southernmost state, is the heartland of Dravidian culture. Its capital, Chennai, formerly Madras, was founded by the British as Fort St. George in the seventeenth century and was one of three centers of British rule in India. However, the British had less influence on Tamil culture or cuisine than in Bengal. The state's population is 89 percent Hindu, 5 percent Muslim, and 5 percent Christian. Tamil Brahmins are strict vegetarians.

Tamil Nadu is bounded by the Bay of Bengal and the Indian Ocean, so fishing is a major industry. The Ghat mountain range to the west is home to coffee and tea plantations. The major crops are rice, millet and other coarse cereals, pulses, sugarcane, peanuts, onions, and oil seeds. Vegetables include eggplant, beans, various kinds of pumpkin and gourds, cabbage, cluster beans, drumsticks (long, thin pods with large seeds), plantain (a large green banana), the stem of the amaranth plant, carrots, green mangoes, yams and potatoes.

Breakfast is the most important meal in a South Indian household and typically is centered around *idlis* and *dosas*. The dough for both is made by soaking rice and *urad dal* (albeit in different combinations) and grinding them into pastes that are left to ferment, usually overnight. To make *idlis*, the batter is poured into special trays with perforated indentations that are stacked on top of each other in a steamer. For *dosas*, the thin batter is poured onto a hot griddle smeared with a little oil. *Idlis* and *dosas* are served with *sambar*—a spicy lentil soup or stew made from *toor dal* and vegetables—and coconut chutney, a paste made by grinding fried coconut with *channa dal*, salt, green chilies, mustard seed, *urad dal*, and lime juice. An alternative is *milakai podi*, a powder made from ground lentils, spices, and chilies. The appropriate drink is strong, filtered coffee mixed with milk that is reminiscent of French *café au lait*.

Sambar (South Indian Lentil Stew with Vegetables)

- 1/2 cup lentils (preferably toor dal)
- 1/2 tsp turmeric powder

- 1 cup mixed vegetables cut into 1-inch cubes (potatoes, eggplant, okra, green pepper, etc.)
- 1 medium onion, roughly chopped

Spices

- 1 1/2 tb coriander seeds
- 3 tsp *channa dal*
- 1 1/2 tsp cumin seed
- 1/2 tsp fenugreek seed
- 1/4 tsp black pepper
- 1 tsp mustard seed
- 4 cloves
- 1/2 piece cinnamon
- 1 to 4 red chilies (to taste) (An alternative is 3 tsp of ready-made *sambar* powder.)
- 1/2 cup grated coconut (unsweetened)
- 1 tb tamarind paste, dissolved in a little warm water
- 1 tsp brown sugar

Tempering

- 1 tb oil
- 1 red chili broken into pieces
- 1 tsp mustard seed
- 3 to 4 curry leaves

Wash the lentils well, drain, put in a saucepan and add two cups of water and the turmeric powder. Cook over low heat for 25 minutes. Add the vegetables. After 5 minutes, add the onions and cook 10 minutes more. Add more water if needed to maintain the consistency of a creamed soup.

Roast the spices in a heavy frying pan over medium heat, shaking frequently, until they start to brown. Cool and grind the mixture (or the *sambar* powder) into a paste with the coconut and a little water. Mix with the tamarind paste and water and sugar and add to the boiled lentils. Heat one tablespoon of oil and fry the chili and mustard seeds until they start to crackle. Add to the lentils with the curry leaves and stir lightly. Serve with *idlis* or *dosas*, made from prepackaged mixes.

Idlis and *dosas* come in many varieties (see Table 2.1). The batter can be made from a mixture of semolina flour, mustard seed, ginger, green chilies, cashew nuts, and yogurt; wheat and rice flours mixed with buttermilk; rice and grated coconut; wheat flour, jaggery (unrefined brown sugar made from brown sap), coconut, and cardamom; or ground *moong dal*. A special saucer-shaped pan is used to make a kind of *dosa* called *addai*. *Dosas* may be filled with spiced potatoes or other vegetables, in which case they are called *masala dosas*. *Dosas* in Tamil Nadu are generally thicker and softer than the thin, crispy ones favored in Karnataka.

South Indian lunch and dinners follow a set pattern. The first course consists of white rice, *sambar,* and a vegetable dish made from seasonal products. Typical dishes are diced mixed vegetables cooked with grated coconut, green chilies, cumin seeds, yogurt, and curry leaves *(avial);* cooked chopped plantains, pumpkin, or ash gourd mixed with a paste of coconut, cumin seeds, green chilies *(koottu);* grated potatoes, coconut and curry leaves *(puttu);* and a dry vegetable dish flavored with mustard seeds, chilies, grated coconut, and curry leaves *(poriyal)*.

The second course consists of rice; *rasam,* a watery hot and sour plain *dal* that is the prototype of mulligatawny soup (the English name comes from Tamil words meaning "pepper water"); and another vegetable. The final course is always plain or flavored buttermilk or yogurt. If guests are present, a sweet may be served in between the last two courses—perhaps fresh fruit or *payasam,* a semi-liquid rice pudding. *Pappadums,* crispy lentil wafers, or a deep-fried lentil bread that looks like a hole-less donut, called *vada,* may also be part of the meal.

A nonvegetarian cuisine of Tamil Nadu is that of the Chettinad or Chettiars, a wealthy trading community famous for their hot, aromatic meat preparations made with onions, garlic, ginger, chilies, peppercorns, and aromatic spices. Typical dishes include *kozhambu,* meatballs in a creamy paste of cashews, poppy seeds, coconut, and fennel seeds; chicken cooked in tamarind water; chettinad chicken, prepared in a gravy of onions and tomatoes flavored with spices and curry leaves; and fried fish marinated in a paste of coriander, cumin, salt, and lime juice.

Karnataka

The state of Karnataka was created in 1956 from the former princely state of Mysore and the Kannada-speaking areas of adjacent states. It borders Maharashtra to the north, Kerala to the south, and Andhra Pradesh and Tamil Nadu to the east. The state capital, Bangalore, the fastest-growing city in Asia, is the center of India's booming computer industries and is known for its Western-style pubs and restaurants.

Karnataka is divided into three regions: a narrow coastal area along the Arabian Sea; the lush, well-watered hills of the Western Ghats; and bare plains to the east. The state grows rice, mangoes, wheat, millet, coconuts, peanuts, oil seeds, wheat, coffee, tea, cashews, and spices, especially peppercorns and cardamoms. Eighty-five percent of the population are Hindus, 12 percent Muslims, and 2 percent Christians. Around 34 percent of the population are vegetarians.

The food has features in common with the cuisines of the neighboring states of Tamil Nadu and Maharashtra. Statewide, people consume equal amounts of rice, wheat, and millet (ragi), although rice is more of a staple in the South and wheat in the North. A distinctive Karnataka dish is mandige, a large wheat paratha that is blended with finely ground sugar and cardamom powder and baked on an upside-down clay pot. The bread is crumbled and mixed with cream, coconut milk, and mango juice; shaped into a ball; and baked in a sealed pot. An essential part of every festival, wedding, and happy occasion is the local sweet Mysore pak, small triangles with a fudge-like consistency made from chickpea flour, ghee, and sugar.

Breakfast could be idli; dosa; a porridge made of ground semolina, onions, and spices called uppuma; or puffed rice cooked with coconut, lemon juice, and seasoning. Lunch and dinner follow the Tamil pattern: a first course of rice, dal, and a vegetable and coconut salad called kosumbri; followed by rice; sambar (called huli); and mixed vegetables; and ending with yogurt.

Coorg, or Kordava, a lush hilly region of coffee, spice, and orange plantations in the Western Ghats, has a distinctive cuisine characterized by pork and chicken curries made with coconut milk, mushroom and bamboo shoot stews, and breads, noodles, and round dumplings made from rice.

The coastal region of Mangalore is famous for its spicy fish and seafood preparations and omnipresence of coconut in the form of oil, milk, or grated. Rice is eaten in many forms: as dosas; sannas, idlis fermented with toddy or yeast; kori rotis, a wafer-thin bread; and adyes, round dumplings made of ground rice and coconut milk. Patrode is a famous Mangalorean dish of colocasia leaves stuffed with rice, dal, coconut, jaggery, and spices rolled and steamed.

Kerala

When the Italian explorer Christopher Columbus set out on his historic voyage five hundred years ago, his destination was India's fabled Malabar Coast, which today is part of the state of Kerala in Southwest

India. From time immemorial, this region had been visited by merchants from Egypt, Greece, Rome, the Middle East, and China who came to buy spices, ginger, ivory, and textiles. Kerala remains a leading exporter of spices, cashew nuts, and shrimp.

The state's lush, green landscape is covered with coconut groves, banana trees, rice paddies, and kitchen vegetable gardens, while its 400 miles of coastline and fresh and saltwater lagoons are teeming with fish and seafood. Cardamom, coffee, and tea grow in the eastern highlands, which in the past protected the kingdoms of Cochin and Travencore from the incursions of the British and helped preserve the region's unique culture and cuisine.

Although 57 percent of the people of Kerala (known as Malayalis) are Hindus, Kerala has sizable proportions of Muslims (23 percent) and Christians (19 percent). The Muslims, called Moplahs, are descendants of Arab traders who married local women. The Christians are a mix of Syrian Christians, who trace their origins back to St. Thomas; Roman Catholics; and other sects. Cochin and other cities once had small but thriving Jewish communities. The two main Hindu castes are the Nairs, or warriors, who eat meat and fish, and the Namboodiris, or Brahmins, who are strict vegetarians. Kerala has India's highest literacy rate and lowest birth rate. Only 6 percent of the state's population is vegetarian.

For all communities, the staple is rice, which is parboiled by soaking the paddy in water, then drying it before milling. Rice flour is used to make many distinctive breads, including *wellayappam*, called *appam* for short. A dough of rice flour is fermented with *toddy* (fermented palm juice) and fried in a little oil in a special pan to make a disk-shaped bread with a soft center and thin crispy edges. *Appams* are eaten for breakfast with coconut milk or a meat stew. Another Kerala bread, called *poottu*, is made by steaming a dough of ground rice and coconut in a bamboo tube. It, too, is eaten for breakfast with mashed bananas. *Idli* and *sambar* or *dosa* and chutney are other breakfast favorites.

The ubiquitous coconut tree was the source of the traditional cooking medium, coconut oil. Grated coconut meat is also used as a thickener for meat, fish, and seafood stews and gravies, and made into chutney. However, in recent years the use of coconut has fallen out of favor because of concerns over its high triglyceride and saturated fat content. As a result, some Malayalis substitute peanut or vegetable oil for corn oil and use condensed skim milk, perhaps adding a little coconut for flavoring.

Characteristic spices are black pepper, ginger, mustard seed, fenugreek, tamarind, cinnamon, cloves, nutmeg, coriander, and curry leaves. Vegetables include plantains (green bananas), a favorite ingredient in curries or stewed in buttermilk, tapioca, okra, beans, and squashes and gourds. A common way of cooking meat or seafood is to sauté black pepper, coriander, cinnamon, cloves, cardamoms, ginger, and onions in oil, then add meat or fish and coconut milk and simmer. The final tempering may include curry and coriander leaves.

A typical meal in a vegetarian Hindu household starts with rice served with plain yogurt or *pullicherry*, a pineapple or cucumber and yogurt salad. This is followed by *sambar* and a vegetable dish, such as lightly spiced cabbage or beans stir-fried in a little oil *(thoren)* or sliced tapioca in an onion-based gravy *(kappa)*. *Avial* is another Kerala favorite. A meal traditionally ends with yogurt and sometimes includes a dessert, such as fruit or a delicately flavored pudding made of rice, brown sugar, raisins, and cashew nuts cooked over a slow fire, called *ada paratham*. Side dishes include *pappadums* and pickles. A typical Kerala feast, served on a banana leaf at weddings and other festive occasions, is called *Sadya* and consists of more than 14 vegetable dishes plus rice.

Nonvegetarians may add a fish or seafood dish, such as *meen moli*—fish or shrimp that is first lightly fried and then cooked in a coconut-based gravy. It is usually served with rice or *appams*. Another favorite is chicken curry, spiced with black pepper.

Moplahs also eat coconut and local spices, but there is evidence of Arab influence in the popularity of rice and meat *biryanis*; delicate meat curries served with a special *paratha*; lamb cooked on a slow fire with garlic, aniseed, and chilies; and a ground wheat and meat porridge (known as *harisa* elsewhere in India).

Kerala-Style Shrimp and Coconut Milk

- 2 pounds large shrimp
- 2–3 tb vegetable oil
- 2 small onions, finely sliced
- 2 tsp garlic paste
- 2 tsp ginger paste
- 2 tsp ready-made coriander powder
- 1/2 tsp chili powder
- 1/2 tsp turmeric
- salt to taste
- One 16-ounce can of tomatoes, with about half the juice drained off
- One 14-ounce can of coconut milk

- 12 curry leaves
- 4 green chilies, sliced into thin strips
- handful of coriander leaves, finely chopped

Sauté the sliced onions in oil in a pot over medium heat until they are transparent. Add the garlic and ginger pastes and stir until the liquid evaporates. Add the coriander powder, chili powder, turmeric, and salt, and stir. Add the tomatoes and cook for several minutes while stirring. Reduce to low heat, add coconut milk and curry leaves and stir for several minutes. Now add the shrimps, bring to a boil, reduce to low heat, and simmer until cooked (about 5 minutes). Garnish with chopped coriander leaves and sliced green chilies. Serve with plain boiled rice.

Andhra Pradesh

One of India's largest states, Andhra Pradesh encompasses the Telugu-speaking parts of South India and the former princely state of Hyderabad, once ruled by descendants of Mughal generals called Nawabs, who were famous worldwide for their fabulous wealth. Ninety percent of the state's population are Hindu and 8 percent are Muslims, who mainly live in the city of Hyderabad, the state capital. The state also has a sizable population of people belonging to scheduled tribes. Andhra Pradesh is a major producer of rice, barley, millet, lentils, bananas, chilies, turmeric, and black pepper.

There are two main styles of Andhra cooking: Hindu cuisine and the rich meat-based cuisine of Hyderabad that has a strong Mughal influence. Although Brahmins are strict vegetarians, other Hindu castes eat meat and fish, especially those living near the coast. Only 16 percent of the state's total population are vegetarian.

Three ingredients are essential in Andhra cuisine: tamarind, red chilies, and *gongura*, the leaf of the rozelle plant. Tamarind,[10] considered cooling to the system and a digestive aid, is used in many different ways: its juice imparts sourness to vegetable and rice dishes, it is mixed with sugar and salt to make a drink, the flowers and leaves are curried, its seeds are ground into a flour, and ripe tamarind fruit can be mixed with jaggery and eaten as a sweet.

Andhra cuisine is reputed to be the hottest in India. According to a legend, there was once a severe famine in the area and all that grew were red chilies, which subsequently became a staple of the Andhra diet. More realistically, chilies are a protection against stomach infection. The hottest chili is called *koraivikaram*, which in Telugu means "the flaming stick." A dry chutney is made by pounding these chilies to a fine powder and mixing it with tamarind pulp and salt. It is preserved year-round and eaten with rice and *ghee*. Perhaps Andhra Pradesh's most famous dish is a green mango chutney called *avikkai*, which is so hot that it has sent some unsuspecting visitors to the hospital. *Gongura* is added to meat, *dal*, and vegetable dishes, and it is also made into a pickle.

Hindu vegetarian cuisine is similar to that eaten in Tamil Nadu and Karnataka, with some unique dishes. The first course consists of rice with two vegetables, one fried and one in a gravy, perhaps a thick tamarind and jaggery (brown sugar) sauce. Two famous Andhra vegetable dishes are eggplants stuffed with coconut, peanuts, and sesame seeds and cooked in a tamarind sauce *(bagara baingan)*, and *mirch-ka-masala*, green chilies cooked in a spicy creamy sauce. A second course features a thick *dal*, either plain or prepared with mango, tomato, or some other vegetable, and a watery vegetable dish called *pullusu*. The meal always ends with yogurt and rice mixed together. Several pickles accompany the meal. Andhra cuisine is famous for its chutneys, made from curry leaves, garlic, raw tamarind, ginger, *dals*, and other ingredients and flavored with red chilies, curry leaves, and mustard seeds. A singular Andhra seasoning comprises various powders made from ground lentils, chilies, coconut, and different spices that are sprinkled on *idlis*, *dosas*, or rice.

At around 5:00 P.M. some people have a light meal (sometimes called tiffin), featuring a semolina porridge *(uppuma)*, a fried lentil *vada*, or a kind of *dosa* made from ground *urad dal*, ginger, and green chilies, and served with onions *(pessaratu)*. Dinner, eaten around 8:00 P.M., is a smaller version of lunch, perhaps consisting of rice, a vegetable, *rasam*, and yogurt. A formal Hindu nonvegetarian meal could include meat *biryani*, tamarind rice, or vegetable *pulao*, chicken or meat curry, a kabab, a *dal*, two or three vegetable dishes, and *rasam*. For poor villagers, a meal might consist of boiled rice with fried *gongura* leaves or a chutney of red chilies, garlic, salt, and lime juice.

Hyderabadi cuisine is a variant of Mughal haute cuisine, transformed by the use of local ingredients and flavorings. A Hyderabadi *korma*, for example, may be made with caraway seeds, ground nuts called *chironji*, poppy seeds, and grated coconut. A traditional Hyderabadi Muslim breakfast is *nihari*, a thick soup-like dish made from sheep's tongue and feet cooked in a very spicy gravy overnight and eaten with a *tandoor*-baked bread called *kulcha*, or *sheermal*, a baked bread soaked in milk and saffron. Today people are more likely to eat *paratha* served with spicy minced meat, or a dish called *tehari* made from yellow rice and potatoes. Lunch and dinner feature plain white rice and *paratha*, a *dal*, and a meat dish, such as kabob, cutlet, beef, lamb, or chicken *korma*, or small strips of meat fried in spices called *pasanda*.

Nihari (Beef or Lamb Stew with Ginger)

- 2 large onions, sliced
- 1 tb oil
- 1 pound of boneless beef or lamb, cut into 1 1/2 inch cubes
- 1-inch piece of fresh ginger
- 3 cloves garlic
- 1 tsp chili powder
- 1 tsp salt
- 2 tsp flour
- 6 cloves
- 1 tsp cumin seed
- 8 black cardamom seeds, removed from pods
- 8 black peppercorns
- One 2-inch piece of cinnamon stick
- Garnish: Sliced ginger, sliced green chilies, chopped fresh coriander leaves

Cook the onions in the oil in a medium-size pot for 5 or 6 minutes until they become golden brown. Add the meat, cook over medium heat for 30 minutes, stirring frequently. Grind the ginger and garlic in a food processor or blender with a little water to make a smooth paste. Add to the meat and cook for 10 minutes. Add the chili powder and salt, and cook another 30 minutes. Meanwhile, grind the spices in a spice or coffee grinder into a fine powder. Mix the flour and spices with a little water, stir into the beef mixture, and add four cups of water. Mix well, and cook, tightly covered, over very low heat for about an hour or until the meat is tender. Before serving, add the garnish and serve with Indian bread.

Hyderabad is famous for its *biryanis*, served on special occasions. One kind is made by marinating pieces of meat in yogurt, chili, spices, and crushed onions while the rice is half-cooked in water flavored with cardamoms, cloves, and cinnamon. The meat is spread at the bottom of a pot and covered with saffron-flavored milk, the rice water, fried onions, mint leaves, chilies, cardamom powder, and other spices. A layer of rice is spread over the meat and sprinkled with the remaining saffron milk, cardamom powder, and lime juice. The pot is sealed with dough and cooked very slowly so that it has a soft texture. This *biryani* is served with a salad of cucumber, yogurt, ginger, garlic, chilies, onions, and yogurt called *boorani*.

During the month of Ramadan, Muslims break their daily fast with *halim*, a porridge-like dish made from whole wheat and sometimes other grains and lentils, meat, onions, spices, and chilies. A well-known dessert is *double-ka-meetha*, a very sweet, fried bread pudding laced with almonds or cashews. Hyderabad has many delicious breads, the best known of which is *kulcha*, a square bread marked with two crossing lines that was embroidered on the old Hyderabad state flag in commemoration of an event associated with the founding of the dynasty.

THE EAST AND NORTHEAST

West Bengal

The populous state of West Bengal borders on the Indian states of Bihar, Orissa, Assam, and Sikkim, the countries Nepal, Bhutan, and Bangladesh, and the Bay of Bengal. West Bengal is 75 percent Hindu and 23 percent Muslim, with minorities of Christians and adherents of tribal religions. Only a very small proportion of Hindu Bengalis are strict vegetarians, and even Brahmins relish fish (sometimes dubbed "vegetables of the sea"). The state is very fertile and well watered by rivers and monsoon rains. The major crops are rice, wheat, chickpeas, tea, potatoes, oil seeds, mangoes, bananas, pineapples, and tomatoes. A standard spice mixture, called *panchphoran*, consists of poppy seeds, cumin seeds, fenugreek, fennel, a tiny black seed called *radhuni*, and mustard seeds.

Historically, the region was part of the Mughal province of Bengal and many local people converted to Islam, especially in the eastern part. The British obtained a stronghold here in the eighteenth century and gradually took over the direct administration of the area from Calcutta (now Kolkata), which remained the capital of British India until 1912. Calcutta was the most anglicized city in India and the British influence permeated many aspects of the life of middle-class Bengalis, including their cuisine. In 1905, the British divided Bengal along religious lines into West and East Bengal. Although this was later reversed, the predominantly Muslim East Bengal became the Pakistani province of East Pakistan in 1947. In 1971, the people of East Bengal rebelled and, with Indian military aid, formed the independent country of Bangladesh. Linguistically, culturally, and gastronomically, West Bengal and Bangladesh have much in common.

Bengalis take food very seriously and reportedly spend a larger portion of their disposable income on food than people elsewhere in India. Two hallmarks of Bengali cuisine are fish and sweets. (So great is the love of fish that poor people will buy fish scales and add them to a dish to impart a fish flavor.) Freshwater fish, including fish from rivers and ponds, are considered desirable while sea fish are not, with the exception of *bhekti*, a delicate cod-like fish.

Bengalis use a number of methods for preparing fish and seafood, including shallow and deep frying, steaming, and stewing. A favorite frying medium is mustard oil, since its pungency is believed to bring out the flavor of freshwater fish. A famous Bengali preparation is *maacher jhol*—a fish stew made by cutting fish (often carp) into large pieces, bones and all, sautéing them with spices in mustard oil, and then simmering the fish in water with vegetables. Yogurt is used in many fish dishes. Fish head, considered a delicacy, is prepared with *dal*, potatoes, and mixed vegetable peelings.

The most coveted Bengali fish is the *hilsa*, a shad-like sea fish that swims upriver to spawn. *Hilsa* is rich and oily in texture and the classic way of eating it is lightly coated with turmeric, chili powder, and salt, and fried. Careful attention must be paid to removing the myriad of tiny bones. *Hilsa* may also be prepared with mustard or tamarind gravy, covered with a mustard and chili paste, and smoked in banana leaves, or steamed with a yogurt and ginger sauce.

Common vegetables are pumpkins and other varieties of squash, green plantains, white radishes, beans, cabbage, cauliflower, mangoes, and jackfruit as well as tomatoes, okra, and potatoes. (The Bengalis are said to be the world's biggest consumers of potatoes after the Irish.) The British contributions to Bengali cuisine include cutlets—breaded and fried patties of ground vegetables, meat, shrimps or fish; chops, which are ovals of minced meat coated with mashed potatoes and deep-fried; soufflés; omelets; and the institution of afternoon tea, complete with cucumber sandwiches, cakes, salty snacks, and carefully made Darjeeling tea—sans spices.

A Bengali meal follows a definite progression of flavors from bitter through salty and sour and ending with sweet. Lunch, the largest meal of the day, traditionally starts with a bitter dish intended to simulate the appetite (just as the French take a glass of bitter vermouth as an aperitif). Called *shukto*, it is made from diced white radishes, potatoes, beans, and other vegetables, plus bitter melon, a dark-green squash that provides the bitter flavor. This is followed by rice and *dal* made from red lentils, accompanied by one or more fried, boiled, and sautéed vegetable dishes. A popular dish is *postho*, a mixture of potatoes and other vegetables cooked in a paste made of white poppy seeds, which imparts a slightly nutty flavor.

If fish and meat are served, they come next. Fish could be fried or served as a *jhol*, a thin curry in which the fish is fried in mustard oil, chilies, and spices; meat might be a mutton *korma*. This course is accompanied by a puffy deep-fried bread made from white flour, called *lucchis*. Next come one or two vegetable dishes and perhaps a rice *pulao* and bread. Plain, boiled rice is always on hand throughout the meal. The next-to-last course is a sweet and sour chutney made with tomatoes, apples, mangoes, or other fruits. Its function is to remove any heaviness from overeating and, like a sorbet in European cuisine, to clear the palate for the pièce de résistance: the sweet or dessert course.

Bengalis are famous for their love of sweets, which borders on an addiction. (In the old days, it was said that very rich landowners survived on a diet of sweets alone.) In Kolkata there is a sweet shop on almost every corner. Incomes permitting, Bengalis eat sweets throughout the day: as desserts at the end of meals (a custom not followed in many other parts of India); at afternoon tea; and as snacks. Sweets are an essential component of Bengali hospitality. Most store-bought Bengali sweets are made of sugar and curds (*chhana*).

Shukto (Mixed Vegetables with Bitter Gourd)

- 6 cups mixed vegetables cut into 1-inch cubes (potatoes, pumpkins, squash, beans, etc.)
- 1 cup bitter gourd cut into 1-inch cubes
- 1 tb vegetable oil
- 1 1/2 tb mustard seed
- 1-inch piece of fresh ginger root
- 1 tsp of salt (or to taste)
- 1/2 cup of milk

Heat the oil in a wok or large pot. Fry the bitter gourd and stir until slightly brown (around 3 minutes). Remove from pan. Meanwhile, grind one tablespoon of the mustard seed, the ginger root (cut into chunks first), and one-quarter cup of water to make a paste.

Fry the rest of the mustard seed for a few seconds, add the other vegetables and fry for five minutes. Then add the paste together with one cup of water. Stir, add the bitter gourd and salt to taste, cover, and cook over slow heat for 15 minutes. The vegetables should be soft but retain their shape. Turn off the heat and add one-half cup of milk and serve with plain boiled rice.

Masur Dal (Lentil Stew)

- 1/2 cup *masur dal* (red lentils)
- 1 medium onion, minced
- 1/2 medium tomato, skin removed and roughly chopped
- 1/2 inch of ginger, sliced
- 1 tsp turmeric powder
- 1/2 tsp chili powder (or to taste)
- 1 tsp cumin seeds
- 3 tb cooking oil or *ghee*

Tempering

- 1–2 dried red chilies
- 2 bay leaves

Rinse the lentils several times in water and soak them in water for an hour. The water should be two inches higher than the lentils. Heat one tablespoon of oil or *ghee* and fry the onions and ginger for around five minutes until they are soft. (Stirring must be constant; otherwise, the onion will burn.)

Add the lentils and 1 1/2 cups of water plus the turmeric powder, and cook until the mixture is soft, around 15–20 minutes. Turn off the heat and mash until the consistency is fairly smooth. Heat one tablespoon of oil or *ghee*, fry the chili powder for a few minutes, and then add the tomatoes and cook until they are soft. Mash a little, add salt to taste, and pour into the lentils. Mix well, boil a few minutes, and remove from the heat. Heat one tablespoon of oil, add a dried red chili, the bay leaves, and the cumin seeds, and fry until the seeds turn brown but do not burn. Pour into the *dal* and serve. The *dal* should have the consistency of a thin broth; add water if needed.

Orissa

Orissa, which borders on West Bengal, Andhra Pradesh, Bihar, and Madhya Pradesh, is one of India's poorest states. More than 90 percent of its population are Hindus; the rest are Muslims and Christians, including a sizable tribal population. Only about 6 percent of its population is vegetarian, perhaps because it has a long coastline, which means fish is available at relatively low cost. For centuries Orissa was under the control of Bengal, so the cuisine has many features in common with Bengali food, especially in the Northeast. Saltwater and freshwater fish and rice are staples of the diet, and prepared much like they are in Bengal. A distinctive dish is fish cooked with dried mangoes. In the southern part of the state, the food is closer to that of South India, and coconut, tamarind, red chilies, and curry leaves are common ingredients.

For poor people, a meal may be vegetable peels and leftovers like cauliflower stems and leaves cooked over a slow fire. *Dals* and vegetables, such as eggplants, yams, and pumpkins, are prepared in yogurt, and mustard seeds are often garnished with coarsely ground cumin seeds and red chilies.

Bihar

Bihar was once the center of India's intellectual and cultural flowering: Buddha attained enlightenment here and Nalanda was the seat of a world-famous university in the fifth century A.D. Today, however, the people of Bihar are among the most destitute on the subcontinent, and many become laborers who migrate to Kolkata and other cities in search of employment. Of the population, 82 percent are Hindus and 15 percent Muslims. Bihari food is rustic and simple. A staple of the diet is roasted chickpea flour (*sattu*). Laborers carry it in a towel to their jobs and mix it with salt and green chilies, while middle-class housewives dip balls made of *sattu*, called *littis*, in *ghee*. Wheat, barley, corn, and other grains are parched by burying them in sand.

Bihari cuisine is in many ways similar to that of Bengal. Mustard oil is the traditional cooking medium. A standard middle-class meal consists of rice, *dal*, and vegetables. A popular dish is *chokha*: Mashed squash, potato, and other vegetables are garnished with mustard oil, onions, and chilies. Sliced vegetables are fried in a chickpea batter to make crispy fritters called *bachka*.

Assam

The state of Assam, which borders on Bangladesh, Arunchal Pradesh, Nagaland, and Mizoram, was once part of a great kingdom ruled by Hindu dynasties and later by the Ahoms who migrated from southern China in the thirteenth century. Under the British, Assam was a separate province. In the 1970s, parts of the state of Assam were broken off to create the states of Nagaland, Meghalaya, Mizoran, and Arunchal Pradesh. Around two-thirds of the population are Hindus, 28 percent are Muslim (many of them immigrants from Bangladesh), and the rest are Christians or adherents of tribal religions. The great majority of Assamese are not vegetarians.

Just as the Assamese language is closely related to Bengali, so too the food of the state of Assam has much in common with Bengali cuisine.

Rice is the staple, served at every meal; *lusis*, the equivalent of Bengali *lucchis*, are fried puffy bread made from white flour. Mustard oil is the traditional cooking medium; and fish, especially carp and *hilsa*, are much in demand.

However, Assamese food has some features that make this one of India's most intriguing cuisines. The Assamese are virtually alone in preserving the six basic tastes of ancient Hindu gastronomy, including sour and alkaline. A national dish is *tenga*, a slightly sour stew made by frying pieces of fish in mustard oil, then simmering them with fenugreek seeds, vegetables, and lime juice. Another sour dish is made of fermented bamboo shoots. Vegetables, potatoes, or fish are mixed with chopped onions, mustard oil, green chilies, and lime juice, and mashed to make a popular dish called *pitika*. All this sourness is counteracted by a dish called *khar* that has an astringent or alkaline taste, probably unique in the world of food. Today the alkalinity comes from baking soda but traditionally the alkaline culinary element was a byproduct of burnt banana-tree stems, which was also sprinkled on *dal* or vegetables as part of a daily meal.

Assam has many versions of *pitha*, a sweet made from rice flour and sugar, associated with its Bihu harvest festivals. They can be filled with coconut, flavored with sesame seeds or aniseed, or mixed with jackfruit pulp. One Bihu specialty, *sunga pitha*, is made by wrapping rice flour and sugar paste in banana leaves, stuffing it in hollowed-out pieces of bamboo, and roasting it over a wood fire.

Breakfast is typically a cup of strong black Assamese tea prepared with milk and sugar. Lunch consists of rice served with one or two vegetable dishes, followed by a fish *tenga* and a *dal khar*. An afternoon tea might feature *lusis* and fried potatoes and onions or wheat bread with omelet. Dinner is similar to lunch.

Lentil and Bamboo Shoot *Khar*

- 1 cup *moong dal*, soaked for one hour
- 1 cup grated bamboo shoots
- 4 tsp baking soda
- 2 tb ginger, finely minced or grated
- 1 clove garlic, thinly sliced
- 2 green chilies, finely chopped
- 1 tsp fenugreek seeds
- 4 tb mustard oil or vegetable oil
- 1 tsp salt

Cook the *dal* in water until it is thick and nearly dry, adding more water if necessary. Cook the bamboo shoots in a little water with the salt and baking soda until
soft. Drain the excess water and mix it with the *dal*. Heat the oil, sauté the fenugreek seeds until they start to crackle, then add the garlic, ginger, and green
chilies. Fry for a minute, then add the *dal* and bamboo shoot mixture and stir
until the water evaporates. Serve with white rice.

Other Northeast States

The states created by the subdivision of Assam (Mizoram, Nagaland,
Arunachal Pradesh, and Meghalaya, as well nearby Tripura and Manipur)
have tribal majorities. The predominant religion is Christianity because
of intensive missionary activity in the area. Many people in the region
have an Oriental appearance, since their ancestors migrated from South
China and Southeast Asia. They speak Tibeto-Burman languages unrelated to India's main language groups.

Their food also has similarities to that of China and Southeast Asia.
The people are mainly nonvegetarians and rice-eaters, preferring a sticky
rice similar to that used in Japan rather than the long-grained type favored in the rest of India. In Nagaland, pork and dog are eaten, and bamboo shoots are essential in curries or pickles. Rice and fish are wrapped in
banana leaves and steamed. Very little cooking oil is used; food is usually
boiled, steamed, or roasted over an open fire. Flavoring comes from garlic,
green onions, ginger, and hot red chilies. People in Tripura and Manipur
dry and ferment small fish and use them in curries, sauces, and pickles, another similarity with Southeast Asian food. Drinks are locally brewed
from millet or rice to make a sake (rice wine)-like drink.

Tribal people who live in the forest eat whatever is available, including
insects, monkeys (although this is illegal), and silkworms, considered a
delicacy. In Mizoram, an animal called a mithun, which is a cross between
a cow and a water buffalo, is killed in a ceremonial sacrifice and eaten in
a community feast. Arunchal Pradesh cuisine features many typical Ti-
betan dishes, including momos, a boiled dumpling stuffed with meat,
dried yak cheese, and salted tea made from barley with yak butter.

NOTES

1. N.P. Narani, "Indian Experience on Household Food and Security," Regional Expert Consultation, FAO-UN Bangkok, August 8–11, 1994. Available
on Web site http://www.fao.org/docrep.

2. K. T. Achaya, *Indian Food: A Historical Companion* (New Delhi: Oxford University Press, 1994), p. 57.

3. "India Food Balance Sheet (Year 2001)," Food and Agriculture Organization of the United Nations (FAOSTAT). Go to the Web site http://apps.fao.org/faostat/collections, and then to Food Balance Sheets.

4. Throughout this chapter, the statistics about religious affiliations in Indian states are taken from the official Census of India 1991, *Table 23: Percentage of Population of Major Religions, 1991*, which can be found on the Web site http://www.censusindia.net/cendata/datatable23/html.

5. For a vivid description of the manners, customs, and cuisine of Lucknow, see Abdul Halim Sharar, *Lucknow: The Last Phase of Oriental Culture*, trans. E. S. Harcourt and Fakhir Hussain (New Delhi: Oxford University Press, 1994), pp. 155–168.

6. J. Inder Singh Kalra, *Prashad: Cooking with Indian Masters* (New Delhi: Allied Publishers, 1989), p. 58.

7. For a collection of recipes from princely families, see Digvijaya Singh, *Cooking Delights of the Maharajas* (Mumbai, India: Vakils, Feffer & Simons, 2002).

8. Hemalata C. Dandekar, *Beyond Curry: Quick and Easy Indian Cooking Featuring Cuisine from Maharashtra State*, Center for South and Southeast Asian Studies, Special Publication No. 3, 1983 (Ann Arbor: University of Michigan, 1983), p. 5.

9. Bhicoo J. Manekshaw, *Parsi Food and Customs: The Essential Parsi Cookbook* (New Delhi: Penguin Books India, 1996).

10. The following story illustrates the wisdom of traditional foodways. In parts of Andhra Pradesh, where the Portuguese introduced tomatoes, people began to use them to replace tamarind in their food. Eventually entire villages began to fall ill with fluorosis, a disease that causes permanent damage to the bones. It was determined that the disease was caused by the chemical fluorine found in the water in the area and that the consumption of tamarind had blocked its absorption. Bilkees I. Latif, *The Essential Andhra Cookbook* (New Delhi: Penguin Books India, 1999), p. xxv.

5

Eating Out

Until the middle of the twentieth century, India did not have a restaurant culture. Eating out was tolerated as a necessity rather than valued as a luxury or a new experience. Every Hindu caste had its own food taboos, and concerns about pollution prevented many Indians from eating in public places, especially orthodox Hindus and Jains. Many wealthy merchants belonged to these two religions and thus had many dietary restrictions—unlike their counterparts in, say, China, where, from the eleventh century on, wealthy merchants patronized restaurants serving sophisticated regional and specialty cuisines and prided themselves on their gourmet taste.

Cooking and entertaining at home were facilitated by the presence of many women in a joint family and, for the wealthy, abundant servants. For all social and religious groups, hospitality was a social and religious obligation. As a result, it was considered virtually an insult to take guests to dinner in a restaurant rather than invite them home.

But times are changing and today eating out is becoming fashionable in Bangalore and other Indian towns and cities.[1] People are discarding their old taboos and India's rapidly growing middle class have the money, time, and inclination to eat out. Trendy restaurants that serve exotic cuisines (Thai and Italian are especially popular) and Western and Indian fast food chains are proliferating. Indian restaurants abroad have also developed in unique ways.

TEMPLE FOOD

From ancient times, Hindu travelers could get a bed and simple meals at inns, called *dharmasalas* (the Sanskrit word for a place where religious duties are performed). They were often connected with Hindu temples, some of which, were very rich, especially in the South, thanks to donations of land by local rulers.

During a Hindu temple service, called a *puja*, priests make offerings to the statues of the deities *(prasad)*, which may include flowers, fruit, rice, *ghee*, yogurt, milk, honey, vegetables, nuts, and sweets. Some deities have favorite foods: Elephant-headed Ganesh, for example, is known for his love of *modaka*, a sweet dumpling. After the *prasad* is offered to the deities, it is considered consecrated and distributed to worshippers as the god's leftovers. Large temples had kitchens that also prepared meals for pilgrims and the indigent. Over the centuries, some temples became associated with certain foods, so some religious pilgrimages assumed a gastronomical dimension, especially in South India. For example, the Padmanabha temple in Kerala is famous for a special *avial*, a mixed vegetable and coconut dish; the Vishnu temple in Kanchipuram, Tamil Nadu, is celebrated for its giant spiced *idlis* weighing three pounds each; while the Balaji temple in Andhra Pradesh offers a thick rice pudding flavored with nuts, cardamom, and saffron. Some temples prepare these dishes on special occasions; others on a daily basis. A temple at Thirupati in South India makes as many as seventy thousand *laddus* each day.

Some temples have enormous kitchen staffs. At the Jaganath temple in Orissa, 400 cooks serve as many as 100,000 people a day. Inside the temple is an enormous chamber with earthen pots piled on top of each other above a fire. The pot with the most water is placed on the bottom, so that its steam goes upward and cooks the other pots. Specialties of this temple include *urad dal*, rice, taro leaves, yogurt, and *kheer* (rice pudding), all cooked in *ghee*. No tomato, garlic, potatoes, cabbage, or cauliflower are used, probably because the temple was built before such vegetables were known in India. The gods are served ritually five times a day, and worshippers can eat in a special room in the temple or buy small pots of *prasad* in a market inside the temple walls to take back to family and friends.

Certain temples celebrate important events in the life of the deity with a food festival. Mount Govardhan in Uttar Pradesh where Lord Krishna once lived is host to several such festivals, the most important being the Mountain of Food, or *Annakuta*, celebrated each year at the end of the rainy season. Members of a local Hindu temple, assisted by outside cooks, prepare a 10-foot-high mountain of rice around which they arrange thousands of breads, sweets, and grain and vegetable dishes in jars and baskets of varying shapes and sizes. The statue of the deity is brought to view the display, followed by the pilgrims, who are given rice, curries, and stewed vegetables on banana leaves. The pilgrims are allowed to purchase sweets and other fried foods to take home and share with their families.[2]

Sikh temples have a large dining hall (*langar*), where volunteers serve vegetarian food to all comers, rich and poor, Sikh and non-Sikh, Brahman and outcaste, as a sacred service and to inculcate the virtue of charity. The Golden Temple at Amritsar, Sikhs' holiest shrine, is visited by 50,000 people each day and 70,000 on weekends. After dinner, they are given consecrated sweets. Sufi Muslims had a similar institution, also called *langar*. Muslim pilgrims who trek to the graves of saints and participants in annual festivals at Muslim shrines are given accommodations at inns called *serais* as well as food.

THE BRITISH LEGACY

In the nineteenth century, Europeans opened restaurants and hotels serving Continental cuisine in Calcutta, Bombay, Madras, and other cities. Initially the clientele were British, but in the twentieth century Westernized Indians began frequenting them. In Calcutta, the most anglicized of all Indian cities, Pelitis, Firpos, and Fleurys were famous restaurants. A 1944 luncheon menu from Firpos (which closed its doors in the 1960s) featured steak and kidney pie, lasagna au gratin, Melton Mowbray pie, sausages with mashed potatoes, roast duck, and fried *bekty* (a local fish) in tartare sauce, along with several kinds of whiskey and gin cocktails. Because they had to prepare all sorts of meat, including pork and beef, cooks at these restaurants were often Christians from Goa or from the Mogh tribe in Bengal who were trained by the Portuguese in the seventeenth century and later worked as cooks on English ships.

The British also brought to India their unique institution: the club, which was the center of social activity and political power in every town and city in British-ruled India. Some, like Delhi's Gymkhana Club, Calcutta's Bengal Club, and Bombay's Byculla Club, catered to high government officials and princes (India was said to be ruled from the Gymkhana Club); others were only for businessmen, who were considered a step down on the social ladder. At first only British were allowed as members, but as more Indians entered the civil service, they too were admitted. Today the clubs, both old and new, continue to prosper and have long waiting lists for membership.

During the days of the Raj (British rule), a formal banquet at a club (with a menu written in French) consisted of ten or eleven courses, mainly Western dishes but with a few Indian touches such as a mulligatawny soup, kabobs, or a curry. Curries were also a favorite dish at British army messes. Today club meals are a combination of Indian and Western dishes. A menu from Delhi's Gymkhana Club, for example, features cream of tomato soup, cheese omelet, assorted sandwiches, chicken stroganoff, and hot dog and hamburgers as well as well as a selection of Indian vegetarian and nonvegetarian dishes, such as chicken *korma*, mutton *kofta* curry, and *channa batora*. On weekends many clubs serve elaborate buffets that include Indian, Western, Chinese, Thai, and Italian food.

Another British legacy is the *dak* (Hindi for post) bungalow. These rest houses for traveling officials were built every fifteen or twenty miles along main roads (roughly a day's march apart) and in many towns and villages. The cooks often had to whip up a meal on the spot, using local ingredients, so omelets, roast chicken, and chicken curry were standard fare. Today more elaborate government rest houses have been built for politicians and tourists, but some of the old bungalows still exist and serve the same kind of food.

CONTEMPORARY INDIAN EATING ESTABLISHMENTS

Indian eating places fall into two broad categories: small, hole-in-the-wall establishments that serve a limited number of inexpensive dishes and upscale restaurants where the décor is more elegant, the menus more extensive, and the prices higher. The first category are frequented by truck drivers, workers living apart from their families, neighborhood people, and students; the second cater to the growing Indian middle class.

Dhabas

Dhabas are Indian truck stops—small wayside stands with a few tables for the convenience of truck drivers and other travelers. Although they can be found everywhere on the subcontinent, their heartland is northern and central India. In old-style *dhabas* the customers sit semi-reclined on handwoven rope and bamboo cots called *charpoys*. Some sell only vegetarian food, especially in Rajasthan; others also sell meat. The typical menu features five or six dishes served from large brass pots. Typical dishes are *palak paneer*, spinach with cheese; *malai kofta*, vegetable balls in a creamy gravy; omelets; and *makani dal*, a rich black bean stew, accompanied by bread, either *chapatis* or *nan*. The standard drink is *chai*, tea that is boiled with milk and spices to produce a strong coarse brew.

Today *dhaba* food is becoming fashionable, especially among young urban professionals who drive out of town on a weekend to visit a favorite *dhaba*. Tables and chairs are replacing the old *charpoys*, the cooking is becoming more sophisticated, and soft drinks and bottled water are sold. In New Delhi, a five-star hotel has even opened a restaurant called *Dhaba* that serves elegant versions of typical *dhaba* dishes. *Dhabas* also operate in Chicago, New York, and other U.S. cities around the clock to provide quick, inexpensive (and often very delicious) meals to Indian and Pakistani taxi drivers.

Udipi Hotels and *Bhojanalaya*

In South India eating establishments are divided into two categories: *Udupi* (also spelled *Udipi*), hotels/restaurants, and military hotels.[3] The first serve only vegetarian food, the latter meat and egg dishes. Their traditional customers were men living away from home, but today they are popular among all levels of society because their food is delicious and their vegetarian menus make them accessible to most diners. (According to a story, so ubiquitous are South Indian restaurants that when Sir Edmund Hilary and Tenzing Norgay reached the top of Mount Everest in 1953, they were greeted by an Udupi restaurant proprietor asking for their order.)

Breakfast is an important meal in South India, so *Udupi* restaurants open very early in the morning. Their menus feature *idlis*, steamed, lens-shaped breads made of fermented rice and lentil flour; *dosas*, large pancakes also made from rice and lentils; *sambar*, a thin, spiced stew of lentils, potatoes, and other vegetables; and coconut chutney. The traditional serving plate is a banana leaf sprinkled with water before each customer sits down. The proper accompaniment is South Indian–style coffee, which resembles French *café au lait*. Finely ground coffee is boiled down into an extract that is mixed with water and hot milk. The waiter raises his arm above his head and pours the mixture into the cup in a long stream in order to create foam, causing some customers to order "a yard of coffee." The same menu is offered for lunch; additional items are added for dinner.

These restaurants are starkly plain, containing little more than a few tables and chairs. In the mid-1930s K. K. Rao opened Woodlands restaurant in Madras to serve South Indian food in a more elegant setting. One of its specialties was an enormous yard-wide, paper-thin *dosa*, which has since become a standard item at South Indian restaurants. The restaurant be-

Eating a *dosa*. Photo © TRIP/H. Rogers.

came very popular, and family members later opened Woodlands restaurants in New Delhi, London, Dubai, and Singapore.

In North India, small cafés and tea stalls, called *bhojanalaya*—halfway between a sweet shop and a modern restaurant—serve vegetarian fare to orthodox Hindus who otherwise would avoid eating outside their homes. Sometimes eating establishments with that name are attached to temples.

Irani Restaurants/Hotels

Located mainly in Mumbai and Hyderabad, these inexpensive nonvegetarian restaurants serve meat and rice dishes cooked in the Muslim style, such as *biryanis*, *pulaos*, and *halims*, omelets, and Western-style breads and pastries. The standard drink is tea made with lots of milk. These homey establishments were opened by Zoroastrian and Muslim Iranians who emigrated to Bombay starting in the seventeenth century and later moved to Hyderabad. A second wave came in the late nineteenth century. Many had their own bakeries that made cakes, breads, and cookies, such as Hyderabad's famous Osmania. In recent years many Irani restaurants have closed their doors as real estate prices have been rising and family members have started entering other professions.

Gujarati Restaurants

Mumbai abounds in small Gujarati restaurants that serve vegetarian *thalis*, a round metal plate with many little bowls filled with salad, vegetable relish, a dry and a wet vegetable dish, *kadhi*, *dals*, crunchy snacks, pickles, and a sweet item served with rice.

Street Food

Indians love to snack, and you can scarcely take a few steps in an Indian town or village without coming across one-person stalls serving one or two items. Oftentimes, people make special trips to buy the wares of a certain vendor. Some offer a single specialty; others have a variety of dishes that can also serve as a quick meal. Usually the food is deep-fried or fried on a griddle. Typical North Indian snacks include *samosas* (savory filled pastries), potato and meat patties, fried vegetables, all kinds of bread, roasted corn on the cob, omelets, and sandwiches. Snacking is a way of life in Gujarat and Maharashtra, where local stalls and shops specialize in crunchy snacks made of deep-fried chickpea flour and roasted, spiced nuts. The most famous are those that line Mumbai's Chowpatti Beach, where the local specialty is *bhelpuri*, a spicy snack made from

Lunch stall, Varanasi. Photo © Art Directors/TRIP.

crispy noodles, puffed rice, tomato, onion, boiled potatoes, coriander, and tamarind chutney.

Sweet Shops

Bengalis, whether in West Bengal or Bangladesh, are famous for their love of sweets, which they eat on every occasion: as desserts, as a snack with tea, to celebrate a happy event, or as part of a religious celebration. Every town and city in Bengal has sweet shops, including thousands in Kolkata (formerly Calcutta) alone, where customers eat a couple of sweets with a cup of tea and take a box home. The basic dough used to make most Bengali sweets is made from *chhana*—casein or curds made by "cutting" boiling milk with lemon juice or some other acid—cooked with sugar, *ghee,* and flavorings. The apogee of the Bengali sweetmakers' art is *sandesh,* made by pressing the dough into pretty molds shaped like flowers, fruit, or shells. There are more than a hundred varieties of *sandesh,* with poetic names such as *Manoranjan* (heart's delight), *Monohara* (captivator of the heart), *Nayantara* (star of the eye), and *Abar Khabo* (I'll have another). Top-quality *sandesh* have a delicate, complex flavor that must be carefully savored. Connoisseurs debate the virtues of their favorite variety and manufacturer with the passion and expertise of a French oenophile.[4]

In Kolkata, some shops that opened in the mid-nineteenth century are still operating today, including B.C. Nag, N.C. Das (inventor of the famous rosogolla, spongy cheese balls in sugar syrup), and Sen Mahasay. Elsewhere in India and abroad, non-Bengali establishments sometimes borrow these names or call themselves "Bengali Sweet Shops." Their products are usually poor imitations of the originals, which do not travel well.

Coffee Houses

Coffee houses in India are often large dimly lit halls where students, intellectuals, and would-be intellectuals, as well as ordinary people, come to drink coffee, eat snacks, talk, and sit for long periods. Kolkata is famous for its coffee houses near the university.

Railroad and Airline Food

An entire book could be written on the food served on Indian's railways, the largest rail system in the world. Until the railways were privatized in the 1950s, a company called Kellner's prepared a wide variety of delicious, mainly Western dishes that were ordered in advance and served from a kitchen at the next station. Today travelers generally bring their own meals with them or eat at a station restaurant, where a standard meal is rice, yellow *dal*, two vegetables, yogurt, and *chapatis*. On the station platforms, vendors sell tea, served in charming little disposable clay pots, as well as snacks. Some stations are famous for certain items: Agra station, for example, is known for its *petha*, a crystallized gourd sweet, while one of the Delhi stations is famous for its *biryani*.

A vivid illustration of the complexity of Indian food is evident in the meal options available on the national airline, Air India. Air India offers more than twenty-five special meals, including Indian vegetarian (dairy products but no meat and eggs), nondairy vegetarian, lacto-ovo (dairy and eggs) Western-style vegetarian, Hindu vegetarian (made with onion and garlic), strict vegetarian (no onions and garlic), Hindu nonvegetarian, Gujarati vegetarian, Jain (no onions, garlic, or root vegetables), raw vegetarian, Muslim, kosher, low cholesterol, low protein, low sodium, low calorie, gluten free, low purine, and high-fiber.

Chinese Food

Chinese restaurants are popular in India and range from small neighborhood establishments to more upscale establishments. Kolkata was the center of Indian Chinese cuisine. In the 1950s, the city was home to more than 80,000 Chinese who first came here in the late eighteenth century. The community grew dramatically in the 1930s and 1940s, when a flood of immigrants, mainly Hakka and Cantonese, arrived from China and Kolkata became home to a bustling China town. Restaurants such as Nanking, Ta Fu Shun, and Beiping were favorite dining spots for cosmopolitan Bengalis. The food ranged from traditional Chinese regional cuisine to a spicy Indian version. Chicken corn soup, chili chicken, sweet and sour pork or lamb, and noodles appeared on most menus.

After the India-China war in the early 1960s, many Indian Chinese emigrated abroad and some family members opened branches outside of India. Delhi, Mumbai, and Bangalore also have many Chinese restaurants, and Chinese dishes are part of the menus of most clubs and five-star hotels. Today Thai food is replacing Chinese food as a fashionable alternative among urban foodies.

Famous Restaurants in India

Until independence the subcontinent had few restaurants where middle-class Indians and tourists could enjoy Indian cuisine in an attractive setting. India's most famous and influential restaurant became New Delhi's Moti Mahal, opened near the Red Fort in 1947 by Kundan Lal, a refugee from Peshawar in Pakistan near the Afghan border. Kundan Lal introduced the tandoori style of cooking in India and created such dishes as *tandoori* chicken, butter chicken, and chicken *tikka* (pieces of chicken marinated in yogurt and spices).

In Kundan Lal's native region, a common method of preparing chicken and goat was to roast pieces of meat with very little spicing on skewers over hot coals in a *tandoor* or *tanoor*, a large clay oven buried in the ground that originated in Iran or Central Asia. In Delhi, he found a *tandoor* maker, a fellow refugee, who experimented with different designs until he came up with an aboveground version that would work in a restaurant kitchen. To make the food more palatable to Indian tastes, Kundan Lal tried different spice mixtures until he settled on the blend used in the restaurant today: ground coriander seeds, black pepper, and a mild red pepper that gives *tan-*

The late Kundan Lal, seated, with family. He was the creator of *tandoori* chicken. Photo by Ashish Sen.

doori chicken its characteristic color. Pieces of chicken were marinated in this mixture and yogurt and roasted in the *tandoor*. To please richer palates (and, some people claim, to use leftover *tandoori* chicken), he created butter chicken: pieces of roasted chicken cooked in a tomato, cream, and butter sauce. The menu at Moti Mahal also included *tandoor*-roasted breads, rice *pulaos*, kabobs, and various curries.

The restaurant became a favorite eating place of Prime Minister Jawaharlal Nehru and, later, his daughter Prime Minister Indira Gandhi, who brought many visiting VIPs there. Today it has several branches in India, plus countless imitators in India and throughout the world. And, in one of the ironies of culinary history, *tandoori* chicken is regarded as the quintessential Indian dish!

Another important landmark restaurant is Karim, also near the Red Fort, that was founded in 1913 by Haji Karimuddin, a descendant of cooks who worked for the Mughal emperors. His goal, according to the menu, was "to bring the Royal Food to the common man." Today the fourth generation operates the restaurant, which has a second branch near a famous Delhi mosque. Karim's menu features richly spiced Moghlai dishes that have been imitated by restaurants in India, the United Kingdom, the United States, and elsewhere. It is famous for its *rogan josh* (a rich lamb stew) and other curries; rice dishes such as *biryani* and *pulaos*; *shammi*, *boti*, and *shish kabobs*; and a variety of breads.

After partition in 1947, the restaurant business in India became a specialty of Punjabis.[5] A hardworking, enterprising people, they arrived in Delhi from Pakistan virtually penniless and branched out into all kinds of small businesses, including setting up food stalls that did not require a lot of capital. By the early 1950s some of these stands had turned into small neighborhood restaurants. Other family members opened branches in other cities and created the restaurant chains Kwality and Gaylord, which later opened branches abroad.

The standard fare in these restaurants, and most Indian restaurants today, is a combination of *tandoori* cuisine, Moghlai food (regarded as haute cuisine in North India because it used expensive ingredients and was the food eaten by princes), and North Indian vegetarian dishes such as *mattar* (peas) *pulao*, *sag panir* (spinach with cheese), and *dals*. This style of cuisine is taught at the catering colleges set up by the government of India, starting in the 1960s, to serve the tourist industry and institutions. As the graduates moved into the workforce, this style became standard in five-star hotels, which in the 1970s and 1980s became centers of dining and social activity for the urban new rich.

In the past it was difficult to find restaurants serving local food in major cities, but this appears to be changing. For example, in Kolkata several restaurants have opened that serve authentic Bengali food (including one called Oh Calcutta!).

Indian Restaurants Abroad

Most Indian restaurants in the United States, Europe, and the Middle East serve either South Indian vegetarian food or the meat-based North Indian/Moghlai cuisine described above. In the United States, Indian food is generally less popular than Chinese or Thai.

In the United Kingdom, however, Indian food has totally permeated the gastronomical culture to the point where curry is now considered the unofficial national dish. Indian food is a $5 billion industry in Britain, accounting for two-thirds of all eating out, and the country has an estimated 8,000 Indian restaurants. More than 90 percent are owned by Bangladeshis, many of whom originally came as sailors.[6]

The first Indian restaurant in London, *Hindoostanee Coffee House*, was opened in London in 1809 by an interesting character named Dean Mahomet, an Indian who served in the British army and married an Irishwoman.[7] The restaurant closed down after a few years. In 1927, Edward Palmer, great-grandson of an Indian princess married to a British general, opened Veeraswamy Restaurant near Piccadilly Square in London, a site it occupies to this day. The restaurant, which followed on the success enjoyed by Indian food at the British Empire Exhibition of 1924–1925, was a favorite of visiting maharajahs and other royalty. The founder of the restaurant was allegedly a South Indian doctor named E. P. Veeraswamy, who was also the author of a famous cookbook, still in print to this day.[8] However, he was in reality Edward Palmer himself.

The food at today's relatively inexpensive, plainly decorated, Bangladeshi-owned restaurants is a kind of hybrid North Indian–Bangladeshi mixture using ready-made curry pastes and food coloring—"Indian food reduced to the lowest common denominator"[9]—a phrase coined by a leading food writer to describe much Indian restaurant food. Many British pubs serve curry, a word that is used for virtually every Indian dish from *korma* and *vindaloo* to *dals*. The drink of choice is beer, a trend helped by a much reported-on study that showed the hot spices in Indian food help people absorb alcohol and can protect against stomach ulcers.

In the past two decades, England has also given rise to its own style of Indian cooking called *balti*. The Hindi word *balti* means a large, iron, wok-like pot or bucket (although some people claim this style of food comes from a region of Pakistan called Baltistan). *Balti* cooking evolved in Birmingham, England, in the late 1970s and 1980s and has become very popular since it is relatively inexpensive and emphasizes the use of fresh ingredients. Dishes are made by sautéing onions, garlic, and spices in oil, then adding meat and vegetables in whatever combinations the customer prefers. The dish is served in the pot, with rice or bread on the side.

Today, at elegant restaurants such as Tamarind, Benares, and Zaika in London, Tabla in New York, and Monsoon in Chicago, Western-trained chefs combine Indian and non-Indian ingredients and techniques to create an elegant (and pricey) fusion cuisine.

Fast Food

Meanwhile, the rapid rise in disposable income among young Indians working in call centers and data processing firms is revolutionizing the Indian restaurant scene. Young Indian yuppies spend half of their annual salaries on shopping, eating out, and other luxury items, and Indians overall spent 55 percent more on eating out in 2002 than in 2001.[10] McDonald's, Pizza Hut, Dominos, Subway, and other Western fast food chains are opening more outlets every year and have adapted their dishes to Indian tastes and customs. The most popular item at McDonald's (which opened its first store in 1996 and now has 48 stores in India) is the McAloo *tikka*, a vegetarian fried potato patty with cheese. It recently introduced McCurry *pan*, a flat pastry filled with spicy broccoli or chicken curry. At Pizza Hut, which has 50 stores and plans to open 100 more by 2005, customized toppings include chicken *tikka masala* (tandoori chicken cooked in a tomato-based sauce) or spicy *paneer* (cheese). It even makes a special pizza without onions or garlic for Jains. India is developing its own fast food chains, including Pizza Corner, Nirulas, and Haldirams, which sells Indian-style sweets and snacks. Barista Coffee Co. is an Indian firm serving high-end coffee at more than one hundred locations around the country.

NOTES

1. An anthropologist tracked the eating patterns of college-educated members of a Brahmin family in Lucknow over a one-year period (1965) to determine how often they ate at home, with relatives, with members of the same caste, with people belonging to other castes, and at restaurants. The changes were dramatic. An older orthodox family member (born in 1908) ate mainly with relatives belong to the same caste, a few times with nonrelatives (and then only *pakka*, or fried food), and several times at a Hindu tea shop. He never ate with people be-

longing to other castes nor would he eat the food served on a train. His son, born in 1929, ate more than a dozen times with nonrelatives from the same caste and several times with people from other castes (although he would not eat with outcastes or Muslims). He was "without scruples" in eating fried food from vendors, tea stalls, and restaurants, which he visited with his coworkers (but not his wife) every two weeks. His son, a student, showed a "glaring disregard for things Brahmanical, including the commensal rules." He often ate with members of other caste groups and communities, and ate both *kaccha* and fried foods at coffee houses and restaurants, which he visited three to four times a week. By 1972, when he became "a nouveau riche," he was taking his wife to social functions where they ate all unrestricted foods, including meat. R. S. Khare, *The Hindu Hearth and Home* (New Delhi: Vikas Publishing House, 1976), pp. 244–252.

2. Paul M. Toomey, "Mountain of Food, Mountain of Love," *The Eternal Food: Gastronomic Ideas and Experiences of Hindus and Buddhists*, ed. R. S. Khare (Albany: State University of New York Press, 1992), pp. 117–145.

3. In Indian English, the word *hotel* denotes "any establishment, even a roadside stall, open to all and serving meals." Nigel B. Hankin, *Hanklyn-Janklyn, or A Stranger's Rumble-Tumble Guide to Some Words, Customs, and Quiddities Indian and Indo-British* (New Delhi: Banyan Books, 1992), p. 88. Udupi is a town in Karnataka famous for its cooks, who started in the kitchens of a famous Krishna temple there.

4. Colleen Taylor Sen, "Sandesh: An Emblem of Bengaliness," in *Milk: Beyond the Dairy, Proceedings of the Oxford Symposium on Food and Cookery 1999* (Blackawton, UK: Prospect Books, 2000), pp. 300–308.

5. Camilla Punjabi, "The Non-Emergence of the Regional Foods of India," unpublished outline of paper presented to the Oxford Food Symposium, "Food on the Move," Oxford, UK, September 1996.

6. Geraldine Bedell, "It's Curry, but Not as We Know it," *The Observer*, 12 May 2002; Nicolas Lander and Iqbal Wahhab, "In Search of the UK's Curry Capital," *Weekend Financial Times*, 31 December 1994–1 January 1995.

7. An account of his unusual life can be found in Michael H. Fisher, *The Travels of Dean Mahomet* (Berkeley: University of California Press, 1997).

8. E. P. Veeraswamy, *Indian Cookery* (Bombay: Jaico Publishing House, 1967).

9. Madhur Jaffrey, "Inching Toward Nirvana," *Food Arts*, July/August 2001, p. 48.

10. "Hey, Big Spenders: India's Booming Middle Class," *Time Online Edition, Global Business*, 27 August 2003.

6

Special Occasions

India is often called the land of feasts, fasts, and festivals. All ethnic and religious groups—Hindus, Muslims, Christians, Jains, Parsis, Sikhs—observe seasonal and harvest festivals, religious holidays, and life transitions, such as weddings, births, and deaths, by eating certain foods, by avoiding them (fasting), or, in some cases, by doing both.

Festivals are also gastronomic affairs, and sweets are an essential element, perhaps because poor people cannot afford to eat them every day. People consume sweets, offer them to guests, and send them to friends and family members as a gesture of affection and goodwill. Most Indian sweets are made with sugar or jaggery (a gritty brown sugar made from sugarcane or palm sap), and dairy products, such as milk and butter. Another common ingredient is chickpea flour, especially in *laddoos*—round balls that are a universal Indian sweet. Popular flavorings include spices, especially green cardamom seeds and sesame seeds, grated coconut, and nuts.

Because of their central role in Indian festive occasions, all the recipes in this chapter are for sweet dishes. Traditionally, sweets were made at home but today most people buy them from professional sweetmakers. Sweet stalls and shops are ubiquitous in Indian cities, towns, and villages, and are open virtually around the clock. Because they are pure vegetarian and fried, everyone, regardless of religion and caste, can enjoy their wares.

Buying sweets for a holiday. Photo © TRIP/H. Rogers.

RELIGIOUS, HARVEST, AND SEASONAL FESTIVALS

Hindu Festivals

Some familiarity with Hinduism is necessary to understand the significance of festivals. Hinduism is often called a path (*dharma* in Sanskrit), a philosophy, or a way of life, rather than a religion. Hinduism has no sacred book comparable to the Bible or the Quran, no precise equivalent to a church, and no single deity worshipped by everyone who calls himself or herself a Hindu. The Hindu pantheon is said to consist of 330 million gods, perhaps because no one really knows how many deities are worshipped. Hinduism grew gradually over five thousand years by absorbing the gods and spirits worshipped by the subcontinent's inhabitants. Eventually they came to be recognized as manifestations of the three major gods who preside over the universe and represent three aspects of the supreme: Brahma, the creator; Vishnu, the preserver; and Shiva, the destroyer. Some Hindus revere only Vishnu or Shiva (Brahma is rarely worshipped), but many worship both gods and some of their incarnations (avatars), wives, children, and animal companions. Vishnu's wife is variously named Uma, Parvati, Durga, and Kali, each representing a particular aspect of the feminine force of the universe. Some deities are worshipped throughout India; others mainly in certain states or regions.

There are no prescribed methods of worship in Hinduism, no equivalent of the Catholic mass or the Muslim Friday service with prayers and sermon. Some people visit a temple daily; some only on special occasions; others never. Hinduism accepts the idea of many ways of reaching the Supreme, so no practice is compulsory for everyone. Spiritual guidance is provided not by the temple priests but by swamis and gurus who are considered to have special insights and powers. They are often associated with spiritual retreats called *ashrams*. Many Hindus have home altars containing statues representing their favorite deities or abstract symbols. The purpose of these statues is to focus devotion; in theory, they are only representations of one or more of the infinite aspects of god.

At the temple, priests conduct daily prayers and offerings as well as special ceremonies on festivals and other special occasions. A worship service typically involves chanting ancient Sanskrit texts and making an offering to the gods. The offering is called *prasad*. It may include flowers, fruits, *ghee*, milk, coconut, or sweets, which the gods are believed to especially enjoy. After being consecrated by this ritual offering, the *prasad* is shared by the worshippers who eat it or take it home to share with family and friends.

All Hindus, devout or not, celebrate annual festivals, which are the occasion for processions, community celebrations, gift giving, and the consumption and distribution of food. Some festivals are connected with the worship of certain gods and goddesses or events in their lives (e.g., the birth of Krishna, the victory of Ram over the demon king Ravana); others celebrate the harvest and the change of seasons.

There are so many ceremonies and festivals on the subcontinent that listing them all is impossible. As a leading scholar comments, "If a Hindu were to perform all [the ceremonies] he would have no time left for anything else in life."[1] The following section describes festivals that are celebrated throughout India or are major regional events. In most cases their date is determined by the Indian lunar calendar, which is based on the phases of the moon.[2] This means that they fall on a different day each year in the Western solar calendar so only the approximate dates are indicated here.

Harvest Festivals

On January 13 or 14, a harvest festival is celebrated throughout India. In North India, crops sown in the fall are starting to grow, hopefully promising a good harvest. In South India, the rice crop is harvested and new seeds are planted for the next crop. This festival coincides with the beginning of the sun's journey to the northern hemisphere, called *Makar Sankranti* in Hindi, and is the only major festival with a date fixed according to the solar calendar. On this day, Hindus are supposed to take a bath in the Ganges or other rivers, worship the gods, give gifts to the poor, and distribute sweets.

In the Punjab, this festival is called *Lohri* and is celebrated by Sikhs and Hindus with bonfires and dancing. Sheaves of newly harvested corn are roasted and eaten along with sweets and snacks, including dried fruits and nuts; *revri*, round flat sweets made of jaggery and sesame seeds; puffed rice; *jalebis*, spirals of chickpea batter, deep-fried and soaked in sugar syrup; *halwa*, a sweet, soft, fudge-like sweet made of carrots and other vegetables; and *ladoos*. One of the most popular Indian sweets, *laddoos* are balls made of flour, *ghee*, sugar or jaggery, and other ingredients, such as nuts, raisins, and sesame seeds. Often they are made from little drops of fried chickpea flour batter that are soaked in sugar syrup and shaped into balls. The following recipe is easy to make.

Laddoos

- 1 cup chickpea flour
- 1/3 cup *ghee* or melted butter
- 1 cup ground jaggery or powdered sugar
- 2 tablespoons chopped almonds, cashew nuts, and/or raisins
- 1/2 tsp cardamom powder (purchased as powder or made by grinding a few green cardamom seeds, shells and all)

Sift the chickpea flour. Heat the *ghee* over high heat until it starts to smoke, then lower the heat to medium and add the flour. Stir it well until the flour starts to turn brown and release a fragrant aroma. Remove from the heat, add the sugar, and mix well. When it cools down slightly, add the cardamom powder and nuts. Mix well and form into small balls around 1 1/2 inches in diameter, using your greased palms. Set aside to harden.

In Maharashtra, people exchange sweets, called *tilguls*, made from sesame seeds, sugar, and jaggery, and greet each other by saying, "Accept these *tilguls* and speak sweet words." In Tamil Nadu, a three- or four-day harvest festival called Pongal starts on January 13. *Pongal* is the name of a special dish prepared on the second day. Married women put newly harvested rice to boil in milk with jaggery, cashew nuts, *ghee*, and coconut. As soon as it begins to boil, they shout "*Pongal*," which means "It is boiling over." A sweet made from the mixture is offered to the Sun and the god Ganesh.

Sweet *Pongal*

- One cup basmati or other long-grain rice
- 1/8 cup *moong dal* (lentils)
- 1 cup milk
- 1/2 cup *ghee* (melted clarified butter)
- 1 2/3 cup brown sugar
- 1/2 tsp cardamom powder (purchased as powder or made by grinding a few green cardamom seeds, shell and all, in a spice grinder)
- 6–8 cashew nuts
- 10 raisins

Cook the rice and *dal* with milk and 1 1/2 cup of water until it is soft and the water is absorbed, adding more water if necessary. Fry the cashews and raisins in half of the *ghee* until they are golden brown, then remove from the pan. Boil the brown sugar in 1/2 cup of water until it thickens. Add the cooked rice and *dal* to the sugar mixture and cook over low heat for five minutes, stirring constantly. Gradually add the remaining *ghee*. Place on a plate, sprinkle cardamom powder over it, and decorate with the nuts and raisins.

Every day during Pongal a lavish lunch is prepared for family members that includes *idli, dosa*, rice cooked in different styles (salty, sweet, mixed with yogurt), coconut chutney, and the sweet *pongal*. On the third day, rice and yogurt are spread outdoors on banana leaves to share the bounty with birds, squirrels, and insects. In Andhra Pradesh, the harvest festival is called *Sankranthi* and it is a must on this day to prepare a *payasam*, a rice pudding made with rice, milk, and jaggery.

The northeastern state of Assam is famous for its festivals, called *bihus*, and the sweet dishes associated with them. At the *Magh* or *Bhogali Bihu* in mid-January, community meals are prepared in thatched huts built for the occasion. The meals feature fried or curried chicken, duck, pigeon, tortoise, goat, and fish. Sweets are an integral part of all *bihus*, especially various kinds of *laddoos* and *pithas*, which are lightly fried pancakes made from rice flour and sugar with various kinds of fillings.

Basant Panchami: *The First Day of Spring*

In North India the end of winter is celebrated on the fifth day in the lunar moon at the end of January or beginning of February. A special offering of the fruit of the ber tree and white radish beans is made to Saraswati, the goddess of learning. These two items are placed on a metal tray (*thali*) with mustard leaves, coconut, yellow *barfi* (a fudge-like sweet made of sugar and milk), or *laddoos*. Everyone wears yellow clothes and the food is dyed yellow. Yellow is an auspicious color and echoes the color of the mustard plants now in full flower. A specialty of this day is sweet rice cooked with almonds, pistachios, cashews, raisins, and milk solids.

Mahashivaratri

In mid-march, Hindus celebrate Mahashivaratri, a festival in honor of Lord Shiva's marriage to Parvati. Devotees fast during the day and spend the night in meditation. The next day, they bathe in the Ganges and worship at a temple or at home. The object of their worship is the *lingam*, a phallic-shaped stone that is a symbol of Shiva. Devotees wash it with water from the Ganges, milk, yogurt, and honey, and make offerings of milk, yogurt, sugar, honey, *ghee*, the leaves and fruit of the bael tree, betel leaves, and flowers. Sometimes little rivers flow outside the main temples from all the excess milk and fruit juice.

Unlike most other festivals, where a feast follows worship, in this case devotees fast throughout the day. At midday they eat a special vegetarian meal consisting entirely of noncereal food. The fast resumes and continues for 36 hours until the morning of the third day.

Mahashivaratri is the major festival of Kashmiri Hindus who celebrate it for 21 days. On the thirteenth day, pots representing Shiva, Parvati, and other deities are decorated with flowers and filled with walnuts. Three days later the walnuts are removed and the pots immersed in a stream or river. The walnuts and rice cakes are distributed to family members and friends.

Holi

The most riotous and colorful of Hindu festivals, Holi is celebrated on the day of the full moon in March and is especially popular in northern and western India. There are no *pujas* or fasts associated with this holiday, which may have originated in an ancient vernal fertility festival, like the Roman Saturnalia. According to one legend, an arrogant king resented his son for worshipping Vishnu and threw him into a large fire to destroy him. The king's sister, Holika, who was immune to burning, sat with the boy who emerged unscathed. On the evening before Holi, bonfires are lit to commemorate this event and to cleanse the air of evil spirits. The holiday is also associated with Lord Krishna, echoing his games as a playful child and adolescent. On the day of Holi, children and teenagers squirt colored water and throw powders on friends, neighbors, and passersby so everyone is forced to wear old clothes.

Holi foods include special sweets and snacks, alcoholic beverages, and *bhang*, the dried leaves of the hemp plant, which is mixed with ground almonds and sugar to make a mildly intoxicating drink called *thandai*. Typical North Indian treats include meat kabobs; *gujiyas*, fried dumplings filled with milk solids (*khoya*), raisins, and spices; *burfi*, a hard fudge-like candy; *laddoos*; *alu kachori*, fried bread stuffed with spiced potatoes; and *malpoa*, a desert made from white flour, milk, sugar, and nuts and raisins. In western India, popular Holi snacks include *puran poli* and *gurpoli*, sweet pancakes stuffed with lentils and jaggery made from the newly harvested sugar.

Badam Burfi (Almond Cake)

- 1 cup almonds without skins
- 4 tb *ghee*
- 1 1/4 cups sugar
- 1/4 cup milk
- 2 pinches cardamom powder

Cover the almonds with water and cook on high in the microwave for six to eight minutes until soft. Grind in a food processor with milk to make a smooth paste. Heat half of the *ghee* in a pan, and stir in the almond paste until it starts to thicken. Add sugar and continue stirring, adding the rest of the *ghee* until it is absorbed and the mixture becomes thick and starts to leave the side of the pan. Add cardamom powder. Put into a greased pan and cut into squares or triangles when cool.

New Year's Day

The Hindu New Year on April 14 is another harvest festival celebrated under various names: *Baisakhi* in North India, *Bohag Bihu* in Assam, *Vishu* in Kerala, *Ugadi* in Andhra Pradesh and Karnataka, and *Bupthandu* in Tamil Nadu. Again, sweets are exchanged and eaten, sometimes with a bitter leaf from the neem tree, symbolizing the mixture of the bitter and the sweet the year will bring. On this day, Hindus believe the goddess Ganga descended to earth, an event commemorated every 12 years with a massive pilgrimage to the town of Hardwar on the Ganges. Sikhs celebrate this as the day on which their leader, Guru Gobind Singh, laid down the basic rules of their religion. In the villages, Sikhs perform the famous *bhangra* dance, which enacts the entire process of the harvest, and enjoy their favorite dish of green vegetables, *sarson ka saag*.

In Maharashtra, New Year's Day is celebrated as the day on which the world was created after a deluge. People enjoy mangoes, jackfruit, melons, and other fruits that begin to appear on the market either raw or made into sherbets and *puranpoli*. In Andhra Pradesh a special chutney is made from sour tamarind juice, sweet jaggery, salt, chili powder, raw mango, and neem leaves.

Janmashtami

Observed in August–September, this holiday commemorates the birth of Lord Krishna, an avatar of Vishnu. The festival is celebrated all over India, especially in Mathur and Vrindaban in Uttar Pradesh where Lord Krishna was born and raised. As a child, Krishna was very fond of milk, *ghee*, and yogurt, so these ingredients play an important role in temple offerings and the festivities. Devotees fast during the day and celebrate Krishna's birthday at midnight by eating *bhog kheer*, a rich rice pudding; *pedhas*, a dry sweet made of milk solids, sugar, and cardamom powder; and *shrikand*, a yogurt, sugar, and cardamom pudding especially popular in western India.

Shrikand (Sweetened Yogurt)

- 2 pounds yogurt
- 3/4 cup powdered sugar
- 1 tb warm milk
- 2 tsp green cardamom powder
- A few strands saffron
- Sliced pistachios and almonds

Hang the yogurt in cheesecloth for 2–3 hours until all the liquid is drained out. Dissolve the saffron in the warm milk, mix with the yogurt, sugar, and cardamom powder in a bowl and beat with a hand blender until it is smooth. Serve garnished with the nuts.

Ganesh Chaturthi

This holiday in August–September celebrates the birthday of Ganesh, the son of Shiva and Parvati, who has a human body and an elephant head. One of the most popular Hindu deities, Ganesh is the god of successful endeavors and so is always worshipped before any important undertaking. The holiday was started in the eighteenth century by the Maratha leader Shivaji to encourage Maharashtrian culture. It is the

Ganesh holding a sweet.

major public festival in the state, lasting 10 days. Clay idols of Ganesh are set up in homes and neighborhoods; on the final day they are taken in a procession to the river or ocean and submerged in the water.

One of Ganesh's endearing qualities is his love of sweets. Statues always depict him holding a *modaka*—a steamed, rice dumpling filled with coconut, sugar, milk solids, and dried nuts. His other favorite dishes are *peras* and *laddoos*. According to a legend, Ganesh once cursed the moon for making fun of him for eating so many sweets, which is why the moon waxes and wanes, regularly losing its beauty and vanishing altogether.

Modaka (Sweet Rice Dumplings)

- 1 cup rice flour
- 1/2–1 cup water
- 1 tsp vegetable oil
- 1 cup grated coconut
- 1/2 cup brown sugar
- 2 tsp of *ghee* (melted clarified butter)
- 1/2 tsp cardamom powder
- Pinch of salt

Bring the water to a boil, add the salt and oil, then the rice flour, and stir until it forms a smooth dry dough. Set aside. Fry the grated coconut in the *ghee*, add cardamom powder and sugar, mix well, and fry until it thickens. When cool, roll the coconut mixture into little balls. Take a small piece of the dough, flatten it on your palm into a circle about three inches in diameter, insert a coconut ball, and wrap it into a little package, squeezed at the top so that it looks like a head of garlic. Continue until all the ingredients are used up. Place in a steamer or colander over boiling water and steam for 7 to 10 minutes.

In North India, an offering is made to Ganesh consisting of *modakas*, rice, *urad dal*, betel nuts, turmeric, milk, incense, coconut, and red flowers. Fasting is not common during this festival. In Rajasthan, a big dish of *laddoos* are kept in houses and offered to guests. In Andhra Pradesh, semolina *laddoos* and *bobbatlu*, a wheat bread stuffed with lentils, jaggery, cardamom, and *ghee*, are popular items.

Dussehra and Durga Puja

The mother goddess, who is believed to possess great power and positive energy, is worshipped throughout India under many different names and manifestations, ranging from the benign (Durga) to the savage (Kali). Two festivals a year, called Navatri (nine nights), are devoted to Durga: one in March–April, the other in September–October. The first is generally a low-key domestic event observed by a vegetarian diet, but the second is celebrated with great pomp and show, especially in West Bengal where it is the state holiday and commemorates the victory of Durga over an evil demon. Neighborhood organizations commission artists to build elaborate shrines and sun-dried clay statues of the goddess, which are carried around in procession for nine days and immersed in a river or pond on the tenth day. The exchange and consumption of sweets is de rigueur, and restaurants and sweet shops do a booming business.

On the final day, called Mahaashtami, a community vegetarian meal is prepared. It might include a special *khichri*; *lucchis*, puffed fried bread made with white flour; vegetables; and many sweet dishes.

Sandesh (Bengali-Style Fudge)
- 1/2 gallon whole milk
- Fresh lemons or condensed lemon juice
- 1/2 cup sugar
- 1 tb finely grated pistachio nuts
- 1 tb *ghee*

Bring the milk to the boiling point in a pot and then add the juice of two lemons or six tablespoons of condensed lemon juice. Stir until the milk curdles and the whey separates. Boil for two minutes, remove from the heat, and strain the milk through cheesecloth. Tie it loosely and hang it for half an hour or so until the water has drained off. (The tap on the kitchen sink is a good place).

Remove the residue from the cheesecloth, squeeze it gently, and knead it into a smooth paste. Mix in the sugar with your hand. Heat the *ghee* in a heavy pan, add the dough, and stir continuously for two to three minutes until it no longer sticks to the pan. Remove from the heat and add a few more drops of lemon juice. When it has cooled enough to handle, put the mixture into little molds or spread it evenly on an oiled plate. Sprinkle the grated pistachio nuts over the *sandesh* and put it in the refrigerator. When it is hard and cold, cut it into diamond shapes one and one-half inches long.

In North India, a festival called Dussehra (ten nights) is celebrated in September–October to commemorate the battle between Lord Rama and the demon King Ravana described in the epic *The Ramayama*. The story is reenacted in street plays; on the final day huge effigies of Ravana and his family are burned and fireworks are lit. The festival begins with the planting of a few seeds of millet, which are watered daily, sprout on the tenth day, and then are eaten in a salad. In North India, it is not a vegetarian festival, and meat dishes are eaten. In South India, where the festival is more religious in nature, a special vegetarian food item is prepared every day for nine days and offered to the goddesses Durga, Lakshmi, and Sarawati in turn. The dishes include *payasam*, *pongal*, tamarind rice, yogurt rice, *vada* (fried breads made from ground rice and lentils), and *vada* soaked in spiced yogurt.

Diwali

The closest equivalent to Christmas is Diwali, the Festival of Lights (called Deepawali in South India), a family festival celebrated nationwide 18 to 20 days after Dassehra in November/December. It celebrates the return of Lord Ram to his kingdom Ayodhya after fourteen years in exile and symbolizes the victory of good over evil, of light over darkness. In the old days houses and buildings were illuminated with little clay lanterns, but today electric lighting is used. During this period Hindus visit friends and family, decorate their houses, buy new clothes and jewelry, and exchange gifts and sweets, sometimes shaped like the lanterns. Animals and toys made of pure white sugar are a distributed to children. In rural areas, farmers honor cattle by feeding them sweets. Some temples prepare elaborate vegetarian feasts featuring hundreds of dishes. A Hindu temple in the United Kingdom made it into the Guinness Book of Records by preparing 1,250 different vegetarian dishes for Diwali.

Diwali is the sweet and snack festival par excellence. In North India, favorite items include *kheer,* a thick rice pudding with raisins and nuts; *nanki,* fried sticks of chickpea batter; *jalebis,* round spirals of chickpea batter soaked in sugar syrup; *kalakand,* mango fudge; different kinds of *burfi;* *narsa,* rice crisps sprinkled with poppy seeds; *misri roti,* little triangles of dough, sugar, pistachios, and almonds; *parwals* (a kind of squash) stuffed with roasted milk solids and nuts, and soaked in sugar syrup; almond *seera,* a thick pudding made from ground almonds, sugar, flour, and milk; various kinds of *khaja,* small deep-fried wafers that can be sweet, spicy, or salty; *lapsee,* a thick pudding of wheat germ, sugar, *ghee,* and chopped nuts; and the inevitable *laddoos.*

In Gujarat and Maharashtra, a festival is held at this time honoring Lakshmi, the goddess of good fortune and the wife of Vishnu. A popular Gujarati sweet is *jagaj,* fudge-like squares of chickpea flour, sugar, milk solids, and nuts. Maharashtrians make *anarsa,* a net-like pancake of rice flour, jaggery, and poppy seeds. Bengalis celebrate Kali Puja at this time by sacrificing goats and other animals at midnight to the bloodthirsty goddess Kali. Statues depict her with a garland of skulls around her neck, holding the head of a demon she has just killed. Kali worshippers eat the meat as part of a feast, often in a thin gravy with rice, called *manksha jhol.* Throughout the year goats are also sacrificed daily at Kolkata's Kalighat Temple and the meat distributed to the poor.

Onam

Observed in December–January, Onam is the national festival of the state of Kerala, where it is celebrated by Hindus, Muslims, and Christians for three days. The government organizes boat races, processions of elephants, and other pageants. The festival honors the memory of an ancient king, Mahabali, whose rule was a golden age and is believed to return to Kerala every year at this time. It also celebrates the rice harvest.

There is no special form of worship associated with Onam. On the third day, families or communities eat a vegetarian meal served on banana leaves. The first course consists of pickles, banana chips, *papads,* crispy breads made of lentils, ginger chutney, and different kinds of yogurt, perhaps mixed with cucumber, fried okra, or coconut. Then rice is served, each time accompanied by *sambar,* a thin spicy lentil soup; *rasam,* a very thin and very hot lentil soup; *avial,* a mixed vegetable stew in a coconut-milk gravy; dried vegetables cooked in mustard seed; and yogurt with vegetables. The meal always includes a sweet dish, such as *payasam*, a rice pudding; *prathaman*, a thick pudding made from rice, brown jaggery, coconut milk, and grated coconut; or banana *erucherry*.

Banana *Erucherry*

- 6 green plantains, peeled and cut into 2-inch pieces
- One or two green chilies, thinly sliced
- 2 cups unsweetened grated coconut
- 8–10 curry leaves
- 1/2 tsp cumin seeds
- 1/2 tsp mustard seeds
- 1/2 tsp turmeric powder
- 1 red chili
- 1 tsp salt (or to taste)
- 2 tb coconut oil

Cook plantain pieces with turmeric, salt, and a little water until soft and mash. Grind half the coconut, the red chili, and the cumin to a fine paste. Add to the bananas and set aside. Heat oil and fry the mustard seeds, green chilies, curry leaves, and the rest of the coconut, and fry until golden. Mix with the mashed plantain and serve hot.

Chaat

In Bihar, the eastern parts of Uttar Pradesh and some parts of Madhya Pradesh, Hindus observe the Chaat festival for six days beginning the day after Diwali. At this time they worship Lord Kartikeya or Skanda, the first son of Shiva and Parvati. It is a very austere festival, involving intense fasting, which parents undertake for their children or their own prosperity and health. During the week people refrain from smoking and gambling and abstain from all meat, onions, and garlic. On the first day there are no restrictions on how much one can eat but on the second day no food at all is allowed for 24 hours. The fast is broken with *puri* made from wheat that is newly ground and *kheer*, a rice pudding.

Hindu Fasts

An important part of Hinduism, fasting is undertaken for many reasons. It can be a mandatory part of a religious festival, a form of worship through self-sacrifice, gratitude for a blessing, a petition to a god for a favor, an instrument of self-discipline, a means of attaining spiritual merit and harmony, or a method of physical cleansing. Ayurveda advocates fasting to cleanse the body of toxic materials and eliminate disease. Women generally fast more than men and have special fast days on which they pray for blessings for their husbands and family. (There is even a day on which unattractive women fast to improve their looks and good-looking women fast to maintain them.) A family member may refuse food to indicate sorrow, frustration, or to force another member to follow or not follow a course of action. Children are not expected to fast.

Fasting has played an important role in Indian politics. The great spiritual and political leader Mahatma Gandhi fasted on many occasions to force the British authorities to take a certain course of action (a hunger strike), to resolve moral dilemmas, or to set himself on a course of personal or political action. Gandhi maintained that a person should not eat more than was necessary to sustain the body for its undertaking, a view that is expressed in the *Bhagavad Gita* and other Indian religious texts. Gandhi wrote:

Food should be taken as one takes medicine in measured doses, at measured times, and as required…A 'full' meal is therefore a crime against God and man.… Hence the necessity for complete fasts at intervals and partial fasts forever.… What is enough [food] is a matter of conjecture, therefore, of our own mental picture…So what we often think is spare or meager is likely to be more than enough. More people are weak through over-feeding or wrong feeding than through underfeeding.[3]

Some Hindus fast on a certain day of the week, often Tuesday, or on the eleventh day of the lunar fortnight, called Ekadashi, which occurs twice a month. Communal fasts are associated with religious holidays such as Ram Navami, Shivratri, and Janamasthami. More than a hundred annual fasts and festivals have been identified in one region of Uttar Pradesh, although no single person observed them all and only twenty were considered major observances.[4]

The Hindi word for fasting, *vrata*, means a vow, and does not usually connote total abstention from food but rather a restricted way of eating. There are many variations, depending on regional, household, and individual traditions and preferences. Fasting always entails the consumption of vegetarian food. At its least rigorous, it may mean cooking dishes in pure *ghee* instead of oil or replacing sea salt with rock salt. Sometimes only boiled foods (*kaccha*) are permitted. Meals might be only taken once a day in the morning. At the most rigorous, no food at all is eaten and only sips of water are allowed.

A common form of fasting involves a category of food called *phalahar*. Food materials are divided into two categories: *anna*, which are harvested with the help of special equipment, such as rice, wheat, barley, and lentils; and *phala*, those that grow without special cultivation, such as wild grains, vegetables, fruits, certain roots and tubers, leaves, and flowers. Only the latter are permitted in a *phalahar* meal. Thus, breads and snacks are made of dried water-chestnut flour or lotus-seed flour instead of wheat and other grains. Other prohibited foods include onions, turmeric, garlic, ginger, sea salt, and *urad dal* (perhaps because it is black and resembles meat and spices).

Fasting may also entail eliminating certain comforts, such as sleeping in a normal bed, washing, and shaving, or talking. At its most extreme, some people make a vow to a deity that they will never eat a certain food again in their life (especially a food they like very much) in return for some favor or blessing.

Jain Fasts and Festivals

Jains have many festivals, some of which they share with Hindus, but their festivals are often marked by abstinence from food rather than feasting. Jain monks, nuns, and devout lay people observe very severe food restrictions in their daily life; for example, they avoid all meat, fish, eggs, garlic, onions, root vegetables, berries, fruit with little seeds, and fermented food. They also exercise self-discipline through vows of silence, sitting in one place without moving, meditation, and other ascetic practices.

The major Jain festival is Paryusanan, an 8- or 10-day period in August–September during which all Jains are supposed to emulate this austere way of life as much as they can. Some totally fast for all eight days, drinking only boiled water; others do so only on the final day of the period. On the final day, they ask forgiveness of those they have offended.

During another fast celebrated twice a year, called Siddha Chakra, Jains drink only water and eat one boiled food each day. In April, Jains observe Akshyatriya, a day on which people offer sugarcane juice to those who have fasted throughout the year.

Jains celebrate the festival Diwali as the day on which their founder Mahavira attained nirvana. *Laddoos* and other sweets are distributed at temples. Mahavira Jayanti in late March commemorates his birthday. On this day, Jains visit sacred sites, visit their temple, and bathe a statue depicting Mahavira, which they carry in a procession around the neighborhood.

A unique Jain custom is the voluntary abstinence from all food and liquids as an honorable way to end one's life and cause the soul to leave one's body. This is done under the guidance of a priest.

Parsi Fasts and Festivals

Parsis are supposed to observe four days of abstinence each month when they do not eat meat, although fish and eggs are acceptable. Meat is also supposed to be avoided during the eleventh month of the Parsi year. Meat is not eaten for three days after the death of a loved one, when the fast is broken with *dhansakh*, a dish cooked with meat, several kinds of lentils, pumpkins, eggplants, cinnamon, cloves, garlic, chilies, and other spices.

Parsis celebrate six *ghambars*—seasonal festivals that last five days each and were originally associated with agricultural activities. After a religious ceremony, a community feast is held to which everyone, rich and poor, contributes. The meal is simple: spiced *dal* and rice with a salad, and perhaps meat cooked with potatoes.

A major event in the Parsi calendar is New Year, or Navroz, which is held at the time of the vernal equinox and observed by lavish feasting. Three sweet dishes are served on this and every other auspicious occasion: *ravo*, a semolina and cream pudding flavored with spices and rosewater; *sev*, fried vermicelli cooked in sugar syrup; and *meethu dhai*, or sweet yogurt. All may have originated in Iran, the Parsis' original home. After breakfast the family goes to the temple to give thanks. Lunch features a rice *pulao* with nuts and saffron, fish in a thick sweet and sour gravy, and spicy chicken curries, plain rice, and *moong dal*. There is a lot of visiting among friends and relatives and each visitor is offered a sweet and a glass of *falooda*—a sweet milky pudding flavored with rosewater and served with vermicelli noodles or ice cream.

Falooda (Sweet Milk Pudding)
- 2 tb cornstarch
- 1 quart whole milk
- 3/4 cup cream
- 1/2 cup condensed milk
- 1/2 cup blanched, peeled, sliced almonds
- 2 tb rosewater
- sugar to taste
- Vanilla ice cream (optional)

Cook the cornstarch in one cup of water until it is thick and translucent. Strain through a colander onto a bowl of ice and cold water to make small noodles. Set aside. Boil the whole milk and cool. Add the cream, condensed milk, almonds, rosewater, and sugar and chill. Mix well before serving, pour into tall glasses, and add a scoop of ice cream if desired.

Sikh Fasts and Festivals

Sikhs celebrate the major seasonal festivals of their native Punjab, including Sankranti, Baisakhi, Lohri, and Holi, and also hold their own festivals in honor of their Gurus, the spiritual leaders who developed the religion between the fifteenth and eighteenth century. Five holidays are especially important: the birthdays of Guru Nanak and Guru Gobind Singh, the creation of the Sikh community, and the martyrdoms of Guru Arjan and Teg Bahadur. On these days Sikhs go to their temple, called a *gurdhwara*, for singing, reading of the sacred book, prayer, worship, and the *langar*, vegetarian lunch in the community kitchen.

Sikhs do not hold services on any particular day of the week and most *gurdhwaras* are open every day for morning and evening services. Reading the scriptures is part of the service and while this is being done, a sweet pudding called *karhah prasad* is made from wheat flour, sugar, and *ghee*. It is later offered to visitors to the temple.

Christian Fasts and Festivals

India's Christians, who are concentrated in Goa, Kerala, and the Northeast, observe Easter, Christmas, and other Christian holidays with special observances and dishes. Christmas is an official holiday in India, and is celebrated by many non-Christians as well. Urban shopping centers are decorated with Christmas trees and Santa Clauses, and families and offices hold holiday parties.

For Goa's Roman Catholics, pork is a must for Christmas lunch, especially *sorpotel*, a hot and sour curry made from pork meat, liver, blood, and fat, flavored with vinegar and spices. A traditional Christmas cake is *bibinca*, composed of 16 layers of egg yolk, flour, and coconut-milk batter that is baked and then turned upside down. Other holiday delicacies are *dodols*, a soft jaggery fudge, and Western-style cakes called *bols* made from almond paste, semolina, sugar, eggs, and brandy. Goa is also home to a lively Carnival preceding Lent.

In Kerala many Catholics fast by avoiding meat and even eggs for 25 days before Christmas. After mass, the priest gives them a piece of cake and a glass of wine to break the fast. Syrian Christians eat an elaborate meal on Christmas day, featuring several meat dishes, including beef and chicken curries made with coconut milk, *appam* (a soft bread made of rice dough fermented with toddy), rice, steamed bananas, vegetables, and ending with rice pudding and English-style fruit cakes purchased from bakeries. Duck was the traditional centerpiece of a holiday meal in both Goa and Kerala. A similar meal is served at Easter. On the day before Good Friday, Syrian Christians observe an unusual custom. A special drink is prepared from coconut milk and jaggery, which the oldest male distributes with a piece of unfermented bread to his family members in what appears to be a replication of the Last Supper.

Muslim Fasts and Festivals

Ramadan or Ramzan, the ninth month in the Islamic lunar calendar, is a period of prayers and fasting. Fasting, one of the five pillars of Islam, commemorates the revelation of the Quran to the prophet Muhammad and is a way of physical and spiritual purification. The fast is very strictly observed: No food or water can be taken between dawn and dusk, although special dispensations are given for pregnant women, children, sick people, and those traveling.

Muslims begin the day with a pre-dawn meal of porridge, bread, or fruit. The fast is broken every day at sunset with a sip of water, dates, and perhaps a little fruit, a custom called *iftar*. People then enjoy sumptuous feasts with their friends and families, centered around meat dishes such as *biryanis*, *kormas*, and *halim*. The end of Ramadan, called *Eid-ul-Fitr*, is marked by the siting of the new moon and is celebrated with great fanfare. People put on new clothes, visit the mosque, and give food and alms to the poor. Special sweet dishes are prepared, such as *sewian*, a vermicelli pudding, and *sheer korma*, a sweet pudding made from vermicelli, milk, saffron, sugar, spices, and *ghee*.

Sewian

- 3/4 cup *ghee*
- 6 crushed green cardamoms
- 3 cloves
- 2 ounces fine vermicelli
- 1 quart milk
- 3/4 cup sugar

- 50 gm dried coconut
- 6 green cardamoms
- 10 drops *kewra* water (a fragrant distillate made from the leaves of a tree)

Break the vermicelli into small pieces and roast them in a heavy frying pan until they are pink. Heat the *ghee* in a frying pan and brown the whole cardamoms and cloves, then add the sugar and milk. When the milk reduces to half its volume, add the vermicelli and dried coconut. Cook until done. Sprinkle with *kewra* water and serve hot or cold.

The second major festival of Muslims is Eid-ul-Zuha or Bakrid, which commemorates Abraham's offering of his son to God, who at the last moment replaced him with a ram (an event also described in the Hebrew Scriptures). On this day Muslims are expected to sacrifice a ram or goat if they can afford it, and distribute one-third of the meat to friends, one-third to family, and one-third to the poor. Every meal includes meat dishes until the animal is eaten. Indian Muslims who belong to the Shia Muslim sect fast for one or more days during the month of Muharram, a period of mourning to commemorate the death of Husain, the grandson of the Prophet who was murdered by Muhammad's enemies. Mourners march in procession barefoot, beating their chests, crying out the name of Husain, and even whipping themselves.

Another holiday is Shabi-I-Barat, the night when God registers men's deeds and determines their fates. People distribute sweets in the name of their ancestors and offer flowers.

LIFE TRANSITION CEREMONIES

Marriages

Indians of all communities spend a great deal of time, energy, and wealth arranging and celebrating marriages for their children. No holds are barred in spending, and celebrations can go on for days. It is not unusual for wealthy and even middle-class people to invite thousands of guests, while the poor borrow money at exorbitant rates to see their daughters off in style. After the wedding, the bride traditionally goes to live with her husband's family.

A marriage is a union not only between the bride and groom, but between their two families. Fascinated by the spectacle, anthropologists have compared South Asian weddings to potlatches (a ceremonial feast of Native Americans living on the northwest coast of North America marked by the host's lavish distribution of gifts), tournaments of rank, and vehicles for social cohesion and competition.[5] There is a lot of jockeying over status between the bride's family and the groom's family, and the amount and quality of the food served at wedding meals becomes symbolic of prestige and respect. People freely discuss the meals they are served and compare them with those at other weddings they have attended.

Pre-wedding Rituals

In all religious and social communities, a series of events precedes the actual wedding. They may include paying respect to the spouse's ancestors, settlement of the terms of the marriage (including the dowry paid by the bride's family to the groom, even though dowries are illegal in India), the announcement of the engagement, the betrothal ceremony, and so on. Many of these occasions are associated with offering snacks and sweets or a full-fledged meal, sending food to the other family, and the exchange of auspicious foods such as sweets made with coconut and sesame seed. In South India, the conclusion of the marriage terms is marked by the exchange of *paan* among the family members negotiating the arrangements.

Fish, considered a symbol of good luck, happiness, and prosperity, play an important part in marriage rituals and festivities. In Tamil Nadu, nine sacred grains are planted in pots, where they sprout and then are fed to fish in a pond so that they may bless the couple. Wedding invitations are often decorated with a fish motif. In West Bengal and Bangladesh, relatives and friends of the bride visit the bridegroom's house, bringing gifts, among them a large carp decorated with flowers that is sometimes even made up with lipstick or a *bindi* (the red dot on a married woman's forehead) to resemble the bride. In Assam, the groom's side presents the fish to the bride's side. In Bengal and Assam it is also customary to distribute fish upon the birth of a son to bring good luck to the newborn.[6]

Muslims in India and Pakistan hold a ceremony one or two days before the marriage at which women decorate the bride's hand and feet with henna (a process called *mehndi*). A light meal is served, which may include a potato curry, kabobs, fish, chutneys, and lots of sweets, including *sharbat*, *laddoo*, and *burfee* (a hard, fudge-like sweet). The following day, the two parties meet and exchange gifts and another meal is served with at least two kinds of *biryani*, meat, fish, and many sweets. On the third day, the bride's family hosts a light meal, with the actual marriage taking place on the fourth day, followed by a large banquet normally hosted by the groom's family.

The Marriage Feast

The focal point of wedding ceremonies is not the religious ceremony but the banquet that follows or is simultaneous with the wedding. The banquet is paid for by the bride's family and prepared by professional caterers who bring their own equipment and ingredients. In a traditional wedding, the banquet is held in a large tent on the family's property or nearby. Guests sit in long rows on the floor, and the food is served on banana leaves placed in front of them. The consumption of *ghee*, poured on dishes by servers, is abundant, even wasteful. Teams of servers go up and down the rows carrying large pots from which they ladle food onto the leaves. Today tables and chairs have become more common, although banana leaves are still used as plates.

Eating from banana leaves poses many pitfalls, as described by an Indian-American writer:

Eating from banana leaves requires the expertise of a civil engineer. The leaf has no rim and therefore no catchment area for fluids such as rasam [a watery dal] or payasam [a thin rice and milk pudding], which therefore flow through the entire leaf and down the table unchecked. Adding to the challenge is the fact that waiters at weddings rush through the line, ladling and pouring hurriedly and insouciantly, without waiting to see if the eater is ready to receive it. . . . When you see waiters bringing out the rasam, you need to quickly build a circular dam with the rice to catch the rasam in the middle. Otherwise it will run in streams all over and out of the banana leaf. . . . The only way to eat payasam . . . is to quickly scoop it up with bare hands and slurp it down. . . . Your hand has to be trained to serve as spoon, fork, knife and scoop, all in one.[7]

If a guest wants another serving, it is considered rude to ask for it directly; rather, he points out that his or her neighbor would like more—whether he does or not. In Bengal, professional eaters were hired so that people would not feel embarrassed about how much they were eating. (In Kolkata, one eater had a nickname meaning "20 kilos"—allegedly, the amount he could eat at one sitting.) Today, it is become increasingly common for wealthy and even middle-class people to hold a reception in a club or a luxury hotel. The food may be served buffet style and in large cities might include a few Thai, Mexican, and Continental dishes as well as cocktails. Alcohol is not served at traditional Indian weddings. The standard drink is chilled buttermilk, perhaps flavored with coriander leaves and salt.

The order of dishes at traditional wedding feasts is fixed, starting with rice and ending with sweet dishes, and always featuring regional special-

People eating on banana leaves, Kolkata. Photo © TRIP/H. Rogers.

ties. Among Brahmins and orthodox Hindus, the wedding banquet is always vegetarian. A typical South Indian wedding meal consists of white
rice, bread, three or four *sambars*, one or two *rasams*, several vegetable
dishes, yogurt rice and other kinds of rice, and two or three sweets. In Maharashtra, it includes rice, *puris*, vegetables in coconut gravy and without
gravy, yellow *dal*, mango chutney, a cucumber and peanut salad and several desserts, such as *basundi, jalebi*, and *shrikand*.

In West Bengal, a Hindu wedding banquet includes fried vegetables,
white rice, one or two *dals*, perhaps a *pulao*, two or three fish dishes, meat
in a liquid gravy served with *lucchis*, chutney, and at least two sweet
dishes, such as sweet yogurt, *rasagoola* (milk balls in a sugar syrup), and
perhaps a *sandesh* or other dry sweet.

A Muslim wedding banquet is a lavish affair featuring as many meat
dishes as the bride's family can afford. Traditionally, it includes at least
one *biryani*, a *korma*, mixed vegetable *navrattan*, *shami* kabob, fish curry or
fried fish (among Bengali Muslims), yogurt and cucumber salad, bread,
and many desserts, including rice pudding *(kheer)* in clay pots, *gulab jama*,
ras malai, wedding cakes, and tea.

Birth and Pregnancy

Generally, a pregnant woman is treated with great care and attention in India. In ayurveda and folk beliefs, pregnancy is considered a "hot" condition. As a result, the pregnant woman is not allowed to eat "hot" foods, such as animal products, spices, eggs, mangoes, papayas, bananas, and sesame seeds, since it is believed they cause abortion. Cold foods such as milk products are considered desirable to ensure strength and a successful delivery. A Hindu woman is fed special foods at certain times of her pregnancy. For example, in parts of North India, her parents send her dried dates, pieces of coconut, and wheat bread and *laddoos* fried in *ghee* in the fifth month, while in Andhra Pradesh, she is fed spicy and sour dishes to tempt her to eat.[8]

A woman usually goes to her parents' house to have the baby. For five days after the birth of a child, the mother is given a semi-liquid diet, including semolina cooked in milk, light chicken broth, and fruit. On the sixth day, she is fed a large meal consisting of a great variety of rich foods, traditionally served in groups of six. The purpose is to give the nursing child strength and also to indirectly expose it to a variety of foods. When a child is six months old, a ceremony called *annaprasana* takes place, in which it is fed solid food for the first time in the form of a sweet rice pudding.

Death Rites

Even the most secular Hindu follows traditional funeral rites when a parent or close relative dies. All eating and cooking activities in a household stop until the body is cremated, which is done as soon as possible. The eldest son of the deceased, the chief mourner, symbolically lights the crematory fire. A household's normal food patterns are suspended for ten to thirteen days, depending on a community's customs. There are wide variations about what is eaten and prepared during this period. In an orthodox Hindu family, only one meal a day may be eaten, frying is prohibited, and spices are eliminated, especially turmeric (a symbol of auspicious events). The chief mourner may have to cook his own food, which might be only boiled white rice, *dal*, and bread. Westernized, meat-eating families may eat only vegetarian dishes during this period. According to an ancient custom, on the thirteenth day after a death, family members feed rice balls to cows and then to crows, who, it is believed, will carry the soul of the deceased to heaven.

The fast ends on the thirteenth day, when a lavish feast is held for family and friends. Every year on the date of the death, a ceremony is held and special vegetarian dishes may be eaten. Hindu widows traditionally become vegetarian and in the old days were expected to lead very austere lives.

NOTES

1. K. M. Sen, *Hinduism* (Baltimore: Penguin Books, 1967), p. 34.

2. The subcontinent has several traditional calendars that are based on different systems of astronomy. Most are lunar; that is, they are determined by the phases of the moon rather than the cycles of the sun. In 1957 in an attempt at standardization, the Indian government adopted the Indian National Calendar based on both lunar and solar years. The start of the year is March 22, except in a leap year, and the start of the entire system is A.D. 78, the first year of the Saka dynasty, when this calendar was invented. The year is divided into six seasons with two months each: spring, summer, rainy season, autumn, winter, and cool. Government documents use both the Western and Saka date, but for business purposes, the standard Western calendar is used.

For religious purposes and determining the date of festivals, the Hindu year is divided into 12 months, consisting of 7 months of 30 days each and 5 months (6 in a leap year) with 31 days. Each month is divided into 2 periods. The first period, called the bright fortnight, begins with the new moon; the second period, the dark fortnight, ends with the full moon. Each position of the moon (called *tithi*) has a special significance for devout Hindus. The eleventh day of each cycle, called *ekadashi*, is considered particularly significant and a day for fasting as a means of mental and spiritual cleansing.

The Islamic calendar is also based on lunar cycles and is 354 days long. However, unlike the Hindu lunar calendar it does not have any leap days or months, so holidays are movable and not consistent with the seasons. The starting point is the migration of the prophet Muhammad to Medina, called the *hijra*, in A.D. 622. Thus, the year 2003 is 1381.

3. Quoted in R. S. Khare, "Food with Saints," in *The Eternal Food*, ed. R. S. Khare (Albany: State University of New York Press, 1992), p. 32.

4. R. S. Khare, *The Hindu Hearth and Home* (New Delhi: Vikas Publishing House, 1976), p. 151.

5. Arjun Appadurai, "Gastro-Politics in Hindu South Asia," *American Ethnologist* 8 (1981): 494–511.

6. Joe Roberts and Colleen Taylor Sen, "A Carp Wearing Lipstick: The Role of Fish in Bengali Cuisine and Culture," in *Fish from the Waters: Proceedings of the Oxford Symposium on Food and Cookery 1997* (Blackawton, UK: Prospect Books, 1998), pp. 252–258.

7. Shoba Narayan, *Monsoon Diary* (New York: Villard, 2003), pp. 188–189.

8. See Moni Nag, "Beliefs and Practices about Food During Pregnancy," *Economic and Political Weekly*, 10 September 1994, 2427–2438; and Chtralekha Singh and Prem Nath, *Hindu Manners, Customs, and Ceremonies* (New Delhi: Crest Publishing House, 2000), pp. 123–136.

7

Diet and Health

In India, as in China, ancient Greece, medieval Europe, and other civilizations, food is inextricably linked to spiritual and physical health. "You are what you eat" is the dominant theme of Indian medical and philosophical systems. Unlike modern Western systems, which take a mechanical approach to treating disease and diet, Indian systems are holistic; that is, they treat the entire individual, including her specific mental, emotional, and physical makeup, rather than her symptoms alone. A person's mental and emotional state is believed to determine his physical health, and these conditions, in turn, are affected by diet. Today alternative systems of medicines, especially ayurveda, are gaining adherents in Western countries and are being studied by the U.S. National Institutes of Health and other organizations.

The Indian government officially recognizes seven systems of medicine and supports colleges, research institutes, and clinics in these disciplines. They are

- Allopathy, or Western medicine
- Homeopathy, a system developed in Germany in the early nineteenth century that uses very small doses of a substance to cure diseases
- Naturopathy, a German system based on the premise that the basic cause of disease is the accumulation of morbid matter and that nature is the greatest healer
- Unani, the Islamic school of medicine with close ties to ancient Greek medicine

- Ayurveda, the ancient indigenous Indian system of medicine
- Siddha, a variety of ayurveda practiced in South India
- Yoga therapy

Many Indians are eclectic in their approach to medicine and health. Patients may seek treatment from physicians belonging to different schools—an estimated 10 percent of Indians use homeopathic medicines—while Western-trained doctors incorporate ayurvedic or yogic medicines and dietary advice into their practices. The official systems of medicine are supplemented and paralleled by homegrown ideas about food and nutrition based on local, family, or even individual beliefs. As an American ayurvedic practitioner puts it:

India's people daily talk, knowingly or not, in the ayurvedic idiom. Even the most illiterate resident of the most remote village knows that yogurt causes phlegm to accumulate in the chest, and everyone makes use of simple herbs like vetiver which removes heat from the body and makes life during the hot season a little more bearable…Ayurvedic thought is part of the conceptual universe of every Indian who thinks like an Indian, and has been part of India's collective consciousness since, probably, prehistoric times…. Medicine in India is not now and never has been the exclusive province of physicians.[1]

AYURVEDA

Ayurveda, Sanskrit for "science of life," has its roots in the *Ajur-veda* ("Science of Longevity"), an appendage to the *Atharva-veda* that was compiled by Aryan priests around 5000 B.C. and written down thousands of years later. Some historians believe it incorporates medicinal ideas from the Indus Valley. It describes such conditions as fever, leprosy, consumption, heart disease, headache, parasites, rheumatism, and epilepsy and their treatments, which include charms and incantations, natural forces like sun and water, and herbs.

The important names in Hindu medicine are Dhanwantari, a deity who is said to have revealed the wisdom of life to a group of sages but was probably a practicing physician; Susruta, a legendary teacher who is believed to have lived in the fifth century B.C. and is considered the father of plastic surgery; and Charaka, who was either a physician who practiced in the second century A.D. or a composite of several physicians who adopted that name. Their writings were reconstructed, expanded, and revised by later physicians.

The primary ayurvedic text is *Charaka Samhita* ("Charaka's Encyclopedia"), a monumental work that is three times as large as extant texts from

Greek medicine. It contains sections on general principles and theories, diagnosis, anatomy, ethics, prognosis, therapeutics, pharmacology, and purification therapy. Another work, *Susruta Samhita*, describes sophisticated surgical procedures, including cesarean section, amputations, the removal of cataracts and bladder stones, the repair of damaged noses and ears, and skin grafting—virtually every major operation performed in modern medicine except ligation of the arteries. The texts emphasize the importance of logic and empirical observation in treating patients and the idea that tradition should be used as a springboard for new research, not a fixed repository of knowledge.

When Alexander the Great invaded India in 326 B.C. he was so impressed by ayurvedic practitioners (called *vaidyas*) that he sent some to Greece, where they may have influenced the development of Greek medicine. During India's golden age from the fifth to the seventh century A.D., medicine and health care flourished. The Gupta kings built hospitals for humans and animals, planted medicinal herb gardens, and regulated the practice of medicine. Research and teaching continued at the great universities, and new diseases and treatments were added to the corpus of knowledge. Hindu works were translated into Arabic and Persian, and Hindu physicians settled throughout the Middle East, where they set up practices and organized hospitals and schools.

In the twelfth and thirteenth centuries, the Islamic invaders brought their own system of medicine to India, called Unani. Both ayurveda and Unani flourished side by side until the arrival of the British, who denigrated traditional wisdom in all areas. Only Western medicine was recognized as legitimate and taught in colleges; Indian medicine was actively discouraged.

The rise of Indian nationalism at the turn of the twentieth century saw a revival of interest in Indian science and medicine, and ayurveda underwent a renaissance that continues today (although Western medicine still receives the bulk of government support). Ayurveda is particularly well developed in the state of Kerala, where ayurvedic hospitals, pharmacies, and health spas flourish. Ayurveda is now being popularized in the West by the writings of Deepak Chopra and others.[2]

Basic Principles of Ayurveda

The basic principle of Vedic thought, of which ayurveda is part, is that the entire cosmos is part of one absolute reality. Everything that exists in the vast external universe, the macrocosm, also appears in the internal cosmos of the human body, the microcosm, which consists of both the relatively unconscious body and the conscious mind and spirit that dwell within it.

All matter is made up of five elements or states of matter: earth, water, fire, air, and ether (the field from which matter is created.) We experience these elements in terms of different qualities, which are classified into 10 pairs of dualities, denoting a continuum: heavy and light, cold and hot, oily/moist and dry, slow and intense, stable and mobile, soft and hard, clear and sticky, smooth and rough, subtle and gross, and solid and liquid. A substance that is heavy, rough, hard, slow, stable, clear, subtle, and gross is made up mainly of the earth element; one that is liquid, oily, cold, slow, soft, and smooth consists mainly of water, and so on.

All body parts, such as bone and cartilage, are mainly earthy in nature. Fat and vital bodily fluids, such as lymph, blood, semen, and mucus, are predominantly watery. Digestive fluids, endocrine secretions, body heat, and substances that produce mental awareness are fiery substances. Everything mobile, including the nervous systems, is air in nature. All channels though which things pass—blood and lymph vessels, pores, the nerves—are ethereal.

In the human body, the elements manifest themselves in three *doshas* (a Sanskrit word meaning "fault" that is sometimes translated as "humors"). They govern all the biological, psychological, and physiological functions of the body, mind, and consciousness. The *doshas* are *vata*, a product of air and ether; *pitta*, which arises from fire and water; and *kapha*, made from water and earth. These *doshas* are invisible, nonphysical forces that can only be detected indirectly in their effects. *Vata* regulates all physical and mental motion; *pitta* is in charge of all transformations, such as digestion and the processing of sensory data; *kapha* stabilizes the living being. Their attributes can be summed up as movement, metabolism, and stability, respectively.

The *doshas* determine not only our basic constitution but our mental makeup, personality, and disposition. People can be defined as *pitta*, *kapha*, or *vata* types, or a combination of two or even all three types. According to standard wisdom, *vata* people tend to be thin, perform actions quickly, and are enthusiastic and imaginative. Mental and physical energy come in bursts, but they have little willpower or confidence and are prone to anxiety. They prefer sweet, sour, and salty tastes and have a variable appetite. Their basic theme is "changeable." *Pitta* types are of medium build and strength, and have an aversion to the sun and heat. They are enterprising and intelligent, but have a tendency toward anger under stress;

their main theme is "intense." Their natural craving is for sweet, bitter, and astringent tastes. Those with a *kapha* constitution have well-developed bodies with a tendency to be overweight. They are tranquil, relaxed, and tolerant but also show traits of greed, attachment, and envy. Their digestion is slow, and they like pungent, bitter, and astringent foods. Their theme is "relaxed."

The basic constitution of an individual remains unaltered during her lifetime, but the combination of elements alters in response to changes in the environment. The three *doshas* keep the body healthy only as long as they continuously flow through and out of it and remain in balance. When the *doshas* are underproduced or overproduced, the body loses vitality and immunity, and disease can result.

For example, if there is excess *kapha*, mucus and other lubricants are overproduced, accumulate, and cause obstructive conditions such as indigestion, lethargy, and cough. Insufficient *kapha* leads to weakness, dryness, body aches, and insomnia. Overproduction and obstruction of *pitta* causes acidity, anger, and excessive hunger and thirst, while insufficient *pitta* can lead to coldness, lack of joy, and stiffness. Excess *vata* promotes weakness, dryness, constipation, and tremors; decreased *vata* reduces all body activities, disturbs the digestion, and encourages nausea and depression.

Many things can affect the balance of the *doshas*: the time of day or season of the year, a person's age and physical activity level, stress, heat and cold, and diet. *Kapha* accumulates in winter and becomes aggravated in spring, whereas *pitta* accumulates in spring and becomes aggravated in summer, a time at which when *kapha* is calmed. People become especially prone to diseases at the junctions of the seasons, and regular purifications and fasts help protect against this. Some of these practices have been institutionalized into the holiday rituals and festivals described in chapter 6.

There are many ways of controlling and adjusting the *doshas*, including massage, exercise, proper sleeping habits, herbal medicines, and diet. Their goal is to increase desirable qualities, reduce negative qualities, and introduce previously absent qualities. The most important way of doing this is by proper eating. As the legendary physician Charaka wrote: "Without proper diet, medicines are of no use; with a proper diet, medicines are unnecessary."[3]

Foods are characterized by their taste—sweet, salty, sour, astringent, bitter, and pungent—and the 10 properties listed earlier. The two categories are related in complex ways. Generally sour, salty, and pungent substances are hot, while sweet, bitter, and astringent substances are cold. A person's choice of food is determined mainly by its taste: Everyone craves the taste they are missing. But you should not follow your predilections blindly; rather, under the guidance of an ayurvedic practitioner, you have to consciously select those tastes and other qualities to help balance your *doshas*.

The proper diet depends on a number of factors, including how you eat, the climate and season, the natural quality of the food, its preparation, the combination of foods you consume, and the amount. Charaka laid down rules for eating that are just as applicable today as they were thousands of years ago.

- Eat properly combined food after digestion of the previous meal to allow a free passage for all substances.
- Eat in a congenial, quiet place—either alone or with affectionate people—so that the mind is not depressed.
- Eat neither hurriedly nor leisurely to appreciate the qualities of the food you are eating.
- Eat without laughing or talking, with concentration, considering your constitution and what is good and not good for you as you eat.
- Do not eat when you are not hungry and do not fail to eat when you are hungry.
- Do not eat when you are angry, depressed, or emotionally distraught or immediately after exercise.
- Keep as large a gap as possible between meals.
- Sit to eat whenever possible facing east.
- Pray, thanking the Creator for the food you are offering your digestive fire.[4]
- Never cook for yourself alone; the gift of food is the best gift at all.
- Feed all five senses: Look at the food and savor its appearance and aroma; listen to the sounds it makes, especially when cooking; eat with your hands to enjoy its texture; chew each morsel many times to extract its flavor.
- Stroll about a hundred steps after a meal to assist the digestive process.
- Do not eat heavy or *kapha*-producing food like yogurt and sesame seeds after sunset and eat nothing within two hours of going to bed.
- Never waste food.[5]

Food should be "alive" in order to give life to the eater. Raw food is more alive than cooked food. Overcooked, undercooked, burned, bad tasting, unripe or overripe, putrified, or stale food should never be eaten. Leftovers should be heated up as soon as possible or, ideally, avoided altogether. Spices should be ground fresh for each use. Cold food and ice water are not considered healthy.

The 10 qualities are innate in all foods. Their presence or absence determines the effect a particular food has on the *doshas*.[6] For example, dry fruits, apples, melons, potatoes, tomatoes, eggplant, ice cream, beef, peas, and green salad have qualities that tend to aggravate *vata*, and thus should not be taken in excess by a person with a *vata* constitution. However, sweet fruits, coconut, brown rice, red cabbage, bananas, grapes, cherries, and oranges are beneficial for *vata* types. *Pitta* is increased by spicy foods, peanut butter, sour fruits, bananas, papayas, tomatoes, and garlic and is inhibited by mangoes, oranges, pears, plums, sprouts, sunflower seeds, asparagus, and mushrooms. Bananas, melons, coconut, dates, papayas, pineapples, and dairy products increase *kapha*; dry fruits, pomegranates, cranberries, basmati rice, sprouts, and chicken inhibit it.

Food combinations are very important. When two or more foods having different taste and attributes are combined, the digestive fire can become overloaded, resulting in incomplete digestion. Generally, a person should avoid eating fruits (especially melons) with any other food or even different fruits at the same time; lots of raw and cooked foods together; fresh foods with leftovers; or milk with bananas, sour fruits, fish, meat, and yogurt. The addition of spices and herbs can help to make foods compatible.

Ayurveda is not vegetarian; in fact, meat is recommended for certain ailments. Charaka calls meat juice "nectar itself" for people who are wasted, emaciated, convalescing, and desirous of increased strength. Even beef has its place as a means of calming an unusually intense digestive fire and for treating diseases caused by *vata* alone. Meat in general is heavy, but meats from animals that live in arid areas are relatively lighter. The meat of very fat, very old, or very young animals should be avoided, as should meat from an animal that was not killed while roaming freely in its natural habitat. Fatty meats are supposed to be eaten in winter and game birds in summer. Venison enjoys a special place in ayurvedic medicine, since it is considered particularly nourishing and beneficial, and can be eaten all year. Still, meat is basically regarded a condiment, better consumed as a broth or soup rather than as a steak or chop.

Fish is generally considered hot (because it lives in cold water) and sweet, so it can strengthen the body without aggravating *kapha*, as most sweet foods do. Fish from a pond are considered preferable to river or sea fish, because they control *pitta*. The opposition to alcohol found in many Hindu texts is absent from ayurveda. Charaka lists 7 sources of wine and 84 liquors, and advocated moderate drinking for its digestive, nourishing, and stimulating effects and as a source of pleasure. Susruta believed that alcohol induced *pitta* but nonetheless listed 30 types of wine that were acceptable to drink.

Garlic and onions, avoided by some Hindus, are remedies in ayurvedic medicine. Garlic, an ingredient in many pills, relieves *vata* and *kapha* and increases *pitta*, and is prescribed for certain ailments, including worms, cough, and asthma. Onion is an astringent and a diuretic.

How can these recommendations be reconciled with Hindu and yogic proscriptions? An ayurvedic practitioner explains it in the following way:

All substances are available to Ayurvedic practitioners as medicine. While the tradition advocates self-realization, one still needs to use whatever is available or necessary to restore balance. The protracted use of otherwise proscribed substances is not implied. Hence garlic may help restore health and thence be unnecessary as a dietary item. The same is true of meat.[7]

Food and Disease

According to the ancient ayurvedic physicians, diseases fall into seven categories: genetic, congenital, metabolic, traumatic (physical or mental), temporal, divine, and natural (hunger, thirst, fatigue, old age). The mind and emotions play a very important role in causing disease, as do dietary imbalances.

Whether or not a disease manifests itself depends on the strength or weakness of the digestive fire, which, in turn, can be affected by many factors: overeating or undereating, overconsumption of heavy food, especially meat; overuse of cold and liquid substances; consumption of food inappropriate for the time of year; the climate; a person's age; and mental causes, especially fear, anger, greed, misery, and sorrow. Poor digestion leads to the production of *ama*, a Sanskrit word that means food that is absorbed into the system without being properly digested.

The ancient physicians were aware of the existence of microorganisms and parasites but believed that exposure would lead to disease only in people whose conditions are ripe for it because of *ama*. The obstructions it causes prevent the *doshas* from flowing freely through the system, so that they accumulate in the body and initially cause lethargy, indigestion, heaviness, and other symptoms. They are easiest to remove at this stage by purification and diet. If they are not removed, they begin to wander around the body, "wreaking havoc in the system wherever they roam." Once they escape their reservoirs, they must be removed or neutralized with medicine and purification techniques, such as enemas, laxatives, and fasting.

It's important to eat the right foods to prevent imbalance and disease, but once a disease has been contracted, food is one of the methods prescribed to cure it. Treatment begins with fasting, "the first and most important of all medicines," in order to unclog the *ama* and restore the appetite. Fasting can mean many things: going without food or water; living on water, liquids, or a single food, such as *khichri*; or eating a number of different foods specific to a particular condition. Vegetables are sometimes avoided during therapy, since they are considered astringent and will cause the channels to close up. The consumption and external application of oil, fat, bone marrow, and *ghee* are considered beneficial for some conditions and people, especially for those who are deprived of love. (The Sanskrit word for fat, *sneha*, also means love.)

Once the acute stage of the disease has passed, the patient is given a pacifying diet accompanied by appropriate medicines. Medicines are always given in a vehicle, such as honey, medicinal wine, fruit juices, jams, butter, *ghee*, or meat soup. They are mainly derived from plants; every plant in the world is said to have an ayurvedic use. Some of these ancient herbal remedies were adapted by Greek and Western medicine; for example, reserpine, extracted from *Wauwolfia serpentina*, is effective for reducing blood pressure while psyllium seed is a popular remedy for bowel problems. The three most important medicinal plants are the fruits called *amalaki*, *haritaki* (myrobalan), and *bibhitaki*. They are combined to make the most popular ayurvedic medicine, *triphala* (Sanskrit for "three fruits").

OTHER HINDU SCHOOLS OF MEDICINE

Yoga therapy and Siddha are closely related to ayurveda. Yoga is more than a series of physical postures; it is a profound philosophy of life that strives to develop a balance between the body and the mind in order to reunite the individual self with the Absolute, or pure consciousness. (*Yoga* means "joining" or "uniting" in Sanskrit.) Paths that lead the yogi (practitioner of yoga) to enlightenment include moral restraints and observances; study of the sacred texts; hatha yoga, which means control of the body through postures; and *pranayama*, correct breathing. The last two methods are means to the end of meditation, the goal of which is to become aware of the unity of the self with the Absolute.

Yoga does not deal with the physical body, but rather with certain invisible sheaths (*kosas*) that parallel the physical organs. Yoga deals with people not on the physical but the mental and astral plane, where three *gunas* (attributes or virtues) determine our fundamental being. The five elements of the universe (earth, water, fire, air, and ether) combine in various ways to create these *gunas*. The first is *sattva*, often translated as lucidity, purity, or dispassion; it is the source of knowledge and enlightenment, and leads to joy and good health. *Rajas*, translated as passion, distraction, or restlessness, leads to action but also to sensuality and suffering if we do not harness and direct its energy. The third element, *tamas*, translated as dark inertia or dullness, is manifested in sloth, lethargy, anger, and ignorance.

All life evolves from the interplay among these forces, and all three are needed for life to continue. *Tamas* gives us the desire to rest and stop our activities. Without it there would be no consistency or solidity in our lives; however, with too much *tamas* we will never do anything. *Rajas* gives us the urge to organize, to work, and to push forward with our projects, but if we have no direction or goal, *rajas* will take us anywhere our uncontrolled senses pull us. *Sattva* enables us to experience our true nature. It also gives us curiosity, the ability to think and reason, and to set higher goals.

Diet is believed to have an intimate connection with the mind, which is formed out of the subtlest portion of the food. Yogis and those aspiring to spiritual advancement should eat *sattvic* foods that render the mind pure and calm, and are conducive to enlightenment and serenity. *Sattvic* foods include fresh fruits and vegetables, wheat, rice, cow's milk, dry ginger, cucumber, green vegetables, honey, kidney beans, nuts, and seeds. *Ghee*, or clarified butter, is considered particularly *sattvic*, since it helps to stimulate the healthy flow of fluids throughout the body.

Rajasic foods stimulate our energy and creativity as well as our passion and aggressiveness. They include items that are sharp, sour, pungent, and hot, such as sesame and mustard oil, fish, yogurt, goat meat, chilies, venison and wild game, fish, eggs, coffee and tea, white sugar, and spices. Some people class garlic as *rajasic*, others as *tamasic*. People trying to lead a spiritual and ascetic life are advised to avoid garlic, which is believed to interfere with meditation and arouse the passions. A vegetarian diet with moderate intake of food is the ideal.

Tamasic foods fill our minds with anger, darkness, confusion, and inertia. These are foods that are rotten, stale, overcooked, and decaying, including red meat, leftovers, fast foods, fried foods, processed foods, plus tobacco, alcohol, and drugs. Practitioners of yoga shun them.

Some writers have tried to equate the three *gunas* with the three *doshas* of ayurveda: *kapha* with *tamas*, *pittha* with *sattva*, and *vata* with *rajas*. However, they cannot be specifically correlated, and probably come from entirely different traditions. Whatever their relationship, an ayurvedic physician is supposed to be familiar with the presence and functioning of the *gunas* and to be able to determine which predominates when he treats a patient.

Siddha (Sanskrit for "pure") medicine may have originated among the ancient Dravidian inhabitants of the subcontinent and developed in South India in the seventh or eighth century. Today it is practiced in Tamil-speaking regions of the South. The principles and doctrines are very similar to those of ayurveda: the human body is considered a replica of the universe, as are food and drugs. The main difference is the extensive use of metals and minerals in treatment, especially sulfur and mercury.

POPULAR FOOD BELIEFS

The most widespread concept is the hot/cold dichotomy, which is strongly entrenched even among people who do not follow ayurvedic practices, especially in North India. This medical theory probably traveled from India to Arabia and the Middle East in the sixth century B.C. and later to Greece and Europe. Today most Indians can tell you whether a food is hot or cold, although the classification varies in different parts of the country. For example, wheat is considered a very hot food in South India (where historically it was not grown), but only moderately hot in the North, where it is a staple. Most varieties of lentils are considered cold in western India and hot in the North. Papayas are regarded as extremely heating in South India but not in the North. Most spices are considered hot everywhere, although a few, such as cumin and fennel seeds, are said to be cold. Jaggery is hot, but sugarcane juice is cold. Because alcohol, yogurt, and honey are all heating, other hot food should not be taken with them lest the *doshas* be thrown out of balance.

Is there some basis to the hot-cold theory? In an experiment in South India, scientists fed one group of volunteers a diet of only cold food and another group only hot food over a period of 10 days. The diets were identical in terms of nutrients. Those who ate the hot foods had highly acidic urine, indicating that the acid-base balance of the body was altered. Those who ate cold foods showed much lower excretion of sulfur and a lower retention of nitrogen.[8]

UNANI MEDICINE

The Unani system of medicine (*Unani tibbia*) was introduced into India by the Muslim conquerors in the fourteenth century. The theoretical framework is derived from the writings of the Greek physicians Hippocrates (460–377 B.C.), who is considered the father of both allopathic and Unani medicine, and Galen (died c. A.D. 200). The Arabic word *Unan* means Greece.[9] Unani practitioners are called *Hakims*.

Over the centuries, the corpus of Greek medicine was enriched and developed by physicians in Egypt, Persia, Iraq, and other Middle Eastern countries, and in China and India. During the golden period of Arab civilization (A.D. 749 to 1258), Greek and Sanskrit texts were translated into Arabic, renowned ayurvedic physicians were invited to Baghdad and other cities to teach and practice, and learned physicians wrote treatises on medicine. When the Mongols invaded Persia and Central Asia in the fourteenth century A.D., many physicians and scholars fled to India. The Delhi Sultans and later the Mughal emperors provided state patronage to physicians and scholars from all over the world and hired them as court physicians. Delhi became a center of Unani medicine, which reached its peak between the thirteenth and seventeenth centuries. During the British rule, Unani medicine suffered because of withdrawal of government support, but official interest returned after Indian independence in 1947 and today India is the world leader in Unani medicine, which has its own licensed physicians, hospitals, and educational and research institutes.

Unani Theory

Unani medicine is based on the humoral theory of Greek medicine, which assumes the presence of four humors in the body: blood, phlegm, yellow bile, and black bile. Humors are applicable to any fluids found in the body, including cellular, tissue, and vascular fluids. These humors are composed of the four basic elements—earth, water, air, and fire—each of which has two qualities: warm and dry for fire, warm and moist for air, cold and moist for water, and cold and dry for earth. The seasons also have qualities, as do an individual's temperament, which can be of four kinds: sanguine, choleric, cold or phlegmatic, and melancholic.

Every person is born with a unique humoral constitution, which represents his healthy state and determines his personality. When the amounts of the humors are changed and thrown out of balance with each other, it leads to disease. Restoring the quality and balance of humors is the goal of treatment, using the body's natural power of self-preservation and adjustment.

The causes of the imbalance can be either external (e.g., excessive heat or cold, a polluted atmosphere, or injuries) or internal. *Hakims* use four kinds of therapies: regimental (exercise, massage, steambaths, emetics, bleeding, and purging; surgery; medicines, based on herbal, animal, and mineral drugs; and diet. Many of the drugs are based on herbs and plants that are cultivated in special gardens.

Digestion plays a central role in the Unani system. Minor and even some major ailments can be prevented by regular, normal digestion; conversely, poor digestion can cause disease. Digestion can be damaged by overeating, eating meals too closely together, eating rapidly, consuming too much water, or insomnia. Certain foods can cause indigestion: those that putrefy quickly (milk and fresh fish), those that take time to digest (such as beef), stale foods, spices and chilies, alcohol, strong tea, coffee, and oily food. However, any food is acceptable in moderation. Aids to digestion include decoctions and teas made from *ajwain* seeds, mint, fennel, and coriander seeds; pomegranate juice; and other herbs and spices.

Diet therapy treats ailments by regulating the quality and quantity of a patient's food. When a disease is advanced, treatment often begins with a total fast, which gives the patient's system a chance to rest, or the restriction of food when the patient needs to regain strength through certain nutrients. A liquid diet, consisting of fruit juices or soups made from meat or vegetables, is prescribed for digestive failure. A semi-solid diet comprising yogurt or *khichri* is recommended in the case of poor or incomplete digestion.

People are also advised to eat foods that have the opposite quality to their temperament. A person who has too much of the sanguine humor, which leads to increased heat, should eat cold food such as barley water or fish and take cooling herbs; if there is a thinning of the sanguine humor, warm and dry foods are prescribed. What is cold and hot is to some extent determined by local and regional beliefs and customs. Some of the cures no doubt reflect folk remedies: for example, a recommended treatment for influenza includes long pepper powder mixed with honey and ginger juice in the early stage and milk and turmeric powder to mitigate the aftereffects. For diabetes, bitter and astringent foods are prescribed, such as bitter gourd juice. Weaknesses of specific organs are corrected by eating the same organ of an animal.

NOTES

1. Robert E. Svoboda, *Ayurveda: Life, Health and Longevity* (New Delhi: Penguin Books, 1993), p. 31. Much of this chapter's discussion of ayurveda summarizes this excellent work.

2. See, for example, Deepak Chopra, *Perfect Health: The Complete Mind/Body Guide* (New York: Harmony Books, 1991).

3. Quoted in K. T. Achaya, *Indian Food: A Historical Companion* (New Delhi: Oxford University Press, 1994), p. 87.

4. In Ayurveda, both the cooking and digestion of food are considered equivalent to offering a substance to the sacrificial fire; the digestive principle is even referred to as fire (*agni*).

5. Svoboda, *Ayurveda*, pp. 118–120.

6. For a comprehensive list of food classifications, see Usha Lad and Dr. Vasant Lad, *Ayurvedic Cooking for Self Healing*, 2nd ed. (Albuquerque: The Ayurvedic Press, 2002), pp. 90–99B; Svoboda, *Ayurveda*, pp. 123–146; and "Food Guidelines for Basic Constitutional Types," on the Ayurvedic Institute Web site www.Ayurveda.com.

7. Mike Dick, Ayurvedic physician, private communication, 2 May 2003.

8. P.S.V. Ramanamurthy, "Physiological Effects of 'Hot' and 'Cold' Foods in Human Subjects," *Indian Journal of Nutrition and Dietetics* 6 (1969): 187. Cited in Achaya, *Indian Food*, p. 81.

9. A proposed alternative derivation is that Unani comes from China's Yunnan province, perhaps because there are many similarities between Chinese and Indian medicine, including the hot-cold classification.

Glossary

Ahimsa   Doctrine of nonviolence.

Ajowain   A slightly bitter seed used in Gujarati cuisine.

Appams   A spongy bread made from rice flour, slightly fermented with *toddy* and steamed. It is especially popular in Kerala, where it is eaten with meat or vegetable curries.

Asafetida (hing)   The resin of a tree, usually in powder form, that adds a truffle-like flavor to *dals* and vegetable dishes; a substitute for garlic for orthodox Hindus.

Atta   Whole wheat flour.

Avial   Vegetables cooked in coconut milk in South India.

Ayurveda   An ancient indigenous system of Indian medicine that is holistic and stresses the connection between body, mind, temperament, and food.

Basmati rice   An aromatic, long-grain rice, grown in the foothills of the Himalayas.

Betel   Hard, brown, dried nuts that area an ingredient in *supari* and *paan*.

Biryani   Rice layered with nuts, meat, and spices; a classic dish of Mughal haute cuisine.

Brahmins   People of a high caste.

Chai   A hot drink made by boiling tea leaves, spices, and milk; popular in North India.

Chapati   Thin, round bread made of wheat flour; a staple in North India.

Chhana   Curds made by bringing milk to a boil and separating it with a souring agent; the basis of most Bengali sweets.

Chickpea flour (besan or gram flour)   A flour made out of ground chickpeas that is used to make snacks and some breads.

Chutney   Originally a freshly ground relish of coconuts, peanuts, *dals*, mangoes, tomatoes, mint leaves, and other ingredients. Under the British, chutney came to denote a preserve, especially of mangoes, in a sugar syrup.

Curry   A generic term for a dish containing meat, fish, and vegetables in a spicy gravy.

Curry leaf   An aromatic leaf that is a common ingredient in South Indian vegetable and lentil dishes.

Dal   A word used loosely for all pulses (legumes), including dried beans and split peas. The word is also used for the boiled, soup-like dish made from them that is an accompaniment of many Indian meals. Some kinds of *dal* are

Channa dal, a small, rather sweetish lentil widely eaten in South India.

Masoor dal, a hulled, salmon-colored, disk-shaped lentil, popular in Bengal.

Moong dal, a small, flat, yellow-colored lentil.

Toor dal, also called toovar dal and arhar dal, an ocher-colored split pea with an earthy flavor.

Urad dal, a lentil sold with a black skin and without the skin; the second is used for breads in South India.

Dhaba   A truck stop, especially in North India.

Diwali   Indian Festival of Lights, celebrated in December with special lights and the exchange of sweets.

Dosa   A crepe-like bread made of fermented rice and lentil flour served for breakfast in South India with sambar and coconut chutney. *Masala dosas* are stuffed with potatoes and onions.

Doshas   Three forces governing all human biological and psychological processes.

Garam masala   A blend of as many as 20 aromatic spices, such as cloves, cinnamon, cardamom, cumin seeds, nutmeg, and the like, added to North Indian meat and rice dishes.

Ghee   Clarified butter, made by heating butter until the milk solids float to the top and are then removed, leaving a clear liquid with a nutty fragrance. For those who can afford it, *ghee* is the preferred cooking medium in Indian food. It is also sprinkled on breads, vegetables, *dals*, and sweets.

Gur   *See* jaggery.

Gurdhwara   A Sikh temple.

Halwa   Soft or hard dessert made from flour, sugar, and different flavorings.

Hilsa   A very bony fish related to the shad; very popular among Bengalis.

Idli   Spongy, disk-shaped, steamed breads made from rice and lentil flour and eaten with *sambar* and coconut chutney for breakfast in South India.

Jaggery   Raw sugar extracted from the sugarcane, date palm, or palmyra palm, and sold in large pieces. It is used to flavor sweets and, in West India, vegetable dishes.

Jains   Followers of a religion founded by Mahavira in the sixth century A.D. Its central tenet is reverence for life, and great care is taken to avoid potential injury to any living creature. Jains are extreme vegetarians who avoid meat, fish, eggs, vegetables that grow underground, certain lentils, small fruits, and honey.

Jati   Guild, sometimes translated "caste."

Kabob   Meat, fish, or vegetables stuck on skewers and roasted over coals or in a *tandoor* oven.

Kaccha   Foods cooked in water that are only served to and eaten by family members.

Kahwa   Kashmiri tea, brewed with milk, sugar, spices, almonds, and saffron.

Khoya   Milk solids made by boiling down milk; used as a base for sweets.

Kichiri   A dish of rice and lentils popular all over India; forerunner of the British kedgeree.

Korma **or** *qorma*   An aromatic North Indian meat dish with a yogurt-based gravy.

Krishna   A popular Hindu deity.

Kulcha   A baked wheat bread popular in Hyderabad.

Laddoos   Sweet balls made from chickpea flour and sugar, and flavored with sesame seeds or nuts.

Lucchis A round, deep-fried, puffy bread made of white flour that is eaten in West Bengal.

Masala A mixture of spices that can be added to a dish at various stages during cooking.

Moghlai food The style of cuisine prepared at the Mughal Court that is a synthesis of Persian and Indian food. It is characterized by a lavish use of aromatic spices, yogurt, cream, nuts, and dried fruits in meat and rice dishes.

Paan A mixture of sliced betel nut, lime paste, spices, and sometimes tobacco wrapped in a betel leaf and eaten as a breath freshener.

Paneer Soft unfermented cheese made from milk curd and used as a vegetable.

Pappadams (South India) or papads (North India) Crispy wafers made from lentil flour, often flavored with spices or garlic.

Parsis or Parsees A small community centered in Mumbai who descended from Zoroastrians who fled Persia for the West Coast of India in the seventh century.

Payasam (South India) or Payesh (North India) A rice pudding with raisins and nuts; sometimes served on special occasions.

Pickles (achar) An essential part of Indian meals as a condiment, an appetite enhancer, and a source of vitamins. They are made from fruit and vegetables, especially raw mangoes, limes, lemons, eggplants, chilies, and garlic, as well as fish and meat that is preserved in spices, salt, oil, and vinegar.

Pongol A harvest festival celebrated in Tamil Nadu; also, a sweet rice dish associated with this festival.

Prasad A consecrated food that is offered to the gods and then distributed to devotees.

Pukka Dishes that are fried in clarified butter and can be shared with people outside the family.

Pulao or Pilau A rice dish incorporating meat, chicken, or vegetables.

Puri A round, deep-fried, puffy bread made of whole-wheat flour.

Raj Period of British rule of India, 1857–1919.

Ramadan The month of fasting in Islam. Muslims break the fast each day at sunset with a special meal.

Roti The general name for bread in North India.

Sambar A spicy vegetable and lentil stew made with *toor dal*, served in South India with *dosas* and *idlis*.

Sandesh A delicate Bengali sweet made of chhana and sugar that comes in hundreds of varieties.

Shiva The Hindu God of Destruction.

Sikhs Followers of a religion created in the fifteenth century as a bridge between Hinduism and Islam. They are identified by their turbans and beards.

Tamarind The seeds and pulp of a tree that add sourness to dishes, especially in South and West India.

Tandoor A large clay oven, originally from Central Asia, used in restaurants to make *tandoori* chicken, bread, and kabobs.

Thali A round, metal tray with a rim and a set of little bowls. Food is traditionally served on a *thali*, especially in western India.

Tiffin A light meal.

Tikka Small pieces of meat (usually chicken) or cheese baked on skewers in a tandoor.

Toddy A strong alcohol beverage made from the sap of the date palm.

Udupi hotel or restaurant A small restaurant serving South Indian vegetarian food.

Unani An Islamic school of medicine, with close ties to ancient Greek medicine, that has many followers in India.

Vedas Four compilations of the oldest and most authoritative Hindu sacred texts composed in Sanskrit.

Vindaloo A hot and sour Goan stew, usually made with pork.

Vishnu A Hindu God, preserver of the universe. He has nine or ten incarnations, including Krishna and Ram.

Wazas Professional cooks who prepare special banquets in Kashmir.

Resource Guide

SUGGESTED READING

K. T. Achaya's groundbreaking scholarly work *Indian Food: A Historical Companion* (New Delhi: Oxford University Press, 1994) is an invaluable introduction to the history of Indian food. Much of the information has been distilled and conveniently organized in the same author's *A Historical Dictionary of Indian Food* (New Delhi: Oxford University Press, 2002).

Although published in the United Kingdom, Alan Davidson's *The Oxford Companion to Food* (Oxford: Oxford University Press, 1999) contains a remarkable amount of information about Indian ingredients, dishes, and culinary history, reflecting the inseparable historical and culinary ties between India and Great Britain. Two good introductions to Indian ingredients are Linda Bladholm's *The Indian Grocery Store Demystified* (Los Angeles: Renaissance Books, 2000) and Monisha Bharadwaj's *The Indian Pantry* (London: Kyle Cathie, 1996). Martin Hughes's *World Food India* (Victoria, Australia: Lonely Planet, 2001), published as part of the Lonely Planet series, offers a lively overview of the entire Indian food scene.

Of the many Indian cookbooks, several stand out. Julie Sahni's *Classic Indian Cookbook* (New York: William Morrow & Company, 1980) provides a sound introduction to Indian cooking methods, ingredients, and recipes, with a focus on North Indian dishes. *Indian Cookery* (New York: Watervane Books, 1972) by Mrs. Balbir Singh, the doyenne of Indian cooking, is not for the novice, but her recipes (again, mainly for North Indian dishes) are excellent. *Cooking with the Indian Masters* by J. Inder Singh Kalra (New Delhi: Allied Publishers, 1989) contains easy-to-follow recipes by India's leading hotel chefs, representing the major regional cuisines. Madhur Jaffrey's classic *A Taste of India* (New York: Atheneum, 1988) provides brilliant descriptions of Indian meals and customs, including some of the lesser known cuisines.

WEB SITES

There are a profusion of recipes and information about Indian food on the World Wide Web. The following Web sites are especially useful:

http://www.welcometoindia.com/cuisine. Short articles and recipes on the major regional cuisines.

www.indianfoodsco.com. Short articles on Indian food culture, cooking techniques, and restaurant menus.

http://www.indiatastes.com/. Recipes, a recipe board, and links to other Indian food web sites.

http://forums.egullet.com. A New-York-based message board. Click on eG Forums, India, China, Japan, and Asia/Pacific, and India and Indian Cuisine for a fascinating exchange of views and information on Indian food topics posted by chefs, writers, and foodies.

Selected Bibliography

Achaya, K. T. *Indian Food: A Historical Companion*. New Delhi: Oxford University Press, 1994.

———. *A Historical Dictionary of Indian Food*. New Delhi: Oxford University Press, 1998.

Ammal, S. Meenakshi. *Cook and See*, Vols. 1 and 2. Madras: S. Meenakshi Amma Publications, 1991.

Andrews, Jean. "Around the World with the Chili Pepper: Post Columbian Distribution of Domesticated Capsicums," *The Journal of Gastronomy* 4, no. 3 (Autumn 1988): 21–36.

Appadurai, Arjun. "How to Make a National Cuisine: Cookbooks in Contemporary India." *Comparative Studies in Sociology and History* 30, no. 1 (1988): 3–24.

———. "Gastro-Politics in Hindu South Asia." *American Ethnologist* 8 (1981): 494–511.

Arora, Neelaxi. *Assamese Cuisine*. New Delhi: Sterling Paperbacks, 1996.

Baljekar, Mridula. *A Taste of Goa*. London: Merehurst, 1988.

Banerji, Chitrita. *Life and Food in Bengal*. New Delhi: Rupa & Co., 1993.

Beals, Alan R. *Gopalpur: A South Indian Village*. New York: Holt, Rinehart and Winston, 1964.

Beeghly, Weyland. *India: Market Development Report Exporter Guide 1999*. GAIN report #IN9054. U.S. Department of Agriculture, August 27, 1999.

Bharadwaj, Monisha. *The Indian Pantry*. London: Kyle Cathie, 1988.

Bladholm, Linda. *The Indian Grocery Store Demystified*. Los Angeles: Renaissance Books, 2000.

Bobb, Eleanor. *The Raj Cookbook*. New Delhi: Piper Books, 1981.

Boxer, Charles R. *The Portuguese Seaborne Empire, 1415–1825*. London: Hutchinson, 1969.

Brennan, Jennifer. *Curries and Bugles: A Cookbook of the British Raj*. New Delhi: Penguin Books, 1992.

Brown, Patricia. *Anglo-Indian Food and Customs*. New Delhi: Penguin Books India, 1998.

Burton, David. *The Raj at Table*. London: Faber and Faber, 1993.

Campos, Joaquim Joseph A. *History of the Portuguese in Bengal*. London: Butterworth, 1919.

Chakravarty, Indira. *Saga of Indian Food: A Historical and Cultural Survey*. New Delhi: Sterling, 1972.

Dalal, Tarla. *The Complete Gujarati Cookbook*. Mumbai, India: Sanjay & Co., 2001.

Das Gupta, Minakshie, Bunny Gupta, and Jaya Chaliha. *The Calcutta Cookbook*. New Delhi: Penguin, 1995.

Davidson, Alan, ed. *The Oxford Companion to Food*. Oxford: Oxford University Press, 1999.

Disney, Anthony R. *Twilight of the Pepper Empire: Portuguese Trade in Southwest India in the Early 17th Century*. Cambridge, Mass.: Harvard University Press, 1978.

Durant, Will. *Our Oriental Heritage*. New York: Simon & Schuster, 1954.

Fernandez, Jennifer. *100 Easy-to-Make Goan Dishes*. New Delhi: Vikas Publishing House, 1994.

Gascoigne, Bamber. *The Great Moghuls*. New York: Dorset Press, 1971.

Hauzel, Hoihnu. *The Essential North-East Cookbook*. New Delhi: Penguin Books India, 2003.

Hughes, Martin. *World Food India*. Footscray, Australia: Lonely Planet Publications, 2001.

Jaffrey, Madhur. *A Taste of India*. New York: Atheneum, 1988.

Kalra, J. Inder Singh. *Prashad: Cooking with Indian Masters*. New Delhi: Allied Publishers, 1989.

Khan, S.N.M. *Indian Muslim Cookery*. London: George Routledge & Son, 1926.

Khare, R. S., ed. *The Eternal Food: Gastronomic Ideas and Experiences of Hindus and Buddhists*. Albany: State University of New York Press, 1992.

———. *The Hindu Hearth and Home*. New Delhi: Vikas Publishing House, 1976.

Latif, Bilkees I. *The Essential Andhra Cookbook*. New Delhi: Penguin Books India, 1999.

Manekshaw, Bhicoo J. *Parsi Food and Customs: The Essential Parsi Cookbook*. New Delhi: Penguin Books India, 1996.

Mathew, Mrs. K. M. *Kerala Cookery*. Kottayam, India: Manorama Publishing House, 1964.

Mehta, Nita. *Punjabi Khaana*. New Delhi: SNAB Publishers, 2002.

———. *Taste of Gujarat*. New Delhi: SNAB Publishers, 2002.

Menezes, Maria Teresa. *The Essential Goa Cookbook*. New Delhi: Penguin Books India, 2000.

Mintz, Sidney W., and Daniela Schlettwein-Gsell. "Food Patterns in Agrarian Societies: The Core-Fringe-Legume Hypothesis." *Gastronomica, The Journal of Food and Culture* 1, no. 3 (2001): 40–52.

Narayan, Shoba. *Monsoon Diary*. New York: Villard, 2003.

Parasramka, Bina. *Marwari Kitchen*. New Delhi: Roli Books, n.d.

Purewal, Jasjit, Karen Anand, and Jennifer Brennan. *The Food of India*. Boston: Periplus, 2000.

Raychaudhuri, Hasi, and Tapan Raychaudhuri. "Not by Curry Alone." In *National and Regional Styles of Cookery, Oxford Symposium on Food History 1981*. London: Prospect Books, 1981.

Roberts, Joe, and Colleen Taylor Sen. "A Carp Wearing Lipstick. The Role of Fish in Bengali Cuisine and Culture." In *Fish from the Waters: Proceedings of the Oxford Symposium on Food and Cookery 1997*, pp. 257–258. Blackawton, UK: Prospect Books, 1998.

Sahni, Julie. *Classic Indian Cooking*. New York: William Morrow & Company, 1980.

Sen, Colleen Taylor. "Dining In: South India Comes to Your Kitchen." *Yoga International*, May–June 1994, 34–40.

———. "Exotic Delights: The Cuisine of West Bengal." *Yoga International*, May–June 1995, 50–56.

———. "In Delhi, It's the Moti Mahal." *Christian Science Monitor*, 5 October 1988.

———. "Indian Blend: The Cuisine of Maharashtra." *Chicago Tribune*, 13 September 1995, Section 7, p. 5.

———. "InfusionFusion: Indian-Style Tea Service Is a Spicy Twist on the Ubiquitous British Ritual." *Food Arts*, January–February 1999, 97–98.

———. "Malabar Meals," *Chicago Tribune*, 8 July 1993, sec. 7, p. 5.

———. "The Marvelous Mango." *Chicago Tribune*, 9 August 1990, sec. 7, p. 3.

———. "Mogul Fare." *Chicago Tribune*, 4 May 1989, sec. 7, p. 3.

Singh, Mrs. Balbir. *Indian Cookery*. New York: Weathervane Books, 1973.

Svoboda, Robert E. *Ayurveda: Life, Health and Longevity*. New Delhi: Penguin Books, 1993.

Toussaint-Samat, Maguelonne. *History of Food*. Trans. Anthea Bell. Cambridge, Mass.: Blackwell, 1992.

Westrip, Joyce. *Moghul Cooking: India's Courtly Cuisine*. London: Serif, 1997.

Wolpert, Stanley. *A New History of India*. 6th ed. New York: Oxford University Press, 2000.

Yule, Henry, and A. C. Burnell. *Hobson-Jobson: A Glossary of Colloquial Anglo-Indian Words and Phrases*. 2nd ed. London and New York: Routledge & Kegan Paul, 1986.

Index

Tables are noted by a t following the page number.

About the Author

COLLEEN TAYLOR SEN is a regular contributor of articles on food and travel to major newspapers and magazines. She specializes in ethnic and Asian cuisines, particularly India's foodways.

**Recent Titles in
Food Culture around the World**

Food Culture in Japan
Michael Ashkenazi and Jeanne Jacob